Springer Series in Cognitive Development

Series Editor
Charles J. Brainerd

Springer Series in Cognitive Development

Series Editor: Charles J. Brainerd

Cognitive Learning and Memory in Children

Progress in Cognitive Development Research

Edited by
Michael Pressley and Charles J. Brainerd

Springer-Verlag
New York Berlin Heidelberg Tokyo

Michael Pressley
Department of Psychology
University of Western Ontario
London, Ontario
Canada N6A 5C2

Charles J. Brainerd
Department of Psychology
University of Alberta
Edmonton, Alberta
Canada T6G 2E9

Series Editor: Charles J. Brainerd

With 14 Figures

Library of Congress Cataloging in Publication Data
Main entry under title:
Cognitive learning and memory in children.
  (Springer series in cognitive development)
  Bibliography: p.
  Includes index.
  1. Memory in children. 2. Memory in children—
Research. I. Pressley, Michael. II. Brainerd,
Charles J. III. Series.
BF723.M4C64 1985   155.4'13   84-23571

⌐9,690

© 1985 by Springer-Verlag New York Inc.

The use of general descriptive names, trade names, trademarks, etc., in this publication,
even if the former are not especially identified, is not to be taken as a sign that such
names, as understood by the Trade Marks and Merchandise Marks Act, may
accordingly be used freely by anyone.

Typeset by Ampersand Publisher Services, Inc., Rutland, Vermont.
Printed and bound by R.R. Donnelley and Sons, Harrisonburg, Virginia.
Printed in the United States of America.

9 8 7 6 5 4 3 2 1

ISBN 0-387-96076-7 Springer-Verlag New York Berlin Heidelberg Tokyo
ISBN 3-540-96076-7 Springer-Verlag Berlin Heidelberg New York Tokyo

Series Preface

For some time now, the study of cognitive development has been far and away the most active discipline within developmental psychology. Although there would be much disagreement as to the exact proportion of papers published in developmental journals that could be considered cognitive, 50% seems like a conservative estimate. Hence, a series of scholarly books devoted to work in cognitive development is especially appropriate at this time.

The *Springer Series in Cognitive Development* contains two basic types of books, namely, edited collections of original chapters by several authors, and original volumes written by one author or a small group of authors. The flagship for the Springer Series is a serial publication of the "advances" type, carrying the subtitle *Progress in Cognitive Development Research*. Each volume in the *Progress* sequence is strongly thematic, in that it is limited to some well-defined domain of cognitive–developmental research (e.g., logical and mathematical development, development of learning). All *Progress* volumes will be edited collections. Editors of such collections, upon consultation with the Series Editor, may elect to have their books published either as contributions to the *Progress* sequence or as separate volumes. All books written by one author or a small group of authors are being published as separate volumes within the series.

A fairly broad definition of cognitive development is being used in the selection of books for this series. The classic topics of concept development, children's thinking and reasoning, the development of learning, language development, and memory development will, of course, be included. So, however, will newer areas such as social-cognitive development, educational applications, formal modeling, and philosophical implications of cognitive–developmental theory. Although it is anticipated that most books in the series will be empirical in orientation, theoretical and philosophical works are also welcome. With books of the latter sort, heterogeneity of theoretical perspective is encouraged, and no attempt will be made to foster some specific theoretical perspective at the expense of others (e.g., Piagetian versus behavioral or behavioral versus information processing).

C. J. Brainerd

Preface

Twenty-five years ago Miller, Galanter, and Pribram (1960) offered *Plans and the Structure of Behavior* to a psychological community that had avoided mentalistic thinking for more than two decades. Miller et al.'s (1960) impact was enormous; the publication of that volume stimulated much of the now classic work in cognitive psychology that was carried out in the 1960s. In developmental psychology the study of cognition was stimulated additionally by Flavell's (1963) masterful summary of Piagetian thinking, as well as Flavell's (1970) initial studies of children's information processing during memorization. The chapters of this volume and its companion [Brainerd, C. J., & Pressley, M. (Eds.), *Basic Processes in Memory Development*] document the enormous progress during the 1970s and 1980s. This volume focuses on memory development and intellectual processing related to memory.

The seven chapters weave conceptual and methodological issues relevant to the development and study of memory. Pressley, Forrest-Pressley, Elliott-Faust, and Miller develop a new model of efficient use of cognitive strategies and review supporting data, especially work on memory strategies. There are many recommendations in this chapter as to how to study efficient strategy use.

Daehler and Greco provide an overview of memory development in very young children. They describe each of the major methods of studying memory in children younger than three years of age, followed by a summary of research on young children's retention. It is a concise, yet thorough, integrative summary of early memory. Daehler's extensive research in this area permits insightful commentary on this challenging area of research.

Paris, Newman, and Jacobs take up the problem of the naturalistic development of memory skills, theorizing that such skills are shaped by children's social interactions. The authors argue that the environment is well suited to developing the child's mind—parents provide support for cognitive processing, withdrawing their assistance gradually as the child matures so as to promote autonomous cognition. Ideas from Soviet theorists are integrated with findings from the cross-cultural literature and western research on cognition, particularly research on everyday cognition.

Rogoff and Mistry explore in detail recent cross-cultural work relevant to memory development. While covering many of the same topics explored by Paris, Newman, and Jacobs, a particular strength of Rogoff and Mistry's contribution is that they provide extensive coverage of the difficulties of cross-cultural research—and many examples of how difficulties can be overcome. Rogoff and Mistry's chapter, especially when combined with Paris, Newman, and Jacob's contribution, provides detailed coverage of how memory can be studied in children's natural environments.

Reyna presents a review of recent research on children's interpretation of metaphors, relating it to other aspects of memory and cognition. Reyna documents that children often provide "magical" interpretations of metaphors; she hypothesizes that magical interpretation is preliminary to mature metaphoric understanding. Her chapter provides sufficient motivation for additional study of this interesting aspect of children's comprehension and interpretation as well as motivation for additional research relating metaphoric competence to other aspects of cognition.

Marx, Winne, and Walsh review a new area of cognitive inquiry, thinking as it occurs in the classroom. These authors have pioneered methodological advances in assessing student cognition during classroom learning, and they describe many of their contributions in this chapter. Marx, Winne, and Walsh identify a number of important variables that influence children's thinking in school—in doing so, this contribution complements well other chapters concerning memory and intellectual development in natural contexts.

The chapter by Joel Levin is a methodological critique of research on learning and cognition. He details many fundamental errors in procedure and analysis that have plagued developmental cognition. Levin also offers many solutions. This chapter is must reading for young cognitive researchers. Most veteran investigators will find worthwhile pointers here as well.

Contents

Contributors

Marvin W. Daehler Department of Psychology, University of Massachusetts, Amherst, Massachusetts 01003, U.S.A.

Darlene Elliott-Faust Department of Psychology, University of Western Ontario, London, Ontario N6A 5C2, Canada.

D. L. Forrest-Pressley Children's Psychiatric Research Institute, London, Ontario N6A 4G6, Canada.

Carolyn Greco Department of Psychology, University of Massachusetts, Amherst, Massachusetts 01003, U.S.A.

Janis E. Jacobs Department of Psychology, University of Michigan, Ann Arbor, Michigan 48109, U.S.A.

Joel R. Levin University of Wisconsin, Department of Educational Psychology, Madison, Wisconsin 53706, U.S.A.

Ronald W. Marx Faculty of Education, Simon Fraser University, Burnaby, British Columbia V5A 1S6, Canada.

Gloria Miller Department of Psychology, University of South Carolina, Columbia, South Carolina 29208, U.S.A.

Jayanthi Mistry   Department of Psychology, University of Utah, Salt Lake City, Utah 84112, U.S.A.

Richard S. Newman   Department of Psychology, State University of New York, Stony Brook, New York 11794, U.S.A.

Scott G. Paris   Department of Psychology, University of Michigan, Ann Arbor, Michigan 48109, U.S.A.

Michael Pressley   Department of Psychology, University of Western Ontario, London, Ontario N6A 5C2, Canada.

Valerie F. Reyna   Department of Psychology, University of Texas at Dallas, Richardson, Texas 75080, U.S.A.

Barbara Rogoff   Department of Psychology, University of Utah, Salt Lake City, Utah 84112, U.S.A.

John Walsh   Faculty of Education, Simon Fraser University, Burnaby, British Columbia V5A 1S6, Canada.

Philip H. Winne   Faculty of Education, Simon Fraser University, Burnaby, British Columbia V5A 1S6, Canada.

1. Children's Use of Cognitive Strategies, How to Teach Strategies, and What to Do If They Can't Be Taught

Michael Pressley, D. L. Forrest-Pressley,
Darlene Elliott-Faust, and Gloria Miller

This chapter is about children's use of strategies. Although the emphasis is on memory, the discussion includes strategies applied in a number of domains. Almost 20 years have passed since Flavell's seminal studies of children's strategies (e.g., Keeney, Cannizzo, & Flavell, 1967), and an enormous amount of research has been reported since then. The present chapter does not survey that work exhaustively, but summarizes current thinking about strategic functioning in children. In doing so, we present a revised definition of strategy, discuss a model of strategy functioning that is more precise than some of its historical predecessors, review recent research relevant to that model, compare two differing tactics to strategy instruction and strategy instructional research, as well as consider alternatives to strategy instruction for children who cannot execute cognitive strategies.

Definition of Strategies

In the spring of 1983 participants at the 18th annual Carnegie Symposium on cognition at Carnegie-Mellon University (Sophian, 1984) frequently used the term strategy, prompting a discussion of the distinguishing features of strategic behavior. Those in attendance had differing viewpoints. Moreover, the Pittsburgh argument is not isolated. In the two-volume set on cognitive strategy

The writing of this chapter was supported by separate grants to the first two authors from the Natural Sciences and Engineering Research Council of Canada.

research edited by Pressley and Levin (1983a, 1983b), many contributors provided definitions of strategy, with no two the same.

Even though there is not general agreement of what constitutes a strategy, there are, however, some widely cited definitions. For instance, Brown (1975) defined mnemonic strategies "as courses of action which are deliberately instigated for the purpose of remembering (p. 110)." Flavell (1977) claimed that mnemonic strategies were "the large and diverse range of potentially conscious activities a person may voluntarily carry out as a means to various mnemonic ends (p. 194)." Despite the common ring to these definitions, the disagreements cited above suggest that these attempts might be missing the mark a bit.

Most observers would agree that strategies must involve more than just the processes that are a consequence of doing the task (Waters & Andreassen, 1983). For instance, looking at words is not a reading strategy. Also, strategies are certainly purposeful in increasing the probability of successfully accomplishing many cognitive goals (e.g., memory, comprehension, writing a coherent paper, losing weight, self-control; Pressley & Levin, 1983a, 1983b). But are strategies "deliberately instigated" in Brown's terms or "voluntary" as Flavell expresses it? When Brown and Flavell proposed their definitions, there was little evidence relevant to the deliberateness issue. There were virtually no studies exploring "why" people deployed strategies when they did. Of course, it had been established that different goals produced different amounts and types of strategy use. For instance, preparation for a memory test elicits more extensive processing than simply looking at stimuli (e.g., Yussen, Gagné, Gargiulo, & Kunen, 1974; Yussen, Kunen, & Buss, 1975). However, it would be farfetched to argue from such goal-strategy use correlations that learners were using strategies deliberately in demanding cognitive tasks. A deliberateness interpretation of such correlations requires converging data, and only recently have studies appeared that provide the multiple measures that are necessary. These recent efforts, some of which will be reviewed in detail in this chapter, reveal that children's use of strategies is not always tied to understanding the strategy's effects (e.g., Ghatala, Levin, Pressley, & Lodico, in press; Pressley, Levin & Ghatala, 1984; Pressley, Ross, Levin, & Ghatala, in press). When learners lack such an understanding, it is hard to argue that they are using a strategy deliberately.

There are other arguments that can be made for eliminating deliberateness as a defining attribute of a strategy. For instance, consider a scholar reading an article in his or her area of expertise. This person might first read the abstract, survey the references, examine the tables, and skim the procedures. In the vernacular of reading specialists, and especially advocates of SQ3R (Robinson, 1961), the expert surveyed the paper. He could ask himself questions as a result of the survey, executing the Q component of SQ3R. If his curiosity were sufficiently peaked, reading the paper would follow. After reading it, mental recitation and review would complete the cycle through the 3Rs. Should this be considered nonstrategic behavior if the scholar carries out these activities almost reflexively? A beginning graduate student reading the same paper might engage in the same SQ3R processing, but do so very consciously as a result of a study skills course. Should the graduate student be considered more strategic for intentionally using the processing that the expert applies automatically? We think not. What matters as far as memory is concerned is not the deliberateness, but the processing that is executed (e.g., Craik & Tulving, 1975; Miller, Galanter, & Pribram, 1960, p. 130). Indeed, it is generally becoming recognized that strategy functioning at its very best has a mindless, reflexive character to it (Brown, Bransford, Ferrara, & Campione, 1983; LaBerge & Samuels, 1974; Torgesen & Greenstein, 1982).

There are many occasions when there is nondeliberate "strategic" processing. For instance, Clark and Clark (1977) described many strategies for constructing utterances and interpreting them. People do not use these strategies after long reflection and careful consideration of cognitive goals—although it would be possible to deploy the Clarks' processing rules deliberately. Also, Siegler and Shrager (1984) documented children's strategies for providing answers to simple addition problems. They first search associative memory. If no answer to the problem is there, they either hold up fingers as computational aids, count on their fingers, or engage in covert processing. Siegler and Shrager provide evidence that these strategies are not deployed deliberately.

Because of these problems with the descriptors deliberate and voluntary, they should not be used in defining strategy. On the other hand, strategies are almost always potentially controllable (cf. Brown, 1978, p. 79)—behaviors that *could be* deployed deliberately. It is this potential conscious control that we choose to emphasize here. For recent commentary on the alternative perspective that deliberateness is an absolutely essential attribute of strategic activity, see Paris, Lipson, & Wixson, 1983; and Chapter 3 in this volume, although in our judgments, the definition of strategy offered by Paris and his associates excludes many behaviors long considered strategic by cognitive, developmental, and educational psychologists.

Cognitive psychologists are much more willing to acknowledge conscious processing and accept learners' reports of it than they were when Flavell (1977) proposed his definition (e.g., Ericsson & Simon, 1980). In the area of memory, humans certainly have the potential to be conscious of both encoding (e.g., Pressley & Levin, 1977a) and retrieval (e.g., Read & Bruce, 1982) processes. Indeed, Think Aloud reports (e.g., Hayes & Flower, 1980; Simon & Hayes, 1976) provide impressive evidence of conscious processing. On the other hand, although there are many sophisticated self-reports of strategy use by children and adults (e.g., Brown & Day, 1983; Meichenbaum, 1977; Pressley, Levin, Kuiper, Bryant, & Michener, 1982), children's consciousness of their strategy use may be difficult to demonstrate in many situations. For instance, young children's language about their internal states is poorly developed (e.g., Johnson & Wellman, 1980; Shatz, Wellman, & Silber, 1983; Wellman & Johnson, 1979). Their vocabularies often fail to include words for describing ongoing processing and strategic activities, lexical entries such as rehearse, group, and rearrange. Words like elaboration are completely out of the question! If assessment problems associated with children's consciousness can be overcome, however, this could be a rich area of developmental study, given theoretical arguments that consciousness about cognitive processes increases with age during childhood and adolescence (e.g., Piaget, 1976, 1978).

Strategy research has evolved tremendously in the last decade. Although there were isolated investigations of complex strategies in the early 1970s (e.g., Egeland, 1974), many more researchers are now focusing on particularly complex strategic interventions. For instance, there is Kendall and Wilcox's (1980) plan for modifying impulsivity. Children are taught to (1) define the problem, (2) focus attention, (3) self-reinforce, and (4) make coping self-statements. Because this chapter includes discussion of many such complex strategies, we specify that strategies can range from single operations (e.g., looking) to complex interdependent sequences.

In summary, a *strategy is composed of cognitive operations over and above the processes that are a natural consequence of carrying out the task, ranging from one such operation to a sequence of interdependent operations. Strategies achieve cognitive purposes (e.g., comprehending, memorizing) and are potentially conscious and controllable activities.* In proposing this definition, we note how similar it is to Miller et al.'s (1960) plans that included interlocking operations, accomplished goals, and were often nondeliberate. Thus, this definition is not a dramatic departure from previous ones, and some readers may react that the definition developed here is no less arbitrary than competing ones. This perception follows because we are trying to define a decidedly "fuzzy" set. For instance, even though most strategies can be reflected on, there are some strategies that might not be conscious or controllable at all (e.g., perceptual strategies; Simon, 1979). Despite some exceptions the proposed definition encompasses most instantiations of processing that researchers consider strategic (e.g., Pressley, Heisel, McCormick, & Nakamura, 1982; Pressley & Levin, 1983a, 1983b).

Three Areas of Strategy Application

In this chapter we showcase three cognitive goals that can be accomplished using strategy variations. These applications are introduced early to motivate continued reading of the chapter. This is necessary because the strategy research best known to many readers involved simple techniques applied to simple tasks, such as rehearsal as a procedure for list learning (e.g., Brown & DeLoache, 1978). If that type of work was the only concern in this chapter, the reader interested in ecologically valid learning could justifiably stop reading. Fortunately, things have changed. Strategy researchers are attacking educational problems such as real-world associative learning, writing, and prose processing. These more complex problems required more complex strategies.

Real-World Associative Learning

Mnemonic techniques for tasks such as vocabulary learning followed directly from basic associative research. Traditional associative learning involves paired items (i.e., paired words, paired pictures, paired objects). Items are learned so they can be recalled given pairmates. Much of the research with children has focused on imaginal elaboration of to-be-associated materials. To learn the pair "cat and apple" using imaginal elaboration, one would generate an interactive image involving a cat and an apple. Elaboration is a critical component in the keyword method, a technique that can be applied to vocabulary learning. An English speaker using the keyword method to learn the unfamiliar English word *carlin*, which means old woman, would first note that part of *carlin* sounds like car, a word already known by the speaker. Then, the learner would generate an interactive image of a car and an old woman.

In addition to studies of single mnemonics, researchers have begun investigations of combined mnemonics for vocabulary learning (Levin, 1981). A recent experiment conducted by Allan Paivio, James Clark, Alain Desrochers, Michael Pressley, and their associates at Western Ontario illustrates this point. The goal was to teach a list of French words so that learners could recall the words and their meanings in order of presentation. To do this, subjects were instructed to use the keyword method to facilitate recall of meaning and to employ 24 mnemonic pegs to learn the order of the words, one corresponding to each list position. In the most demanding condition of the study, subjects created interactive images that included the meaning of the vocabulary item, its keyword, and the pegword corresponding to the list position. Although the results were complex, in general, when adults used both keywords and pegwords, recall of both meanings and order was enhanced (i.e., benefits of both strategies were obtained). On the other hand, many subjects experienced difficulty executing both components because of the complex processing involved in this combined mnemonics procedure.

Text Processing

There are many strategies that can be employed before, during, and after processing a text (Levin & Pressley, 1981). In preparation for reading one can overview materials, question oneself about headings in text, retrieve from memory everything one knows about the topic, and examine sample questions carefully (see, for example, Anderson & Armbruster [1980], Davidson [1976], and Robinson [1961] for discussions). As one reads one can make images representing the prose content (e.g., Pressley, 1976), ask oneself questions, and answer questions posed in text. For additional discussion of these latter two approaches, see Pressley and Forrest-Pressley (in press). There are strategic reactions that can be invoked when readers "sense" (monitor) that something is wrong with their reading, such as looking back (e.g., Clay, 1974; Garner & Reis, 1981; Just & Carpenter, 1980), rereading, seeking external confirmation, self-correcting, and deploying more attention to problem areas of text (e.g., Baker, in press; Baker & Brown, 1984; Wagoner, 1983). After a text is completed, one can do many things, perhaps most prominently recite and review the text (Robinson, 1961).

Good readers deploy strategies appropriate to the reading task at hand. For instance, skillful readers adjust their reading to the goals of the reading task (e.g., DiStefano, Noe, & Valencia, 1981; Forrest & Barron, 1977; Forrest-Pressley & Waller, 1984; Rothkopf & Billington, 1975, 1979). Capable readers underline appropriately and take notes that aid memory and comprehension (e.g., Brown & Smiley, 1978). People spontaneously use imagery to remember prose (e.g., Sadoski, in press).

Bird and Bereiter (1984) provided an especially penetrating analysis of the types of strategies that mature readers use during reading. Those investigators required ten good adult readers to "think aloud" about their strategic processing as they read. Four strategies were apparent: (a) Subjects executed strategic restatements of text including replacing unfamiliar terms with inferred synonyms, simplifying complex text, restating to incorporate interpretations, and summarizing. (b) Readers backtracked and reread confusing aspects of text. (c) Readers actively looked for information that complemented text that was presented earlier. (d) Problem solving to resolve inconsistencies or obscurities in text was common.

There are other text processing goals besides comprehension and memory. Brown and Day's (1983) work on summarization is a good illustration of this point. They discovered that highly proficient summarizers use five rules to produce adequate condensations: (a) they delete trivial and redundant information; (b) they replace lists of items with superordinate terms; (c) they select a topic sentence; (d) they invent one if there is none in the text; and (e) they combine across paragraphs.

Writing

The gist of one popular approach for improving prose composition skills consists of three phases: (a) planning, (b) translating, and (c) reviewing (Flower, 1981; Hayes & Flower, 1980). Planning includes generating, organizing, and goal setting. Generating involves retrieving and finding information relevant to the writing task and producing rough drafts of comments to be included in the essay. Organizing is placing these comments in an outline. Goal setting is establishing criteria to judge whether the text is meeting its purpose as well as planning writing so that the text satisfies the intent of the writer. Translating is taking the products of planning and transforming them into acceptable prose—sentences, paragraphs, and sections. Reviewing the results and editing the paper follows. Editing includes grammatical corrections and evaluating whether the test accomplishes its purpose. There can be many trips through this planning–translating–editing loop during the course of preparing an essay.

Concluding Comment

A main thrust of strategy research has been to train techniques such as the ones discussed in this section. Use of strategies is multicomponential and goes beyond teaching the strategic operations *per se*. The next section identifies the components that interact to produce proficient strategy use.

The Components of Proficient Strategy Use

What is the nature of efficient strategy execution? We briefly outline the architecture of the memory strategy system, and then explore how that architecture affects strategy deployment, as well as how strategy use produces changes in the strategy system. Strategy use includes strategies, knowledge about strategies, and monitoring, and the dynamic interaction of these components. The model presented here shares characteristics with other attempts to specify the relation of metacognition to cognition, although we believe the present effort to be more explicit than other attempts (e.g., Brown, 1980; Büchel, 1982; Flavell & Wellman, 1977; Paris et al., 1983; Pressley, Borkowski, & O'Sullivan, 1984, in press). The model follows on the heels of correlational research documenting strong relationships between metacognition and cognition. See Schneider (in press) for a summary of that literature. An important contribution of models of this type is that they can lead to experimental research, some of which will be covered later in the chapter.

Strategy Representations and Associated Abilities

The most fundamental units in the system are strategy representations and associated abilities to execute those strategies. The expert strategy user has a large array of these, perhaps including the vocabulary, text processing, and writing strategies detailed previously. Experts' strategy representations and abilities are complete. For example, an expert's summarization strategy includes all five components detailed by Brown and Day (1983), although experts do not always produce the entire strategy. Low motivation may result in incomplete use of a strategy. When the expert is feeling lazy, he or she may produce a series of topic sentences for a summary but not use the deletion and across-paragraph integration rules. State variables (e.g., being tired or drunk) can have the same effects. Also, some goals may require only partial strategy activation. An accomplished writer producing an outline might go through only the planning part of the Hayes and Flower (1980) writing strategy. Both goals and motivational requirements of strategies will be taken up again in the discussion of metamemory about strategies. Suffice it to conclude at this point that experts do not always display their competence.

Specific Strategy Knowledge

Experts possess specific strategy knowledge for each strategy in their repertoire. Specific strategy knowledge includes information about materials to which the strategy can be applied, goals the strategy can help to meet (i.e., means–end, utility information), time constraints associated with the strategy, effort requirements, personal satisfaction derived from use of the strategy, and information about strategy modification. Thus, experts know that a Brown and Day (1983) summarization strategy can be applied to expository materials when one is trying to reduce the prose. They also know that it takes only a few minutes to do a page and is fairly easy to do once one grasps the material. Experts know to produce only topic sentences and integrate them across paragraphs when trying to reduce a very long prose passage to *Reader's Digest* form—that is, experts know how to shortcut the strategy for materials much longer than the ones studied by Brown and Day. Such specific strategy knowledge is a part of metamemory and plays a critical role in the orchestration of strategy use.

Monitoring

Monitoring is keeping track of cognition and is an important part of cognitive processing. Much research on the topic is within the general paradigm used in Markman's (1977, 1979) seminal demonstrations of deficiencies in children's comprehension monitoring. In those experiments children heard prose passages that included inconsistencies. Children often failed to note such problems—they did not monitor whether their understanding of a presentation made sense. Since the initial Markman investigations, children have been presented prose containing nonsense words, anomalous sentences, internal logical contradictions, and content that clashes with world knowledge (see Baker [in press] for an overview). In general, children frequently do not report problems with flawed materials (Baker, in press). An important discovery, however, is that even though children do not report inconsistencies, they may still detect them. Children may exhibit nonverbal signs such as body movements and signs of confusion, yet not verbalize their feelings. See Beal and Flavell's (1982) and Patterson, Cosgrove, and O'Brien's (1982) research with young children for examples that substantiate as well that young children do not translate these feelings of miscomprehension into action strategies. More mature learners do by reexamining difficult-to-understand material (e.g., Alessi, Anderson, & Goetz, 1979), making self-corrections (e.g., Pace, 1980), and increasing attention (e.g., Rothkopf & Billington, 1979).

Efficient cognition requires monitoring: (a) Is the match between the strategy and the task appropriate? Is the cognitive goal being accomplished? Questions such as these are central to monitoring per se. Such keeping track of cognition permits on-line executive decisions, such as should the strategy be reapplied, or perhaps another strategy deployed? (b) As learners monitor strategy functioning, their long-term knowledge about the strategy may change, with the incremented knowledge base instrumental in future strategy use. In short, monitoring takes strategies as input and produces strategy shifts and new metamemory about strategies (cf., Campione, Brown, & Ferrara, 1982).

There are many examples of monitoring in the psychological literature. For instance, adults sense when their current comprehension is out of synchrony with their world knowledge (e.g., Tikhomerov & Klochko, 1981). People continuously and automatically monitor their speaking, noting speech errors and making corrections with ease (Levelt, 1983). When acquiring a second language, people monitor the adequacy of their language productions, with different speaking tactics associated with different amounts of monitoring (e.g., Krashen, 1978; Krashen & Pon, 1975). Good mathematicians possess internal "critics" that guide their problem solving (Davis, 1983). Mature learners also monitor actively how well their strategies are working as they execute complex memorization tasks such as the learning of prose (e.g., Smirnov, 1973, Chapter 6), with strategy shifts determined by such monitoring.

Summary: Interrelationships Between Strategies, Specific Strategy Knowledge, and Monitoring

Strategies, specific strategy knowledge, and monitoring are tightly tied in the sophisticated strategy user. There are often several possible strategies for attacking a problem. If it is a familiar problem, he or she may select a strategy witout thinking. With less familiar problems, specific strategy knowledge plays a larger role. The sophisticated learner possesses knowledge about when various strategies are appropriate. Presumably, a challenging cognitive task is analyzed regarding goals, materials, time constraints, and other factors, with a strategy selected that best matches the situation. In such demanding circumstances metacognitive–cognitive correlations are expected (Borkowski, in press). The more known about a strategy, the more likely its appropriate use.

What happens once a strategy is invoked? The learner may make progress, may enjoy the strategy, or may have difficulty executing the strategy. Mature strategy users monitor effectiveness, enjoyableness, and difficulty of strategies as they execute them. This monitoring directs continued use of the initial strategy or selection of another strategy—it is the main mechanism of midcourse corrections (cf., Norman & Shallice, 1980). A second function of monitoring is to generate new specific strategy knowledge. For example, users may encode that strategy X is not appropriate for situation 1, but that strategy Y is, or they may note that the first strategy was difficult to execute, and the effort was not worth the gain. When similar memory problems are encountered in the future, the present memorization task affects subsequent strategy selection through these changes in the learner's specific strategy knowledge.

What can be gained from efforts to validate this model? Potentially a great deal. Children do not always deploy strategies effectively. Although there is ample speculation that these failures are somehow tied to metacognitive deficiencies (e.g., Flavell & Wellman, 1977; Borkowski, in press), progress in documenting such linkages has been slow (e.g., Pressley, Borkowski, & O'Sullivan, 1984, in press). The present analysis of strategy deployment logically suggests a number of specific deficiencies, some strategic, some metacognitive, and some both metacognitive and strategic, that could result in production deficiencies.

A child may not produce a strategy in an appropriate situation, because of the following factors: (a) The child does not possess the strategy, with several alternative versions of this type of production deficiency. The learner may not possess any version of the strategy that they fail to produce. Alternatively, the child may possess some of the strategic components, but not all of them. Even if all of the components are there, they may not be integrated into an efficient strategic sequence. (b) A second source of production deficiencies may be inadequate specific strategy knowledge. Children may not know that strategies they possess are appropriate in particular situations or that the learning techniques they possess could be modified to fit current intellectual tasks facing them. Alternatively, the child may possess metamemory about the strategy that argues against strategy deployment, such as motivational information; for instance, that the strategy is not fun to execute in the current situation or requires more effort than the learner desires to expend at the moment. (c) The child may fail to monitor, with several possible versions of this problem. While executing strategy X, the learners might fail to continue using X because learners do not monitor that more deployment of X is required to accomplish the goal. While executing strategy X, learners may fail to bring in strategy Y, which would be more appropriate and effective, because they do not realize that there is a problem using X. Another possibility is that learners may monitor that a strategy is not working, but they do not use this product of monitoring to modify processing. (d) The learner may possess a combination of deficient strategies, insufficient metamemory about strategies, and flawed monitoring, or they might coordinate these components very inefficiently.

How would production deficiencies be remedied according to this model? One could initially diagnose exactly what deficiency underlies a failure to produce a strategy on a particular occasion. First, is the strategy present in the learner's repertoire? The whole strategy or only part of it? Are the components of the strategy properly integrated? Also, how facile is the learner in executing those components? If the strategy is not present at all, one need not worry about specific strategy knowledge, for it is hard to have information about a concept without possessing the concept! If the strategy is present in rudimentary form, either part of the strategy or a less than optimally organized version of the technique, the learner's metamemory about the strategy could be assessed. Determine as well if the learner knows how to monitor, when to monitor, and in fact, does monitor. Determine also if the learner realizes that awareness produced by monitoring is important in strategy regulation and in the modification of specific strategy knowledge.

With such an exhaustive analysis, one ought to be in a good position to plot an instructional course. If the learner had the strategy but seemed not to know when to apply it, teach some metamemory about the strategy. If the learner possessed fix-up strategies (such as looking back in text) but did not monitor, teach monitoring skills such as checking, reflecting on one's performance, and comparing current strategic efforts with usual performance on such tasks. Of course, the problem with this instructional course is that cognitive diagnosis is frequently more problematic and expensive than cognitive interventions (cf. Flavell, 1971). Still, given a learner who seems "close" to strategic competence, but not quite there, it might be more efficient to do some probing to see if problem components can be identified quickly. If so, then focus the treatment on that particular problem.

Nonstrategic Knowledge and Memory

Readers may have the impression that strategy use is the main thrust of cognitive activity and memorization, simply due to neglect of nonstrategic factors until this point in the discussion—most prominently, neglect of learner's nonstrategic knowledge. There are important interactions, however, between strategy use and the knowledge base.

1. Although unfamiliar materials may require strategic intervention for efficient learning, material consistent with what learners know may be acquired easily without strategic intervention. For instance, if a little girl is presented the letters "YNJEA" to memorize, greater strategic effort is required than if the letters are ordered to spell her name (JANEY), a sequence well integrated in her knowledge base (Lodico, Ghatala, Levin, Pressley, & Bell, 1983).
2. One strategy may be deployed when knowledge is high, another when the knowledge base is low. For instance, consider the behaviors of two different entertainment critics. While watching *King Lear* to prepare a review for a prestigious drama magazine, an advanced literary scholar reviews his long-term memory about the play, but does little more during the performance than correct his knowledge base where it was flawed. While watching the same play to prepare a review for the school paper, the freshman English major makes copious scribblings in the margin of the Cliff's Notes. One might see a reversal of roles, however, if a Fleetwood Mac concert were the object of review, with the English prof scribbling in the margins of a *Rolling Stone* and the student sitting back and enjoying the music (cf. Akin, 1980; Charnass, 1979; Chiesi, Spilich, & Voss, 1979; Egan & Schwartz, 1979).
3. A rich knowledge base provides "gist" for the strategy mill. If one knew nothing about a topic, it would be tough to write an essay, even by dutifully applying the Hayes and Flower (1980) writing strategy. Also, instructions to use associative mnemonics more certainly promote associative learning when relationships between the to-be-learned pairs are readily retrievable from the learner's knowledge base (e.g., Pressley & Levin, 1977b).
4. Monitoring and consequent shifts in processing are critically dependent on the knowledge base. Consider reading comprehension strategies. To decide

whether a strategy is producing miscomprehension, one must have a knowledge base that conflicts with what one thinks one just read! A main mechanism of comprehension monitoring is detection of such mismatches. The deployment of fix-up strategies depends on a well-developed knowledge base.

Because research on strategy-knowledge base interactions is in its embryonic stage, and because such research is covered in detail elsewhere (Chi, 1978), we do not consider it further here. Even though the search for strategy × knowledge interactions continues, the emphasis on strategies as a main effect in this chapter is defensible because children are called upon so often to learn materials that are very unfamiliar to them (e.g., new vocabulary words), or they are presented tasks that cannot be accomplished by using the knowledge base alone (e.g., efficient summarization). We recommend as recent examples of strategy × knowledge-base interactions studies such as those reported by Rohwer, Rabinowitz, and Dronkers (1982) and Siegler and Shrager (1984), but will confine our subsequent commentary to strategy use, specific strategy knowledge, and strategy monitoring.

Strategy Instructional Research

Although an important goal of all strategy instruction researchers is to discover how to produce efficient strategy users, researchers have differed in their tactics for achieving this goal. On the one hand, there are intensive studies of individual components of efficient strategy use (i.e., strategies, monitoring, and to a much lesser extent, specific strategy knowledge). There also have been examinations of packages containing all of these elements. The differences between these two research tactics and the advantages and disadvantages of each are pronounced.

Intensive Study of the Individual Components of Strategy Use: Strategies, Specific Strategy Knowledge, Monitoring

Most strategy researchers have focused their attention on one of the components of strategy use considered critical to efficient strategy functioning (or at least on one component at a time). Consequently, work on efficient strategy functioning has been fragmented, although a great deal has been learned about each of these components.

Strategy research. A few strategies have been studied intensively, ones that are theoretically and/or practically important. We now possess detailed information on rehearsal (e.g., Ornstein & Naus, 1978), organizational strategies (Moely, 1977; Lange, 1978), imagery-elaboration approaches to associative learning (e.g., Pressley, 1982), and imaginal approaches to text memory and comprehension (e.g., Levin & Lesgold, 1978), as well as some others. Each of the strategies proved to have complicated and different developmental courses; also, strategy instructional recommendations vary across strategies/processes. For instance, although rehearsal is easy to teach to nonusers (e.g., Flavell, 1970), instruction in imaginal elaboration is sometimes difficult (e.g., Bender & Levin, 1976). The success of elaboration instruction often depends on the mode of materials (e.g., Pressley & Levin, 1978), whereas the effects of rehearsal and organizational strategies do not seem to vary with mode of presentation (Moely, 1977). Instructing children to use imagery in associative situations is easier than instructing them to use it in memorizing prose (cf. Pressley, 1977), with benefits much greater in associative tasks. These differences in outcomes make obvious that one cannot do research on one strategy/process and generalize the pattern of outcomes to another strategy with any confidence. Attempts to do so must necessarily be very gross (cf. Paris & Cross, 1983), lacking detail that is absolutely necessary in order to make useful instructional recommendations.

A main conclusion that follows from research on particular strategies is that strategy instructional effects are very situationally specific. Understanding these specificities is critical before educational dissemination of a strategy can occur. The many potential dimensions of specificity are illustrated by considering research on the keyword method.

Early keyword research identified developmental constraints associated with the strategy. Although imagery-generation versions of the strategy were difficult for young grade-school children to execute (e.g., Pressley & Levin, 1978), alternative versions of the strategy based on verbal elaboration and mnemonic pictures did benefit young children (e.g., Pressley, Samuel, Hershey, Bishop, & Dickinson, 1981; Pressley, Levin, & McCormick, 1980). How far can the strategy be stretched as an aid to learning? It is helpful in learning second-language vocabulary (e.g., Atkinson & Raugh, 1975), first-language vocabulary (e.g., Levin, McCormick, Miller, Berry, & Pressley, 1982; Pressley, Levin, & Miller, 1981), prose (e.g., Shriberg, Levin, McCormick, & Pressley, 1982), and a variety of science and social studies factual materials (e.g., Jones & Hall, 1982; Levin, Dretzke, McCormick, Scruggs, McGivern, & Mastropieri, 1983; Mastropieri, 1983; Pressley & Dennis-Rounds, 1980). The method benefits recall of meanings without debilitating comprehension of vocabulary (Dretzke, Levin, Pressley, & McGivern, 1983; Pressley, Levin, & Miller, 1981), although going from the meaning to the word using a keyword mediator can introduce problems (Pressley & Levin, 1981). The method is more effective than alternative procedures, many of which are widely recommended in the literature (e.g., Levin, Jonson, Pittelman, Hayes, Levin, & Shriberg, 1983; Pressley, Levin, Kuiper, Bryant, & Michener, 1982; Pressley, Levin, & Miller, 1982). In addition, the method can be taught successfully in grade-school classrooms (Levin, Pressley, McCormick, Miller, & Shriberg, 1979), although classroom benefits with older learners are more elusive (Levin et al., 1979). This latter finding is consistent with other data suggesting that keyword effects with adults may be highly constrained, especially so with very good adult learners who are strategic without instruction (e.g., McDaniel & Pressley, 1984).

In summary, the detailed evaluation of the keyword method has provided a wealth of critical information for moving the keyword method out of the laboratory and into actual educational settings. See Pressley, Levin, and Delaney (1982) and Levin (in press) for more complete summaries of this data base.

Although there exist detailed analyses of a few strategies, such as the keyword method, there are many other strategies with potential for educational application that either have not been investigated or have been given insufficient study. These include strategies based on theoretical conceptions of memory, such as meaningful orientation strategies (e.g., Waters & Waters, 1979; Pressley & Bryant, 1982) which follow from depth-of-processing analyses (Craik & Lockhart, 1972); schematically guided encoding and retrieval strategies (e.g., Gordon & Braun, 1983; Singer & Donlan, 1982) which are products of schema-based theories of prose representation (e.g., Rumelhart, 1980); and attentional strategies (e.g., Pressley & Bryant, 1982) based on traditional notions of relationships between attention and performance. Strategies have also been derived from analyzing the performances of expert learners, with Brown and Day's (1983) summarization strategy being a prime example of this genre. A third source of strategies is the traditional curriculum and instruction literature. Strategies such as SQ3R (Robinson, 1961) are well known and widely recommended, but not well studied (Johns & McNamara, 1980). Given the increasing recognition of the potency of cognitive strategies (e.g., Pressley & Levin, 1983a,b), it is likely that many more strategies will be evaluated systematically in the near future.

Monitoring research. Initial work on monitoring was concerned with documenting monitoring deficiencies (e.g., Markman, 1981) and understanding the significance of those deficiencies (Flavell, 1979, 1981). A more recent concern is determining how monitoring can be established in children who do not do it spontaneously. The monitoring training studied most widely to date involves teaching children explicit criteria for deciding that something is wrong with a passage. Markman and Gorin's (1981) version of this approach illustrates training of this type.

Markman and Gorin (1981) presented 8- and 10-year-olds with a series of passages, some of which were flawed. Defective passages contained falsehoods, including statements such as, "They sleep on tree tops, where cool, soft grass grows." Passages with inconsistencies included conflicting statements such as, "[Koalas] will sleep only high up on the tops of trees," and "[Koalas] sleep on the ground in the cool, soft grass." Subjects were assigned to one of three types of instruction. In the falsehood set training condition children were alerted to look for falsehoods and were provided examples of them. Sample inconsistencies were presented in the inconsistency set training condition as subjects were alerted to look for sentences that contradicted one another. Children in the neutral set condition were told only to look for problems. Detection of problems was higher in both of the training set conditions than in the neutral set condition. More inconsistencies were detected in the inconsistency set condition than in the falsehood set condition, and more falsehoods were detected in the falsehood set condition than in the inconsistency set condition. Detection of both types of errors was better in both instructional conditions than in the neutral condition. Thus, Markman and Gorin (1981) substantiated that simply providing more explicit directions and criteria for monitoring can increase detection of problems, an outcome consistent with other findings relevant to this approach (e.g., Pratt & Bates, 1982).

Recent training efforts included more extensive instruction than Markman and Gorin's (1981) work and resulted in greater gains. Elliott-Faust and Pressley (1984) presented grade-school children with passages similar to the ones used by Markman (1977, 1979), again with some passages containing inconsistencies. The study included control conditions in which children were told only to find the errors, conditions in which children were presented standards of evaluation in a fashion similar to that employed by Markman and Gorin (1981) in the inconsistency set condition, and conditions in which children were given more elaborate training. In one of these latter conditions, children were taught to compare contiguous sentences of the passages against one another to determine if they made sense. This instruction involved extensive practice and feedback. In an even more elaborate instructional condition, children were instructed explicitly to evaluate each sentence against the whole meaning of the passage. Again, much practice doing this and feedback were provided. In the most elaborate instructional condition, subjects were taught a self-instructional scheme for comparing the meaning of individual sentences against the meaning of the entire paragraph that it was embedded in. In general, the most elaborate instructions produced better monitoring than occurred in the control conditions or when learners were only provided the appropriate standard of evaluation. Miller (in press) has also examined self-instructional training procedures for comprehension monitoring and has obtained positive results as well, both immediately following training and on 3-week delayed assessments.

Progress is being made in identifying ways to increase children's monitoring. We expect a plethora of research on a variety of monitoring processes including checking, determining if what one reads makes sense, reviewing, comparing one's interpretation of an event against world knowledge, comparing performance on the current occasion with previous performances, self-interrogation, and self-testing. When such research is completed, it should be possible to specify much better how monitoring can and should be developed.

Specific strategy knowledge. Specific strategy knowledge is the most novel aspect of the present model, and is also the component that most resembles a black box. It is easy to construct a list of what can be known about strategies— one can know when the strategy is appropriate, how easy it is to carry out the technique, and which parts of the strategy are mandatory and which optional. The more challenging questions pertain to the importance of the various facets of specific storage knowledge for cognitive regulation. What metamemory should be trained to promote effective strategy deployment? To date there has been very little research on any aspects of metamemory about strategies, except that adding utility information to an instruction increases strategy maintenance (e.g., Black & Rollins, 1982; Borkowski, Levers, & Gruenenfelder, 1976; Cavanaugh & Borkowski, 1979; Kennedy & Miller, 1976; Lawson & Fuelop, 1980; Ringel & Springer, 1980).

Determining how adding specific strategy knowledge affects strategy regulation should be a high priority. Virtually all discussions of sophisticated strategy use accept as axiomatic that the more that one knows about a strategy, the more likely the generalized use of the strategy (e.g., Brown, 1978; Brown et al., 1983; Flavell, 1979). One of the more complete commentaries was offered by Belmont, Butterfield, and Ferreti (1982). Those authors analyzed studies of strategy instruction that had produced durable strategy use versus those that had not. Successful instructions included self-management components, such as directions to evaluate the strengths and weakness of a strategy and to evaluate whether a trained strategy actually worked—activities that should lead to increased specific strategy knowledge. Belmont et al.'s (1982) across-experiment comparisons of training procedures varying in completeness suggested that bare-bones strategy instructions are much less effective than ones that include when, where, and how information.

A recent study provided a within-experiment evaluation of the effects of adding specific strategy knowledge to instruction, permitting cause-and-effect conclusions not possible from comparisons across studies such as the analysis reported by Belmont et al. (1982). O'Sullivan and Pressley (1984) hypothesized, based on long-standing analyses of transfer (e.g., Gagné, 1977; House, 1982; Thorndike & Woodworth, 1901), that adding information about how and when to use a strategy would increase transfer of the keyword method. Children in grades 5 and 6 and adults were presented two memory tasks during the study, first learning pairings between cities and their products and then acquiring definitions of Latin vocabulary words. Control subjects learned both sets of materials with no strategy instructions. Subjects in all other conditions learned the city–product pairs using the keyword method, which is effective with such materials (Pressley & Dennis-Rounds, 1980). These keyword training conditions varied with respect to how explicitly subjects were told how and when keyword mnemonics are helpful. In the most explicit conditions, such information was conveyed verbally and illustrated with multiple exemplars. In the least explicit keyword training condition, where and when information was not presented at all, with "how" information presented without the embellishment that occurred in the more explicit conditions.

The most important dependent variable in the study was whether subjects transferred the keyword strategy to the Latin vocabulary task, which also benefits from keyword application (e.g., Pressley & Dennis-Rounds, 1980). In general, with children transfer was greater when the keyword instruction explicitly contained a lot of information about how and when to use the strategy. Adults' transfer was high regardless of the explicitness of strategy information included in the instructions. Adults probably abstract more knowledge about a strategy from simple instructions and practice than do children, making the explicit provision of such information much more crucial with children (cf. Pressley, Levin, & Ghatala, 1984).

Although the O'Sullivan and Pressley (1984) study allowed stronger cause-and-effect conclusions than previous work, it did not provide fine-grained conclusions about particularly critical aspects of specific strategy knowledge, nor did it provide extensive insights into optimal ways of inducing that metamemory, except to suggest that children need more explicit tuition than do adults. Much more work is needed on these themes. What O'Sullivan and Pressley (1984) provided was preliminary evidence that increasing information about a strategy during instruction makes an important difference in children's generalized strategy use. In doing so, it provides motivation for additional study.

Summary. Research on strategies, monitoring, and specific strategy knowledge continues, with most workers who are interested in strategies focusing on one of these three aspects of efficient strategy use. Although much has been learned about these components, and especially about strategies (e.g., Pressley, Heisel, McCormick, & Nakamura, 1982), the disconnectedness that results from studying the individual components of strategy use is disturbing given the integrative nature of the present model.

What is needed ultimately are higher-order frameworks that provide meaningful integrations of strategies, specific strategy knowledge, and monitoring. Learners need to be taught to coordinate the three components. A main assumption of those studying individual components is that the design of such higher-order integrations will be facilitated by knowing a lot about the individual components. Thus, there is no rush to study higher-order treatment packages. Alternatively, others have designed higher-order training packages given what is currently known about strategies, metamemory about those strategies, and monitoring.

Training Packages

There are many strategy training procedures that combine strategies, monitoring, and specific strategy knowledge. Packages exist for training memory (e.g., Asarnow & Meichenbaum, 1979), for improving math skills (e.g., Neilans & Israel, 1981), for treating impulsivity (e.g., Egeland, 1974; Kendall & Wilcox, 1980), and for improving complex motor skills (e.g., Kirschenbaum, Ordman, Tomarken, & Holtzbauer, 1982), to mention but a few. Campione et al. (1982) labeled such multicomponent treatments as self-control training. This label followed from the hypothesized outcome of such instruction, self-regulated and appropriate use of the trained strategy. Campione et al. (1982) consider self-control training the preferred approach to strategy instruction, based largely on training successes generated in their laboratories. A review of two of these studies provides a flavor of this approach.

Palincsar and Brown's (in press, Experiment 1) study involved seventh-grade poor readers who were either provided a type of self-control training or who served as control subjects not receiving training. Instruction was intended to increase reading comprehension. The self-control training included teaching the children to summarize what they read, to question as they read along, to predict what might be coming in the story, and to clarify meaning. These skills were taught through one-to-one student–teacher interaction in the form of a game in which student and teacher took turns leading a dialog. These dialogues contained a number of mechanisms to induce summarizing, questioning, predicting, and clarifying. When a new passage was presented, the teacher asked the learner to predict passage content based on the title and to predict how the passage might relate to prior knowledge. After reading the passage, the student was asked to recall the topic and several important points. Teacher and student asked each other questions, summarized, and offered predictions and clarifications throughout the course of reading the passage. Predictions were sometimes obtained by asking, "What question do you think the teacher might ask?" Summarizing was prompted with, "Remember a summary is a shortened version, it doesn't include detail." Praise and feedback were provided throughout the teacher modeling activities when the learner appeared to have difficulty.

Thus, the multicomponent package included many strategies, some of which were monitoring techniques. Learners were made aware that if one can summarize or predict what questions will be asked, that is a good sign that one has understood the passage. Knowledge about the strategies and the total package was explicitly provided as well. Subjects were told that the purpose of these activities was to aid comprehension. They were also explicitly instructed to use the strategies taught to them as they read. The 10–13 days of modeling and feedback afforded many opportunities for the teacher to provide information about the strategy.

The results of the Palincsar and Brown (in press) study supported the conclusion that the self-control training lead to general improvement. Reading comprehension increased after training was initiated, and the comprehension scores of trained subjects following instruction exceeded those of control learners. Comprehension gains transferred to in-the-classroom tasks related to reading. Comprehension of social studies and science materials presented during class time was better in the trained children than in the control children. The trained children also could provide better summaries of texts than control children and could generate better questions about a text than control children. Finally, trained children's detection of text incongruities improved as a function of training. There was no doubt that the instruction had an important impact on children's reading.

Other studies of comprehensive training have been reported by the Illinois group (e.g., Brown & Barclay, 1976; Brown, Campione, & Barclay, 1979), with such training producing generalized increases in strategy use. Just as in the reading comprehension study, however, there was no way of identifying the active ingredients of training, a shortcoming of this research approach that Brown and her associates acknowledge (Palincsar & Brown, in press). Those investigators feel it essential first to identify effective treatment packages before trying to decompose them into effective and ineffective components. See Pressley (1979) for commentary on this research approach.

To their credit the Illinois group has initiated research that analyzes some of their multicomponent packages. Day (1980) illustrates this type of experimentation. Day trained adults who had difficulty with efficient summarizing to summarize using the five-part strategy identified by Brown and Day (1983). In the most elaborated treatment condition summarization-rule training was taught along with knowledge about the strategy and monitoring. The subjects were trained to use the five summarization rules, and they were taught to monitor the adequacies of their summaries. For example, subjects were taught that topic sentence generation should be accompanied with a check that the topic sentence accurately reflected the meaning of the paragraph. It was emphasized in this condition to check and double check the summarization product to assure that it reduced the material and did so accurately. Although the training included explicit presentation of a substantial amount of information about the strategy, feedback about the summaries should have increased learners' specific strategy knowledge even further. In addition to this very complete training condition, Day (1980) included three other conditions, each consisting of a subset of the input included in the most complete condition. One condition involved rules training and self-management training, although strategy rules, metamemory, and monitoring were not as well integrated as in the most complete condition. A third group was taught the five summarization rules only; a fourth monitoring skills only (e.g., to check summaries as proceeding along).

Monitoring training alone did not result in improved summaries between pretest and posttest. Improvement did occur in the other three conditions, with the most noticeable change being improvement in one of the more complex aspects of summarizing, that is, finding or inventing a topic sentence. Although the posttest differences in performance between the three conditions that included strategy rules were not large, they were in the predicted direction with summaries in the most comprehensive condition better than in the other two conditions.

Day's (1980) study is a good example of how to determine if adding monitoring instruction to strategy training enhances the use of a strategy. Other aspects of the comprehensive condition could have been evaluated with the addition of a few other conditions. For instance, the amount of knowledge provided about the summarizing strategy could have been varied systematically. Nonetheless, Day's (1980) experiment was an ambitious test of her hypothesis that adding monitoring to summarization training enhances effects with low-ability learners.

In summary, self-control training includes all of the components assumed necessary for efficient strategy use. This comprehensive approach has been evaluated in training populations who are known to be highly deficient in cognitive processing (e.g., impulsive children, retarded children, low-ability adults). It is reasonable to assume, as Campione et al. (1982) do, that these disadvantaged subjects would fail to monitor strategy effectiveness even if they were in possession of an effective strategy for a task. Also, it would be expected that they would be less likely than higher-ability learners to abstract specific strategy knowledge from strategic experiences. Thus, much effort is devoted to self-control training to enhancing monitoring and learners' knowledge of how, when, and where to use strategies. That that effort can pay off is documented amply by the generalized gains in performance obtained in these experiments.

Studying Components of Efficient Strategy Use Versus Studying Self-Control Training Packages

Given that the goal of strategy instruction is to produce efficient strategy users, why study the instruction of individual components of efficient strategy use? Why not study only efficient strategy use in toto—study only self-control training packages?

1. Extensive self-control training is not always needed. Self-control packages were developed specifically for use with deficient populations. Strategy instruction alone is sufficient for sophisticated subjects in some situations. For instance, when adults are given keyword method instructions, they monitor strategy utility even without explicit instructions to do so (Pressley, Levin, & Ghatala, 1984). Also, even very simple keyword instructions, ones that are almost devoid of knowledge about the strategy, produce generalized use of the technique with adults (e.g., O'Sullivan & Pressley, 1984; Pressley & Dennis-Round, 1980). Thus, for some groups self-control training would be a waste of instructional resources.

   As discussed earlier, production deficiencies can be due to massive deficiencies in strategy deployment, monitoring, and specific strategy knowledge or be due to problems in any one component. For maximum efficiency training should be adjusted accordingly.

2. The specific components combined into self-control training packages may not be the best components that could be placed in such training. Through study of the individual components, unconfounded with other aspects of training, it may be possible to isolate powerful strategies, monitoring

techniques, and aspects of specific strategy knowledge that make important differences in cognition. That is a main strength of studying individual components. After thorough study of components, it should be possible to piece together training packages in a much more intelligent fashion.
3. A corollary of point 2 is that little is learned about the characteristics of specific components from evaluation of a self-control training package, except that strategy X works well when trained with monitoring procedure Y and knowledge A, B, and C.

Closing Comment

In closing, it is encouraging that both approaches to strategy research specify that strategies, monitoring, and specific strategy metamemory are important, with the assumption that efficient learners have an optimal mix of all three. It is a safe bet that both types of research will fill the pages of scholarly journals in coming years given the apparent commitments of the researchers contributing to these efforts. This is a good situation. Although we have reservations about the analytical gains that follow from self-control training, there is no doubt that such research provides a clear reminder of an important goal of strategy training—producing strategy users who by keeping track of their performances and being well informed about strategies, use them to maximum advantage. On the other hand, the efforts of researchers studying the instruction of individual components should provide information as to when self-control instruction is overkill, as well as provide knowledge about types of strategies, monitoring procedures, and pieces of information that can be added to packages most profitably.

Although we view all of the research on strategy instruction discussed in this section in a positive light and relevant to the model of efficient strategy deployment presented earlier, none of the research discussed so far provided systematic analysis of strategies, specific strategy knowledge, and monitoring within single studies. A program of research being carried out at the University of Western Ontario, the University of Wisconsin, and the University of Houston has begun to fill in that important empirical gap.

Research on Strategy Shifts, Specific Strategy Knowledge, and Monitoring

Strategy Shifts During Associative Learning

One of the main assumptions of the strategies/specific strategy knowledge/monitoring model is well supported by data. Learners change strategies as they proceed through intellectual tasks (e.g., Battig, 1974; Butterfield & Belmont, 1977; Butterfield, Siladi, & Belmont, 1980; Paivio & Yuille, 1969; Sommerville & Wellman, 1979), although most studies documenting this phenomenon did not provide information relevant to all aspects of the model considered here. The research program discussed in this section was designed to accomplish that goal.

Pressley, Levin, Ghatala and their associates recently completed a series of studies that elucidate relationships between memory strategy use, specific strategy knowledge, and memory strategy monitoring. In all of these experiments, as learners tried various strategies, their monitoring of strategy efficacy was assessed. Shifts in metamemory about strategy potency were related to strategy use decisions.

Pressley, Levin, & Ghatala's (1984) Adult Study. Pressley, Levin, and Ghatala (1984) required adults to acquire the meanings of foreign vocabulary items. On initial vocabulary-learning trials, subjects were instructed to alternate between two strategies for learning vocabulary items. Learners used the keyword method for half of the items and a verbal rehearsal strategy for the rest. The keyword method is much more potent than rehearsal for this task (e.g., Atkinson & Raugh, 1975; Raugh & Atkinson, 1975). Subjects either received no strategy efficacy information from the experimenter during instruction or were deceived by him or her, being told that rehearsal was the better strategy. After studying one vocabulary set using the two methods, subjects took a meaning recall test. Either immediately preceding or immediately following this test, subjects were asked to select one of the two strategies to learn a second list of vocabulary.

Subjects were faithful to the strategy execution instructions, elaborating and rehearsing appropriate items on the first list, with keyword recall exceeding control recall. In general, subjects making strategy selections after the recall test chose the elaboration strategy even if the experimenter told them rehearsal was the superior strategy. Subjects who were provided no strategy recommendations and who made their selection before the test chose the keyword strategy at a slightly greater than chance level; subjects given the repetition recommendation and who made their selections before the test chose the rehearsal strategy. The choice data were complemented by a variety of measures tapping the learner's awareness of strategy efficacy. These revealed that taking the test was an important metacognitive experience (Flavell, 1979)—understanding that the keyword was superior increased as a function of taking the test. After taking the test (but not before), adults made their strategy choices on the basis of relative strategy potency.

How do these results fit the model of strategy use summarized earlier? Subjects making choices after the test had had opportunity to monitor the relative recall of keyworded versus rehearsed items and did so (cf. Brown & Lawton, 1977; Moynahan, 1973). The product of that monitoring, relative strategy utility information, which is a form of specific strategy knowledge, was used to direct subsequent strategy selection. Pressley, Levin, and Ghatala's

(1984) adults were highly sensitive to their recall performances and realized that such information is of considerable value.

Strategy practice, monitoring, and future strategy decisions are not as tightly interwoven in children as in adults. Data generated in four recent studies illustrate that children's monitoring and use of relative strategy utility is far from optimal. Each study, however, identified methods for improving effective strategy selections. We present a brief synopsis of the four research efforts and then an integrative commentary on the significance of the child studies.

Pressley, Levin, & Ghatala's (1984) Child Study. Pressley, Levin, and Ghatala (1984) included a sample of fifth and sixth graders. In contrast to the adults, child learners given the rehearsal recommendation selected rehearsal, even after taking the test. The complete pattern of results (choice data, interview data) suggested that although children's monitoring of strategy efficacy was not as accurate as adults, they did detect the keyword superiority during the test. They did not use the relative utility information that was monitored to make their strategy decisions—the product of monitoring was not used in an executive fashion. However, if children were told their exact recall of keyword and rehearsal items before strategy selection (i.e., they were provided feedback), they elected the keyword strategy despite the experimenter's rehearsal recommendation.

Lodico, Ghatala, Levin, Pressley, and Bell (1983). Lodico, Ghatala, Levin, Pressley, and Bell (1983) first trained 7–8-year-old children in their experimental condition to monitor performance when using different approaches to a problem. Training was given with materials and tasks quite different from the criterion memory tasks. For instance, the first training task was to draw a circle, with children first drawing freehand and then using a round cookie cutter. Then subjects were asked to evaluate which method produced the better circle, specify why it worked, and decide which method they would use if asked to draw another circle. These training procedures were repeated with a letter-learning task, with letters presented either randomly or so as to spell the child's name. Throughout this training feedback about the adequacy of answers was provided to the children. During the period corresponding to training in the experimental condition, control subjects played the circle and letter games and practiced the same strategies as experimental subjects except that no monitoring instructions were provided. After training the children were told they would be playing more games, with experimental subjects reminded to keep track of their performance so they would select the better game-playing strategy. The children then learned two practice lists of paired associates and were tested on the pairings. They used a potent elaboration strategy to learn one list and an ineffective rehearsal strategy to learn the other one. When given a third paired-associate list to learn, the experimental children were more likely to select elaboration than the control condition, despite the fact that both experimental and control subjects realized that their recall of the elaborated practice list was higher than their recall of the rehearsal practice list. What training accomplished was not to increase awareness of relative strategy efficacy, but to increase use of the information derived from monitoring in making the executive decision of choosing the elaboration method.

McGivern, Levin, Ghatala, and Pressley (1983). Children and adults watched a videotape of a person learning paired associates, with half of the items studied with an overt verbal elaboration strategy and half studied with an overt rehearsal procedure. Immediately after the videotape of studying ended, control subjects chose one of the two strategies for learning another list of paired associates. Children in the congruent condition made a choice after watching the model study and seeing the model take a recall test, with greater recall for elaborated than rehearsed pairs, congruent with the actual effects produced by the strategies. In the incongruent conditon strategy choice followed viewing a tape in which the model's recall clashed with real-world outcomes—more rehearsal than elaborated items were recalled. After making strategy choices, subjects' perceptions of the model's performance were assessed, with the main focus the determination of whether subjects realized which type of pairs were better recalled by the model.

Utility monitoring of the model's performance did not guide children's strategy choices. At the second-grade level, about one fourth of the subjects did not even encode which pair type was recalled better; even when the model's relative performance was noted, there was no relationship between these perceptions and the children's strategy choices. Choice of the elaboration strategy was actually lowest in the congruent condition, although the proportion of subjects choosing elaboration did not differ significantly between the three conditions (congruent = 19%, incongruent = 44%, and control = 31%). At the fifth-grade level, most subjects encoded the model's performance with the two pair types, but the between-condition effects were small, again with 56% choice of elaboration in the congruent condition, 50% elaboration usage in the incongruent condition, and 31% elaboration in the control condition. Since the chance level of elaboration selection was 50%, the conclusion that follows is that strategy selection was not influenced by the model's performance.

After watching the videotapes and making strategy selections, subjects were tested on their memories of the paired items studied by the model. Recall of elaborated pairs exceeded recall of rehearsed pairs as expected. After taking this test, selection of elaboration was higher than before the test with 69% of Grade 2 subjects choosing elaboration and 79% of Grade 5 children doing so, with no significant between-condition differences in the proportions of subjects choosing elaboration at either age level. This increased selection of the more effective strategy after subjects were tested suggested that monitoring that occurs as one takes a test has more impact than monitoring of someone else's performance on a test.

Consistent with the adult outcomes in Pressley, Levin, and Ghatala (1984), McGivern et al.'s (1983) adults coordinated monitoring and strategy choices better than children did. Particularly impressive after viewing the congruent model was that 81% of subjects selected elaboration, with chance level strategy selection in the other two conditions. Accurate, modeled feedback affected the strategy choices of adults even though it had no effect on children's strategy choices.

Children's failure to use observationally gained utility information is not restricted to the situation studied by McGivern et al. (1983). For instance, Brown (1980, pp. 461–462) reported ongoing research in her laboratory in which children watched models using both effective and ineffective strategies for list learning. Just as in McGivern et al. (1983), children discerned which strategies were more effective, but used ineffective strategies to perform the same tasks themselves.

Pressley, Ross, Levin, and Ghatala (in press). Grade-school children practiced learning vocabulary using the potent keyword method and a meaningful context strategy that is widely recommended and familiar to children, but ineffective (e.g., Pressley, Levin, Kuiper, Bryant, & Michener, 1982)—a context method that the preponderance of children select over the keyword method when given a choice between the two techniques without an opportunity to practice them. After practice study combined with a test on the practice items, the children were required to select one of the two methods for use on another list of vocabulary. The majority of children selected the context strategy unless (a) they had been told just before strategy selection to think back to the types of words (keyword or context) they had just recalled on the test, or (b) they were given explicit feedback on the number of keyword and context words remembered. In those two cases almost all children selected the keyword technique. Consistent with the Pressley, Levin, and Ghatala (1984) child data and Lodico et al.'s (1983) data, more than 75% of the subjects in Pressley, Ross, Levin, and Ghatala (in press) realized that keyword was better after doing the practice list and taking the test. Unless prompted to do so, however, children did not use this information in strategy selection. Children often produce knowledge as a function of experience, and yet fail to use that knowledge in directing subsequent cognition (cf. Bransford, Stein, Shelton, & Owings, 1981).

Ghatala, Levin, Pressley, and Lodico (in press). One reasonable criticism of the studies discussed thus far in this section is that the strategy choice paradigm is a bit unusual. Most strategy instructional research involves training of single strategies which are presumed to be effective. Ghatala et al. (in press) remedied this deficiency by examining the training of single strategies.

Second-grade subjects in Ghatala et al. (in press) were given three study/test trials on a paired-associate task with a different set of items on each trial. On the first study/test trial (baseline) children studied paired associates without strategy instructions. On the second study/test trial, half of the children were required to use elaboration and half were instructed to count the letters in the paired items, a very ineffective strategy even relative to baseline levels. Immediately following the second study/test trial, subjects were given a third study/test trial and were told that they could learn the pairs any way that they wished, but that they were to try to remember as many pairs as possible. Following the third test trial, subjects were asked to explain why they used particular strategies. Several delayed tests of strategy maintenance were given to the subjects who had been required to use elaboration on the second trial.

Prior to the three study/test trials on the paired-associate task, one third of the children had been taught to monitor strategy effectiveness and use strategy utility information following procedures used in Lodico et al. (1983). Another third of the children were trained to monitor whether strategies are fun. The rest of the children, referred to as control learners, received no monitoring training. The "fun" monitoring condition was included because fun monitoring requires reflection on and making judgments about strategic behaviors, thus controlling for these aspects of training. Performance differences between the utility and fun monitoring conditions would be due to type of monitoring and not monitoring training per se.

The 3 (levels of monitoring training) × 2 (levels of strategies) experiment provided straightforward results. On trial 1 recall levels in all six conditions were comparable, as would be expected since none of the children had been taught strategies for learning. The differences in strategy training at this point involved only monitoring strategies, and since second-grade children do not possess effective strategies for associative learning, they possessed no effective strategy to remedy learning difficulty even if they did monitor learning problems.

On trial 2, recall was higher than baseline in all elaboration training conditions; recall was lower than baseline in counting conditions. Trial 2 recall did not vary as a function of monitoring training—again not unexpected, since what learners did on trial 2 was strictly limited to the trained strategy.

Trial 3 recall was higher in the elaboration-training conditions than in the counting-strategy conditions, because subjects trained to use elaboration continued to use it. The counting strategy was abandoned by subjects trained to use it on trial 2. There was clear evidence of monitoring of strategy effectiveness. All children taught elaboration realized that they remembered more items on the second trial than on the first trial; most children taught counting knew that they remembered more on trial 1 than on trial 2. Despite accurate monitoring, children often failed to interpret the recall differences as due to the use of strategies! Only learners trained to monitor utility attributed differential recall to the use of strategies. Also, only these subjects reported making third trial decisions based on how the strategy affected memory. In short, without strategy-utility training, monitoring was not tied tightly to third-trial strategy use. Once again, optimal executive decisions did not follow from monitoring automatically.

One could argue based on the third-trial data that this failure of children to relate prior recall to strategy choices is inconsequential, since effective strategy use on trial 2 invariably leads to effective strategy use on trial 3. However, it did not do so on 1-week and 9-week maintenance trials. Long-term maintenance of elaboration was higher when strategy-utility monitoring training preceded elaboration instruction.

Summary. The general methodology was the same in Pressley, Levin, and Ghatala (1984), Lodico et al. (1983), McGivern et al. (1983), Pressley, Ross, Levin, and Ghatala (in press), and in Ghatala et al. (in press), a methodology apropos to the model of strategy use proposed in this chapter. In all studies possession of the strategies of interest was guaranteed—subjects were instructed explicitly in their use. One particular aspect of specific strategy knowledge was assessed—understanding the relative potency of the strategies. All experiments included an executive decision—choice of a strategy.

Results across studies were consistent and complementary. Pressley, Levin, and Ghatala (1984) documented that monitoring of keyword potency occurred during a test on a practice list that was studied using the two strategies. The knowledge of relative strategy efficacy gained during monitoring of test performance determined adults' subsequent strategy decisions. With children, monitoring, strategy knowledge, and strategy use are not coordinated nearly as well. Although children note relative strategy potency during practice study/ testing and while observing others study/test, their use of that information is more variable than is the case with adults. More positively, explicit feedback about recall with the two strategies increases use of the more effective strategy (Pressley, Levin, & Ghatala, 1984); training learners to abstract relative effectiveness information and to use that information in decision making (Ghatala et al., in press; Lodico et al., 1983) and teaching children to attend to relative strategy efficacy information that they possess (Pressley, Ross, Levin, & Ghatala, in press) also increases the likelihood of effective strategy selections.

In closing this section, we emphasize that determining relationships between strategy use, metacognition, and monitoring requires within-experiment study of strategy use, changes in strategy use, specific strategy knowledge, and monitoring. Although few studies in the area of memory have tapped all of these dimensions, such comprehensive documentation of strategy dynamics is even rarer in other strategy domains, although such work certainly could be carried out. Research on the important problem of reading strategies is a good case in point.

Strategy Shifts During Reading

In terms of the model developed in this chapter, when sophisticated learners are first presented a text and a particular goal (e.g., comprehending the most important information in the text), they elect some subset of the prose-learning strategies they possess. As reading and comprehension proceeds, the reader monitors performance including adequacy of decodings, comprehension, congruence between what is read and world knowledge, and whether the strategy is enjoyable and easy to execute. When readers monitor that learning is going poorly, they switch to other prose-comprehension techniques. As a result of monitoring, the metamemory about the initial strategy also may change, perhaps annotated with information that the technique is not so good with the type of passage just read or given the amount of time allotted for the present task.

Models of reading which include strategy, monitoring-, and specific strategy knowledge-type components similar to the ones outlined here have been around for a long time (e.g., Huey, 1908; Thorndike, 1917). See Forrest-Pressley and Gilles (1983) for additional commentary on this point. However, there are few single studies that tap information about all three main components. Forrest-Pressley and Waller (1984) was one that did provide such comprehensive information. The project was concerned with cognitive and metacognitive aspects of reading, with separate investigations of decoding, reading comprehension, language, attention, and memory. Due to space limitations, only work on comprehension is considered here.

Third-grade and sixth-grade children were presented passages to read, under four different instructional sets. Children "read for fun," "read for a title," "read to find one specific piece of information (skim)," and "read to study." Reading was followed by questions about the passages. After responding to a question, the child indicated whether he or she was sure or not sure about whether the answer was correct. Such feelings, when combined with actual performance, provided a measure of monitoring. In general, the older children better predicted recall than younger children. Good readers made better predictions than average readers, who predicted better than poor readers. Predictions were less accurate for skimmed materials than when reading for other purposes.

Children were probed about their knowledge of comprehension and comprehension monitoring. Responses to, "How would you know when you were ready to write a test?" were more adequate with increasing age. With increasing age and ability children offered better answers to, "How would you know if the test was hard or easy?" Good readers and older readers were more likely to cite cues such as the length of time to finish, the number of items that you are sure of, etc., which indicate the difficulty of the test. In response to, "How could you tell when you knew enough about the game to teach someone else how to play a new game?," there was an increase with grade in the frequency of specific responses. In summary, sophisticated verbalizations about how one monitors one's own comprehension increased with age more than with reading ability, although on every question there was always the same direction of effect with regard to reading ability, with more able readers providing at least slightly more sophisticated responses than poorer readers.

The study also included interview measures of strategy use and what learners know about strategies. "What do you do when you read and you know that there will be a test on the story later?" Older/better readers were slightly more likely to be aware of the need for rehearsal before a test. "Can you do anything as you read that would make what you read easier to remember?" Only the older/better readers tended to indicate that strategies such as taking notes, remembering main points, and self-testing make it easier to remember what you have read. "What would you do to find the name of a place in the story?" Older/better readers were much more likely to suggest a "skim" strategy; younger/poorer readers were more likely to opt for a "just read" strategy. "What would you do so that you could remember a story to tell it to your friend?" Younger/poorer readers often suggested writing down the whole story; older/better readers suggested trying to remember the important parts.

In summary, older/better readers were aware of many more strategies than younger/poorer readers, with awareness defined as providing an appropriate strategy given a particular learning task. The older/better readers not only knew strategies, they knew when to deploy them (i.e., possessed some specific strategy knowledge).

The Forrest-Pressley and Waller (1984) research admittedly had short-comings from the point of view of the present model. Far more detailed measures of metacognition about strategies could have been gathered. On-line shifts of strategy use were not obtained. The monitoring data were not correlated with strategy use in a fine-grained fashion. Nonetheless, there was a great deal of evidence in the study consistent with the conceptualization detailed here.

The older/better readers reported more strategies and were more likely to report strategies appropriate to particular learning tasks. The older child was also more aware of how to monitor, with many third graders claiming that they would be ready to write a test after reading the story once and that they would not have any idea of how well they had done before getting the marked test back from the teacher. The reactions of Grade 6 subjects were much different. When asked how she would know when she was ready to write a test, one Grade 6 good reader replied, "Uh, well, when I, if I read the story a few times, and I got the people to ask me questions, and I couldn't answer them all, or had trouble with them, I'll probably wait a while and read some more, and try to remember everything else; and then, once I could, um, remember everything important in it, I'd probably be ready to do the test." That Grade 6 youngster knew about monitoring, as did many of the older subjects in Forrest-Pressley and Waller (1984).

Even if young/poorer readers monitor comprehension failures, the Forrest-Pressley and Waller (1984) data suggest that they would have no idea what might be done to correct the situation. For example, many young/poor readers indicated that they would practice for a test (e.g., read the story several times) but that there was nothing more that they could do to make the information easier to remember. In addition, many indicated that they read the same way for fun as they did when preparing for a test. In contrast, the older/better readers were more likely to put several strategies together in plans of attack. Based on the answers to the monitoring questions, the older/better readers also knew better when to deploy these skills. For additional examples of research documenting linkages between strategies, monitoring, and knowledge about reading strategies, see Olshavsky (1976–77) and Baker and Anderson (1982).

Closing Comment

The most novel aspect of the present model is specific strategy knowledge. Although experiments discussed here included some strategy knowledge information, efforts to date to delineate metamemory about strategies have been very constrained, with utility information studied much more frequently than any other piece of specific strategy knowledge (cf. Paris, 1978; e.g., Kennedy & Miller, 1976). What is needed is more exhaustive within-experiment efforts aimed at delineating various types of metamemory about strategies, determining how the richness of metamemory about strategies affects strategy use, and specifying how strategy use and monitoring alters specific strategy knowledge.

In comparing Brown's (1978, 1980; Brown, Bransford, Ferrara, & Campione, 1983) discussion of strategy use with the present conception, it might be argued that the Brown descriptions are richer and that the present framework is very limited. Nonetheless, the model offered here is richer than the most comprehensive research efforts to date, some of which were just reviewed. We feel that the complexity of theoretical models should not exceed greatly the complexity of research efforts. In support of this view, we can cite impressive programs of research on memory development that evolved in response to miniature models of memory processing (e.g., Flavell, 1970; Ornstein & Naus, 1978; Rohwer, 1973). Consistent with this plea for more focused theorization, we note Brown et al.'s (1983) call for research on particular metacognitive components and how these components affect very specific aspects of cognition. As a consequence of Brown et al.'s compelling arguments for more circumscribed metacognitive work, we are sure that the present effort is only one of the first of many miniature metacognitive-action models. One outcome of this shift in metacognitive theory and research will be a decreased use of the general term metacognition and increases specification of the particular metacognitive constructs and processes of interest (Brown et al., 1983). Our separation of specific strategy knowledge and monitoring is completely consistent with this approach.

What to Do for Learners Who Cannot Be Taught Efficient Strategy Use

Until this point in the chapter the emphasis has been on learners performing strategies for themselves, self-regulated strategy use, and how to develop that skill. This orientation reflects the clear stance of a number of leaders in cognitive development that efficient cognition at its very best is autonomous processing (e.g., Belmont et al., 1982; Brown, 1980; Brown & DeLoache, 1978; Campione et al., 1982). Unfortunately, self-regulated strategy deployment that is maximally effective does not always occur, even among sophisticated adult learners (e.g., Day, 1983; Gick & Holyoak, 1983; Rohwer, Raines, Eoff, & Wagner, 1977), although with high-ability, mature learners, such as college students, there is reason for optimism that adequate and flexible use of single strategies can be induced rather easily through instruction (e.g., O'Sullivan & Pressley, 1984; Pressley & Dennis-Rounds, 1980). This same optimism does not hold when dealing with retarded children (e.g., Belmont et al., 1982; Bender & Levin, 1978) and very young children (e.g., Bender & Levin, 1976). Most notably lacking are training programs for the development of extensive and well-regulated multiple-strategy repertoires in adults or children, normal or disadvantaged. Even if flexible strategy use can be trained, it may be very expensive to do so (e.g., Palincsar & Brown, in press). Thus, the training of truly efficient and extensive strategy use in some populations is a distant goal, not a present reality, and even in the future, such training may require a lot of effort.

Does that mean that available strategy and strategy training research is irrelevant to the current generation of learners who cannot become autonomous cognizers? We think not. In fact, many recommendations can now be derived from the strategy training literature to improve children's learning and performance. There is every reason to be extremely enthusiastic about the fruits of strategy research for these populations, as long as one does not put too much emphasis on autonomous performance.

Consider the illustrative strategies presented at the beginning of the chapter. Does it really matter that a child uses keyword methods autonomously? If one's goal is to increase children's associative learning, spontaneous strategy use is only important if there is nobody or nothing in the environment to cue the child to use keywords and elaboration. Associative learning per se is equivalent whether children spontaneously use elaboration or do so only under an instruction (e.g., Rohwer & Bean, 1973). When children are performing naturalistic associative tasks (e.g., vocabulary learning), they are often in settings that could provide such cuing (e.g., school). Also, there are many ways that texts presenting materials with an associative component could be modified to promote elaborative usage. For instance, the keyword method could be taught explicitly with keywords accompanying new vocabulary in text.

What about writing? Is it so important that people use writing heuristics without help? The real concern is the production of high-quality essays, not whether a person had many cues in front of them as they wrote. Consider the case of researchers writing APA manuscripts. Many frontline scholars cannot remember the order of subsections or details to be presented in methods sections. The solution to this deficiency is keeping a copy of the APA Manual at hand during the composing of articles. Does it make a difference that APA authors use this "crutch?" The article is what is important, not the means used to produce it.

What about summarization? People rarely construct summaries for their own sake. They are usually produced in response to a need; a student may require a good set of notes on an article in order to prepare for a test, or a debater may need a condensation of a newspaper story for presentation during a competition. Does it matter if students or debaters have Brown and Day's (1983) five rules in front of them as they summarize rather than use the rules without external prompting? Does it matter that they themselves think to use the summarizing rules or that a teacher or debate partner reminds them? Many times it does not. What matters for the student is that the summary allows retrieval of enough information from the article to permit successful mastery of a course requirement. For the debater the summary must allow accurate presentation of the points raised in the article.

As these examples illustrate, the products of strategy use are important, even if learners do not use strategies on their own to produce those products. Of course, relevant to this point is the massive literature documenting performance gains when strategies are carried out in response to direct instruction (e.g., Pressley, Heisel, McCormick, & Nakamura, 1982; Pressley & Levin, 1983a,b). We do not want the emphasis on efficient strategy use in this chapter to be interpreted to mean that instruction that produces such autonomous cognition is the only desirable type of instruction or the only desirable cognitive intervention. If learners do not or cannot become autonomous, instruction in strategy deployment and generous cuing of strategy use should occur. Indeed, we support as explicit prompting as necessary, including in some cases the provision of a proxy for the strategic product. Researchers interested in writing strategies have provided data on the gains associated with a variety of prompts that can be provided to young writers who do not possess an elaborated writing strategy and who probably could not develop one given current instructional technology. That work will be reviewed briefly because it illustrates a diversity of ways to cue strategy use in the context of an important educational task. Work on elaborative mnemonics will then be reviewed to illustrate gains from providing children proxies for strategic products.

Prompting Writing Strategies in Children

Children's naturalistic writing does not include the use of elaborate writing strategies such as those detailed by Hayes and Flower (1980) and discussed earlier. Also, instructional research has not advanced to the point of training children to use these types of global strategies. Nonetheless, progress in writing instruction has been steady, principally in the identification of procedures aimed at improving particular aspects of the writing process.

Bereiter and Scardamalia (1982) and their associates have recognized that a key difficulty that children experience in writing is executive in nature. When children do not plan, translate, and review as they write, it is not because they cannot perform these components of effective writing, but rather they simply fail to produce these strategies on their own. In order to test their hypothesis, Bereiter and Scardamalia studied cuing as a facilitator of children's writing.

For instance, children's essays often are notably devoid of content. An example of an opinion essay illustrates this point: "I don't think boys and girls should play on the same teams because the boys are stronger and the girls might get hurt." Working on the assumption that this expositional brevity was not due to complete ignorance of the subject matter but rather due to failure to retrieve information, Scardamalia, Bereiter, and Goelman (in press) studied simple prompts to children to say more as they wrote. Such prompting dramatically increased the amount of content generated. Other approaches intended to increase prose volume are promising as well. If before they write an essay, children are asked to write down all relevant single words on a topic that they can retrieve, the subsequent compositions are longer with more elaborated arguments.

A second deficiency is failure to plan the whole text. Bereiter and Scardamalia have studied this problem as well, and identified one procedure that promotes greater planning by children. If young writers are given the last sentence of an essay, they can construct reasonably coherent essays leading up to that sentence, especially if the last sentence involves ideas that are complex enough so that there is a lot of planning to do—a concluding sentence such as, "And so, after considering the reasons for it and the reasons against it, the duke decided to rent his castle to the vampire after all, in spite of the rumor he had heard."

Other approaches to promoting more complete essays have been examined, each involving contentless prompts that might suggest classes of materials that could be added to the essays. Bereiter, Scardamalia, Anderson, and Smart (1980) presented children a list of discourse elements in the form of imperative sentences, for example, "Give a reason for an opinion," and "Tell more about the reason." Children were instructed to write essays by choosing a directive, writing a sentence in response to it, returning to the directive menu to choose another imperative, writing to fulfill the directive, etc. The results were essays with a greater variety of discourse elements. On a more disappointing note, the judged quality of the essays and the quantity were not affected. Along a similar line, the OISE group have provided children with sets of sentence openers such as, "I think . . . ," "For example, . . . ," and "Even though . . . ," with the direction to choose one of the openers to begin each sentence in an essay. Again, some data with this technique suggest that it is promising, although Bereiter and Scardamalia (1982) also provide examples of very defective essays that followed from application of this procedure.

In addition to exploring ways to increase the amount and organization of materials in essays, methods for improving revision skills have also been explored (Scardamalia & Bereiter, in press). One approach is to have children revise sentence by sentence, selecting an evaluation for each sentence from a list of evaluations provided to the children (e.g., "People won't see why this is important," "I think this could be said more clearly," and "This is good"). In response to the evaluation, the children then choose from a list of directives (e.g., "I'd better give an example," "I better leave this part out," and "I think I'll leave it this way") and follow through on the directive. Children are adept at choosing evaluations, with their evaluations in close agreement with expert raters. Unfortunately, they often follow an adequate evaluation with an . inadequate directive. In addition, children experience difficulty composing sentences that "said it a different way," usually generating a form very much resembling the original flawed sentence.

Although Bereiter and Scardamalia have made progress in improving children's composition skills, there is still very much to be done. What is important in the present context is that children's writing can benefit from removal of executive requirements, accomplished by prompting effective strategy use. This is especially noteworthy because school offers so many opportunities for the types of cuing that Bereiter and Scardamalia have studied. Also, with the addition of computers to school environments, opportunities for prompting are increased. There already exist computer programs for promoting composition based on presenting series of prompts to writers (e.g., Burns & Culp, 1980; Rubin, 1980; Woodruff, Bereiter, & Scardamalia, 1981).

Although cuing writing involves explicit directions compared to when children are left to their own devices to tackle academic tasks, even more explicit interventions are possible and should be employed in certain situations. Attention now turns to one programmatic effort involving the explicit provision of mediators to children.

Providing Keyword Mediators to Children

As detailed earlier the keyword strategy is a very effective mnemonic procedure that can be applied to a variety of materials that possess an associative component. In particular, the technique has been applied with prose materials that are more complicated in structure than the vocabulary-definition linkages for which the method was originally developed. Prose requires more complex mediating images, images with more components and more intricate relationships. Keyword researchers recognized that children might experience difficulty producing these types of images. If that were the case, maximum keyword effects might occur only if learners were provided keyword-mnemonic pictures, rather than if they generated them on their own.

Shriberg et al. (1982) set out to determine if the keyword method could be applied to prose materials, as well as to determine the necessity of providing mnemonic pictures versus having learners generate mnemonic images for prose on their own. Although only Experiment 2 in the series is described, other relevant data in the study were consistent with conclusions highlighted here.

Eighth-grade students were presented a dozen passages to learn, each about a "famous" person and each five sentences in length. The first sentence contained a person's name and the individual's accomplishment. The rest of the paragraph elaborated this information, as in the passage about Charlene McCune:

Animal owners all over the world are impressed that Charlene McCune has taught her pet cat how to count. The cat can count to 20 without making any mistakes. Moreover, the remarkable cat can do some simple addition. It took many months of patient training to teach the cat these skills, and Ms. McCune rewarded him with a large bowl of spaghetti after every successful session. Finally, last week, the local university presented the cat with an honorary diploma.

In the pictures plus condition subjects were shown a mnemonic picture as each passage was read by the experimenter. The picture included a keyword referent representing the name of the famous individual (e.g., racoon sounds like McCune). Thus, as racoons jumped over a fence in the picture, a cat in academic garb tallied them on a blackboard. A plate of spaghetti sat waiting for the cat. Children in the imagery condition were provided keywords for each passage and were instructed to construct interactive pictures such as the ones used in the pictures plus condition, with some practice at imagery construction included in the instructions. As passages were presented to control subjects, they were presented the printed version of the prose but were provided no pictures nor were given any imagery instructions.

After the passages were presented, subjects answered a series of questions tapping memory of the name–accomplishment associations as well as recall of the other information. Picture plus subjects had high recall (79%) of accomplishments given names relative to both imagery (55%) and control (23%) learners. In addition, recall of other information was significantly higher in the pictures plus condition (83%) than in the imagery condition (66%), with control recall (76%) of the other information intermediate between imagery and pictures plus. In summary, eighth graders were not as facile at generating mnemonic images for prose as had been hoped, with the performance of imagery subjects well below that of pictures plus learners. In such a situation it is perfectly reasonable to recommend that learning not be made victim of children's information processing shortcomings.

Levin, Shriberg, and Berry (1983) have shown that the benefits of mnemonic pictures can be obtained even when prose is not as concrete as in Shriberg et al. (1982). Such a situation would be expected to pose even more difficulties if learners had to generate their own images, since a preliminary step to constructing a mnemonic image given abstract prose is translating abstract elements into concrete referents.

The specific task in Levin et al. (1983) involved learning attribute information about various towns, including the town of Fostoria:

> *Fosteria* has a lot to offer its people. People have *considerable wealth*, and everyone lives comfortably. Many of the townsfolk also become quite prosperous because the land has *abundant natural resources*. In addition, the town is especially well known for its *advances in technology*, for just about everything is run by computer. The progress has attracted many new residents, and statistics show a growing population.

In the mnemonic picture for Fosteria, everything was covered with frost, the referent for Fostoria's keyword. A large crowd of people, many of whom clutched handfuls of money, were gathered around an oil well and a computer terminal. Thus, all of the abstract attributes were concretized in this interactive picture. Providing such pictures almost doubled eighth graders' recall of town attributes from the town names.

In addition to prose learning, there are a number of other tasks that are susceptible to mnemonic learning, but require mnemonics sufficiently complicated that children should not be expected to produce mediators on their own. For instance, the order of U.S. presidents can be taught using a set of mnemonic pictures (e.g., Levin et al., 1983; Levin, McCormick, & Dretzke, 1981). Materials have also been devised for teaching U.S. state capitals (Levin, Berry, Miller, & Bartell, 1982; Levin, Shriberg, Miller, McCormick, & Levin, 1980). In addition, there are occasions when provided mnemonic pictures are required even with learning of simpler materials such as vocabulary. For example, preschool children experience difficulty generating any type of interactive images, and thus, self-generated, keyword-mnemonic images are out of the question with 3–5-year-old children. However, when Pressley, Samuel, Hershey, Bishop, and Dickinson (1981) provided keyword-elaborated pictures to preschoolers, learning increased as much as 1000%! For more examples of mnemonic pictures and discussion of their use, see Levin and Pressley (in press) and Levin (in press).

Concluding Comments

In the best of all possible cognitive worlds, learners would have a well-developed repertoire of strategies, they would possess sufficient metamemory about those strategies so that they would know when to deploy each one, and they would know how to modify the strategies, as well as when it was appropriate to do so. Learners would keep track of their cognitive activities, with such monitoring directing strategy shifts. The education of immature learners would be straightforward. Educators would teach strategies that are known to be effective; they would know what metamemory about strategies should be included in instruction; and they would know how to teach monitoring so that cognitive regulation could be carried out almost effortlessly.

Needless to say, we are not in the best of all possible worlds, but rather far from it. First of all, although there are many extant strategy recommendations (e.g., Pressley & Levin, 1983a,b; Tierney, Readence, & Dishner, 1980), there are very few strategies that have been widely tested and demonstrated to enhance learning and performance (cf. Pressley, Heisel, McCormick, & Nakamura, 1982). A major challenge is to test the many existing strategy recommendations to determine which learning techniques are effective. In the past there has been too much acceptance of armchair analyses of strategies and their effects (cf. Pressley, Levin, & Bryant, 1983). Progress is also required in the development of new strategies designed to meet contemporary educational challenges (e.g., strategies for teaching efficient computing skills). Understanding of monitoring is even less complete, with only a handful of reports on the training of monitoring (e.g., Elliott-Faust & Pressley, 1984; Miller, 1984; Markman & Gorin, 1981). Evaluation of the critical components of specific strategy knowledge is also in its early stages (e.g., O'Sullivan & Pressley, 1984).

Despite this grim evaluation of current knowledge, we are optimistic that a wealth of information about strategies, specific strategy knowledge, and monitoring will accumulate in the next decade—so much work on these topics is ongoing that it is almost impossible to open an issue of any cognitively oriented journal without encountering at least one report on strategy functioning. Nonetheless, the greatest challenges lie somewhat down the road—we know almost nothing about how to produce the learner who is automatically strategic, who generally uses strategies and can do so by expending little cognitive effort, freeing the bulk of cognitive resources for other cognitive activities (cf. LaBerge & Samuels, 1974; Schneider & Shiffrin, 1977; Shiffrin & Schneider, 1977). If strategies are ever to be integrated into complex information processing such as reading, such automaticity is required (Torgesen & Greenstein, 1982).

As we await the best of all possible worlds, however, it is likely that cognitive psychologists will make many contributions that improve learning and performance. Recommendations for altering materials so that they are more memorable have followed from strategy research (see Pressley [1983] and Gagné & Bell [1981] for a host of examples). Also, study environments can be modified so that people are cued to use strategies that they would not produce spontaneously. Teachers can tell children to use strategies; texts can provide hints to do so; and educational computer programs can provide explicit prompts for users to produce particular strategies. Such cueing of effective strategies will lead to efficient acquisition of curriculum content, a main goal of educators. Although some (e.g., Brown et al., 1983; Paris et al., 1983) have claimed that such materials modification and cueing do not contribute to the loftier enterprise of creating autonomous learners who know how to learn (i.e., learners like those in the best of all possible worlds), that claim is not defensible empirically. In fact, a reasonable alternative hypothesis is that autonomous use of strategies might develop as a function of the substantial strategy experience provided by the modified materials and cueing to use strategies. Learners would have ample opportunities to learn the components of strategies, to discover that strategies are effective, and to observe strategies applied in many different situations. It is hard to imagine how these experiences could impair the development of autonomous cognition. Indeed, restructuring the environment so that strategic mediators and cued strategic processing are prominent may be a reasonable first step to developing the best of all possible cognitive worlds. See Pressley (1983) for amplificaiton of this final theme.

References

Akin, O. (1980). *Models of architectural knowledge.* London: Pion.

Alessi, S., Anderson, T., & Goetz, E. (1979). An investigation of lookbacks during studying. *Discourse Processes, 2,* 197–212.

Anderson, T. H., & Armbruster, B. B. (1980). *Studying* (Tech. Report 155). Champaign-Urbana, Illinois: University of Illinois.

Anderson, V., Bereiter, C., & Woodruff, E. (1980). *Activation of semantic networks in writing: Teaching students how to do it themselves.* Paper presented at the annual meeting of the American Educational Research Association, Boston.

Asarnow, J. R., & Meichenbaum, D. (1979). Verbal rehearsal and serial recall: The mediational training of kindergarten children. *Child Development, 50,* 1173–1177.

Atkinson, R. C., & Raugh, M. R. (1975). An application of the mnemonic keyword method to the acquisition of Russian vocabulary. *Journal of Experimental Psychology: Human Learning and Memory, 104,* 126–133.

Baker, L. (in press). How do we know when we don't understand? Standards for evaluating text comprehension. In D. L. Forrest-Pressley, G. E. MacKinnon, & T. G. Waller (Eds.), *Metacognition, cognition, and human performance.* New York: Academic Press.

Baker, L., & Anderson, R. I. (1982). Effects of inconsistent information on text processing: Evidence for comprehension monitoring. *Reading Research Quarterly, 17,* 281–294.

Baker, L., & Brown, A. L. (1984). Metacognition and the reading process. In P. D. Pearson (Ed.), *Handbook of reading research* (pp. 353–394). New York: Longman.

Battig, W. F. (1974). Within-individual differences in "cognitive" processes. In R. L. Solso (Ed.), *Theories in cognitive psychology: The Loyola symposium* (pp. 195–228). New York: John Wiley & Sons.

Beal, C. R., & Flavell, J. H. (1982). Effect of increasing the salience of message ambiguities on kindergarteners' evaluations of communicative success and message adequacy. *Developmental Psychology, 18,* 43–48.

Belmont, J. M., Butterfield, E. C., & Ferretti, R. P. (1982). To secure transfer of training instruct self-management skills. In D. K. Detterman & R. J. Sternberg (Eds.), *How and how much can intelligence be increased?* (pp. 147–154). Norwood, N.J.: Ablex Publishing Corp.

Bender, B. G., & Levin, J. R. (1976). Motor activity, anticipated motor activity, and young children's associative learning. *Child Development, 47,* 560–562.

Bender, B. G., & Levin, J. R. (1978). Pictures, imagery, and retarded children's prose learning. *Journal of Educational Psychology, 70,* 583–588.

Bereiter, C., & Scardamalia, M. (1982). From conversation to composition: The role of instruction in a developmental process. In R. Glaser (Ed.), *Advances in instructional psychology* (Vol. 2, pp. 1–64). Hillsdale, N.J.: Erlbaum.

Bereiter, C., Scardamalia, M., Anderson, V., & Smart, D. (1980). *An experiment in teaching abstract planning in writing.* Paper presented at the annual meeting of the American Educational Research Association, Boston.

Bird, M., & Bereiter, C. (1984). *Use of thinking aloud in identification and teaching of reading comprehension strategies.* Manuscript submitted for publication. Toronto, Ontario: Ontario Institute for Studies in Education.

Black, M. M., & Rollins, H. A. (1982). The effects of instructional variables on young children's organization and free recall. *Journal of Experimental Child Psychology, 31,* 1–19.

Borkowski, J. G. (in press). Signs of intelligence: Strategy generalization and meta-cognition. In S. Yussen (Ed.), *The development of reflection.* New York: Academic Press.

Borkowski, J. G., Levers, S. R., & Gruenenfelder, T. M. (1976). Transfer of mediational strategies in children: The role of activity and awareness during strategy acquisition. *Child Development, 47,* 779–786.

Bransford, J. D., Stein, B. S., Shelton, T. S., & Owings, R. A. (1981). Cognition and adaption: The importance of learning to learn. In J. Harvey (Ed.), *Cognition, social behavior and the environment.* Hillsdale, N.J.: Erlbaum.

Brown, A. L. (1975). The development of memory: Knowing, knowing about knowing, and knowing how to know. In H. W. Reese (Ed.), *Advances in child development and behavior* (Vol. 10). New York: Academic Press.

Brown, A. L. (1978). Knowing when, where, and how to remember: A problem in metacognition. In R. Glaser (Ed.), *Advances in instructional psychology* (Vol. 1, pp. 77–165). Hillsdale, N.J.: Erlbaum, 1978.

Brown, A. L. (1980). Metacognitive development and reading. In R. J. Spiro, B. Bruce, & W. Brewer (Eds.), *Theoretical issues in reading comprehension* (pp. 453–481). Hillsdale, N.J.: Erlbaum.

Brown, A. L., & Barclay, C. R. (1976). The effects of training specific mnemonics on the metamnemonic efficiency of retarded children. *Child Development, 47*, 71–80.

Brown, A. L., Bransford, J. D., Ferrara, R. A., & Campione, J. C. (1983). Learning, remembering, and understanding. In J. H. Flavell & E. M. Markman (Eds.), *Handbook of child psychology: Vol. III*. Cognitive development (pp. 177–266). New York: John Wiley & Sons.

Brown, A. L., Campione, J. C., & Barclay, C. R. (1979). Training self-checking routines for estimating test readiness: Generalization from list learning to prose recall. *Child Development, 50*, 501–512.

Brown, A. L., & Day, J. D. (1983). Macrorules for summarizing texts: The development of expertise. *Journal of Verbal Learning and Verbal Behavior, 22*, 1–14.

Brown, A. L., & DeLoache, J. S. (1978). Skills, plans, and self-regulation. In R. S. Siegler (Ed.), *Children's thinking: What develops?* (pp. 3–35). Hillsdale, N.J.: Erlbaum Associates.

Brown, A. L., & Lawton, S. C. (1977). The feeling of knowing experience in educable retarded children. *Developmental Psychology, 13*, 364–370.

Brown, A. L., & Smiley, S. S. (1978). The development of strategies for studying text. *Child Development, 49*, 1076–1088.

Büchel, F. P. (1982). Metacognitive variables in the learning of written text. In A. Flammer & W. Kintsch (Eds.), *Discourse Processing* (pp. 352–359). Amsterdam: North-Holland.

Burns, H. L., & Culp, G. H. (1980). Stimulating invention in English composition through computer-assisted instruction. *Educational Technology, 20*, 5–10.

Butterfield, E. C., & Belmont, J. M. (1977). Assessing and improving the executive cognitive functions of mentally retarded people. In I. Bialer & M. Sternlicht (Eds.), *Psychological issues in mentally retarded people*, Chicago: Aldine.

Butterfield, E. C., Siladi, D., & Belmont, J. M. (1980). Validating theories of intelligence. In H. W. Reese & L. P. Lipsett (Eds.), *Advances in child development and behavior* (Vol. 15). New York: Academic Press.

Campione, J. C., Brown, A. L., & Ferrara, R. A. (1982). Mental retardation and intelligence. In R. J. Sternberg (Ed.), *Handbook of human intelligence* (pp. 392–490). Cambridge, England: Cambridge University Press.

Cavanaugh, J. C., & Borkowski, J. G. (1979). The metamemory–memory "connection": Effects of strategy training and maintenance. *Journal of General Psychology, 101*, 161–174.

Charnass, N. (1979). Components of skill in bridge. *Canadian Journal of Psychology, 33*, 1–50.

Chi, M. T. H. (1978). Knowledge structure and memory development. In R. Siegler (Ed.), *Children's thinking: What develops?* (pp. 73–96). Hillsdale, N.J.: Erlbaum.

Chiesi, H., Spilich, G. J., & Voss, J. F. (1979). Acquisition of domain-related information in relation to high and low domain knowledge. *Journal of Verbal Learning and Verbal Behavior, 18*, 257–273.

Clark, H. H., & Clark, E. V. (1977). *Psychology and language*. New York: Harcourt, Brace, & Jovanovich.

Clay, M. (1974). The development of morphological rules in children with different language backgrounds. *New Zealand Journal of Educational Studies, 9*, 113–121.

Craik, F. I. M., & Lockhart, R. S. (1972). Levels of processing: A framework for memory research. *Journal of Verbal Learning and Verbal Behavior, 11*, 671–684.

Craik, F. I. M., & Tulving, E. (1975). Depth of processing and the retention of words in episodic memory. *Journal of Experimental Psychology: General, 104*, 268–294.

Davidson, R. E. (1976). The role of metaphor and analogy in learning. In J. R. Levin & V. L. Allen (Eds.), *Cognitive learning in children: Theories and strategies* (pp. 135–162). New York: Academic Press.

Davis, R. B. (1983). Complex mathematical cognition. In H. P. Ginsburg (Ed.), *The development of mathematical thinking* (pp. 254–290). New York: Academic Press.

Day, J. D. (1980). *Training summarization skills: A comparison of teaching methods*. Unpublished doctoral dissertation. Champaign-Urbana, Ill.: University of Illinois.

DiStefano, P., Noe, M., & Valencia, S. (1981). Measurement of the effects of purpose and passage difficulty on reading flexibility. *Journal of Educational Psychology, 73*, 602–606.

Dretzke, B. J., Levin, J.R., Pressley, M., & McGivern, J. E. (in press). In search of the keyword method comprehension link. *Contemporary Educational Psychology*.

Egan, D. E., & Schwartz, B. (1979). Chunking in recall of symbolic drawings. *Memory and Cognition, 7*, 149–158.

Egeland, B. (1974). Training impulsive children in the use of more efficient scannning strategies. *Child Development, 45*, 165–171.

Elliott-Faust, D. J., & Pressley, M. (1984). *The "delusion of comprehension" phenomena in young children: An instructional approach to promoting listening comprehension monitoring capabilities*. Presented at the annual meeting of the American Educational Research Association, New Orleans.

Ericsson, K. A., & Simon, H. A. (1980). Verbal reports as data. *Psychological Review, 87*, 215–251.

Flavell, J. H. (1970). Developmental studies of mediated memory. In H. W. Reese & L. P. Lipsitt (Eds.), *Advances in child development and behavior* (Vol. 5). New York: Academic Press.

Flavell, J. H. (1971). Stage-related properties of cognitive development. *Cognitive Psychology, 2*, 421–453.

Flavell, J. H. (1977). *Cognitive development*. Englewood Cliffs, N.J.: Prentice-Hall.

Flavell, J. H. (1979). Metacognition and cognitive monitoring: A new area of cognitive-developmental inquiry. *American Psychologist, 34*, 906–911.

Flavell, J. H. (1981). Cognitive monitoring. In W. P. Dickson (Ed.), *Children's oral communication skills*. New York: Academic Press.

Flavell, J. H., & Wellman, H. M. (1977). Metamemory. In R. V. Kail & J. W. Hagen (Eds.), *Perspectives on the development of memory and cognition* (pp. 3–33). Hillsdale, N.J.: Erlbaum and Associates.

Flower, L. (1981). *Problem-solving strategies for writing*. New York: Harcourt, Brace & Jovanovich.

Forrest, D. L., & Barron, R. W. (1977). *Metacognitive aspects of the development of reading skill*. Paper presented at the annual meeting of the Society for Research in Child Development, New Orleans.

Forrest-Pressley, D. L., & Gillies, L. A. (1983). Children's flexible use of strategies during reading. In M. Pressley & J. R. Levin (Eds.), *Cognitive strategy research: Educational applications* (pp. 133–156). New York: Springer-Verlag.

Forrest-Pressley, D. L., & Waller, T. G. (1984). *Reading, cognition, and metacognition*. New York: Springer-Verlag.

Gagné, E. D., & Bell, M. S. (1981). The use of cognitive psychology in the development and evaluation of textbooks. *Educational Psychologist, 16*, 83–100.

Gagné, R. M. (1977). *The conditions of learning* (3rd ed.). New York: Holt, Rinehart & Winston.

Garner, R., & Reis, R. (1981). Monitoring and resolving comprehension obstacles: An investigation of spontaneous text lookbacks among upper-grade good and poor comprehenders. *Reading Research Quarterly, 16*, 569–582.

Ghatala, E. S., Levin, J. R., Pressley, M., & Lodico, M. G. (in press). Training cognitive-strategy monitoring in children. *American Educational Research Journal*.

Gick, M. L., & Holyoak, K. J. (1983). Schema induction and analogical transfer. *Cognitive Psychology, 15*, 1–38.

Gordon, C. J., & Braun, C. (1983). *Teaching story schema: Metatextual aid to reading and writing*. Presented at the annual meeting of the American Educational Research Association, Montreal.

Hayes, J. R., & Flower, L. (1980). Identifying the organization of writing processes. In L. W. Gregg & E. R. Sternberg (Eds.), *Cognitive processes in writing* (pp. 3–50). Hillsdale, N.J.: Lawrence Erlbaum Associates.

House, B. J. (1982). Learning processes: Developmental trends. In J. Worell (Ed.), *Psychological development in the elementary years* (pp. 187–232). New York: Academic Press.

Huey, E. B. (1968). *The psychology and pedagogy of reading*. Cambridge, Mass.: MIT Press. (Originally published by MacMillan, 1908).

Johns, J. L., & McNamara, L. (1980). The SQ3R study technique: A forgotten research target. *Journal of Reading, 23*, 705–708.

Johnson, C. N., & Wellman, H. M. (1980). Children's developing understanding of mental verbs: Remember, know, and guess. *Child Development, 51*, 1095–1102.

Jones, B. G., & Hall, J. W. (1982). School applications of the mnemonic keyword method as a study strategy by eighth graders. *Journal of Educational Psychology, 74*, 230–237.

Just, M. A., & Carpenter, P. A. (1980). A theory of reading: From eye fixations to comprehension. *Psychological Review, 87*, 329–354.

Keeney, T. J., Cannizzo, S. R., & Flavell, J. H. (1967). Spontaneous and induced verbal rehearsal in a recall task. *Child Development, 38*, 953–966.

Kendall, P. C., & Wilcox, L. E. (1980). Cognitive-behavioral treatment for impulsivity: Concrete versus conceptual training in non-self-controlled problem children. *Journal of Consulting and Clinical Psychology, 48*, 80–91.

Kennedy, B. A., & Miller, D. J. (1976). Persistent use of verbal rehearsal as a function of information about its value. *Child Development, 47*, 566–569.

Kirschenbaum, D. S., Ordman, A. M., Tomarken, A. J., & Holtzbauer, R. (1982). Effects of differential self-monitoring and level of mastery on sports performance: Brain power bowling. *Cognitive Therapy and Research, 6*, 335–342.

Krashen, S. D. (1978). Individual variation in the use of the monitor. In W. C. Ritchie (Ed.), *Second language acquisition research: Issues and implications* (pp. 175–183). New York: Academic Press.

Krashen, S., & Pon, P. (1975). An error analysis of an advanced ESL learner: The importance of the Monitor. *Working Papers on Bilingualism, 7*, 125–129.

LaBerge, D., & Samuels, S. J. (1974). Towards a theory of automatic information processing in reading. *Cognitive Psychology, 6,* 293–323.

Lange, G. (1978). Organization-related process in children's recall. In P. A. Ornstein (Ed.), *Memory development in children.* Hillsdale, N.J.: Erlbaum.

Lawson, M. J., & Fuelop, S. (1980). Understanding the purpose of strategy training. *British Journal of Educational Psychology, 50,* 175–180.

Levelt, W. J. M. (1983). Monitoring and self-repair in speech. *Cognition, 14,* 41–104.

Levin, J. R. (in press). Educational applications of mnemonic pictures: Possibilities beyond your wildest imagination. In A. A. Sheikh (Ed.), *Imagery and the educational process.* Farmingdale, N.Y.: Baywood.

Levin, J. R. (1981). The mnemonic '80s: Keywords in the classroom. *Educational Psychologist, 16,* 65–82.

Levin, J. R., Berry, J. K., Miller, G. E., & Bartell, N. P. (1982). More on how (and how not) to remember the states and their capitals. *Elementary School Journal, 82,* 379–388.

Levin, J. R., Dretzke, B. J., McCormick, C. B., Scruggs, T. E., McGivern, J. E., & Mastropieri, M. A. (1983). Learning via mnemonic pictures: Analysis of the presidential process. *Educational Communication and Technology Journal, 31,* 161–173.

Levin, J. R., Johnson, D. D., Pittelman, S. D., Hayes, B. L., Levin, K. M., & Shriberg, L. K. (1983). *A comparison of semantic- and mnemonic-based vocabulary-learning strategies.* Paper presented at the annual meeting of the American Research Association, Montreal.

Levin, J. R., & Lesgold, A. M. (1978). On pictures in prose. *Educational Communication and Technology Journal, 26,* 233–243.

Levin, J. R., McCormick, C. B., & Dretzke, B. J. (1981). A combined pictorial mnemonic strategy for ordered information. *Educational Communication and Technology Journal, 29,* 219–225.

Levin, J. R., McCormick, C. B., Miller, G. E., Berry, J. K., & Pressley, M. (1982). Mnemonic versus nonmnemonic vocabulary-learning strategies for children. *American Educational Research Journal, 19,* 121–136.

Levin, J. R., & Pressley, M. (1981). Improving children's prose comprehension: Selected strategies that seem to succeed. In C. M. Santa & B. L. Hayes (Eds.), *Children's prose comprehension: Research and practice.* Newark, Delaware: International Reading Association.

Levin, J. R., & Pressley, M. (in press). Mnemonic vocabulary instruction: What's fact, what's fiction. In R. F. Dillon & R. R. Schmeck (Eds.), *Individual differences in cognition* (Vol. 2). New York: Academic Press.

Levin, J. R., Pressley, M., McCormick, C. B., Miller, G. E., & Shriberg, L. K. (1979). Assessing the classroom potential of the keyword method. *Journal of Educational Psychology, 71,* 583–594.

Levin, J. R., Shriberg, L. K., & Berry, J. K. (1983). A concrete strategy for remembering abstract prose. *American Educational Research Journal, 20,* 277–290.

Levin, J. R., Shriberg, L. K., Miller, G. E., McCormick, C. B., & Levin, B. B. (1980). The keyword method in the classroom: How to remember the states and their capitals. *Elementary School Journal, 80,* 185–191.

Lodico, M. G., Ghatala, E. S., Levin, J. R., Pressley, M., & Bell, J. A. (1983). The effects of strategy-monitoring on children's selection of effective memory strategies. *Journal of Experimental Child Psychology, 35,* 263–277.

Markman, E. M. (1977). Realizing that you don't understand: A preliminary investigation. *Child Development, 48*, 986–992.

Markman, E. M. (1979). Realizing that you don't understand: Elementary school children's awareness of inconsistencies. *Child Development, 50*, 643–655.

Markman, E. M. (1981). Comprehension monitoring. In W. P. Dickson (Ed.), *Children's oral communication skills* (pp. 61–84). New York: Academic Press.

Markman, E. M., & Gorin, L. (1981). Children's ability to adjust their standards for evaluating comprehension. *Journal of Educational Psychology, 73*, 320–325.

Mastropieri, M. A. (1983). *Mnemonic strategies with learning-disabled students.* Unpublished doctoral dissertation, Arizona State University, Arizona.

McDaniel, M. A., & Pressley, M. (in press). Putting the keyword method in context. *Journal of Educational Psychology, 76*, 598–609.

McGivern, J. E., Levin, J. R., Ghatala, E. S., & Pressley, M. (1983). *Developmental differences in the vicarious acquisition of an effective learning strategy.* Paper presented at the annual meeting of the American Educational Research Association, Montreal.

Meichenbaum, D. H. (1977). *Cognitive behavior modification.* New York: Plenum.

Miller, G. E. (in press). The effects of self-instructional and didactic training on young children's comprehension monitoring. *Reading Research Quarterly.*

Miller, G., Galanter, E., & Pribram, K. (1960). *Plans and the structure of behavior.* New York: Holt, Rinehart & Winston.

Moely, B. E. (1977). Organizational factors in the development of memory. In R. V. Kail & J. W. Hagen (Eds.), *Perspectives on the development of memory and cognition* (pp. 203–236). Hillsdale, N.J.: Erlbaum.

Moynahan, E. D. (1973). The development of knowledge concerning the effect of categorization upon free recall. *Child Development, 44*, 238–246.

Neilans, T. H., & Israel, A. C. (1981). Towards maintenance and generalization of behavior change: Teaching children self-regulation and self-instructional skills. *Cognitive Therapy and Research, 5*, 189–195.

Norman, D. A., & Schallice, T. (1980). *Attention to action: Willed and automatic control of behavior* (CHIP Tech. Rep. 99). LaJolla, California: University of California.

Olshavsky, J. E. (1976–77). Reading as problem solving: An investigation of strategies. *Reading Research Quarterly, 12*, 654–674.

Ornstein, P. A., & Naus, M. J. (1978). Rehearsal processes in children's memory. In P. A. Ornstein (Ed.), *Memory development in children* (pp. 69–99). Hillsdale, N.J.: Erlbaum.

O'Sullivan, J. T., & Pressley, M. (1984). Completeness of instruction and strategy transfer. *Journal of Experimental Child Psychology.*

Owings, R. A., Petersen, G. A., Bransford, J. D., Morris, C. D., & Stein, B. S. (1980). Spontaneous monitoring and regulation of learning: A comparison of successful and less successful fifth graders. *Journal of Educational Psychology, 72*, 250–256.

Pace, A. J. (1980). *The ability of young children to correct comprehension errors: An aspect of comprehension monitoring.* Paper presented at the annual meeting of the American Educational Research Association, Boston.

Paivio, A., & Yuille, J. C. (1969). Changes in associative learning over trials as a function of word imagery and type of learning set. *Journal of Experimental Psychology, 79*, 458–463.

Palincsar, A. M., & Brown, A. L. (in press). Reciprocal teaching of comprehension-fostering and monitoring activities. *Cognition and Instruction.*

Paris, S. G. (1978). Coordination of means and goals in the development of mnemonic skills. In P. A. Ornstein (Ed.), *Memory development in children* (pp. 259–273). Hillsdale, N.J.: Erlbaum Associates.

Paris, S. G., & Cross, D. R. (1983). Ordinary learning: Pragmatic connections among children's beliefs, motives, and actions. In J. Bisanz, G. Bisanz, & R. Kail (Eds.), *Learning in children*. New York: Springer-Verlag.

Paris, S. G., Lipson, M. Y., & Wixson, K. K. (1983). Becoming a strategic reader. *Contemporary Educational Psychology, 8*, 293–316.

Patterson, C. J., Cosgrove, J. M., & O'Brien, R. G. (1980). Nonverbal indicants of comprehension and noncomprehension in children. *Developmental Psychology, 16*, 38–48.

Piaget, J. (1978). *Success and understanding*. Cambridge, Mass.: Harvard University Press.

Piaget, J. (1976). *The grasp of consciousness: Action and concept in the young child*. Cambridge, Mass.: Harvard University Press.

Pratt, M., & Bates, K. (1982). Young editors: Children's evaluations and productions of ambiguous messages. *Developmental Psychology, 18*, 30–42.

Pressley, G. M. (1976). Mental imagery helps eight-year-olds remember what they read. *Journal of Educational Psychology, 68*, 355–359.

Pressley, M. (1977). Imagery and children's learning: Putting the picture in developmental perspective. *Review of Educational Research, 47*, 585–622.

Pressley, M. (1979). Increasing children's self-control through cognitive interventions. *Review of Educational Research, 49*, 319–370.

Pressley, M. (1982). Elaboration and memory development. *Child Development, 53*, 296–309.

Pressley, M. (1983). Making meaningful materials easier to learn: Lessons from cognitive strategy research. In M. Pressley & J. R. Levin (Eds.), *Cognitive strategy research: Educational application*. New York: Springer-Verlag.

Pressley, M., Borkowski, J. G., & O'Sullivan, J. T. (1984). Memory strategy instruction is made of this: Metamemory and durable strategy use. *Educational Psychologist, 19*, 94–107.

Pressley, M., Borkowski, J. G., & O'Sullivan, J. T. (in press). Metamemory and the teaching of strategies. In D. L. Forrest-Pressley, G. E. MacKinnon, & T. G. Waller (Eds.), *Metacognition, cognition, and human performance*. San Diego: Academic Press.

Pressley, M., & Bryant, S. L. (1982). Does answering questions really promote associative learning? *Child Development, 53*, 1258–1267.

Pressley, M., & Dennis-Rounds, J. (1980). Transfer of a mnemonic keyword strategy at two age levels. *Journal of Educational Psychology, 72*, 575–582.

Pressley, M., & Forrest-Pressley, D. (in press). Questions and children's cognitive processing. In A. C. Graesser & J. B. Black (Eds.), *The psychology of questions*. Hillsdale, N.J.: Lawrence Erlbaum Associates.

Pressley, M., Heisel, B. E., McCormick, C. G., & Nakamura, G. V. (1982). Memory strategy instruction with children. In C. J. Brainerd & M. Pressley (Eds.), *Progress in cognitive development research: Vol. 2. Verbal processes in children* (pp. 125–159). New York: Springer-Verlag.

Pressley, M., & Levin, J. R. (1977a). Developmental differences in subjects' associative learning strategies and performance: Assessing a hypothesis. *Journal of Experimental Child Psychology, 24*, 431–439.

Pressley, M., & Levin, J. R. (1977b). Task parameters affecting the efficacy of a visual imagery learning strategy in younger and older children. *Journal of Experimental Child Psychology, 24*, 53–59.

Pressley, M., & Levin, J. R. (1978). Developmental constraints associated with children's use of the keyword method of foreign language vocabulary learning. *Journal of Experimental Child Psychology, 26*, 359–372.

Pressley, M., & Levin, J. R. (1980). The development of mental imagery retrieval. *Child Development, 51*, 558–560.

Pressley, M., & Levin, J. R. (1981). The keyword method and recall of vocabulary words from definitions. *Journal of Experimental Psychology: Human Learning and Memory, 7*, 72–76.

Pressley, M., & Levin, J. R. (1983a). *Cognitive strategy research: Educational applications*. New York: Springer-Verlag.

Pressley, M., & Levin, J. R. (1983b). *Cognitive strategy research: Psychological foundations*. New York: Springer-Verlag.

Pressley, M., Levin, J. R., & Bryant, S. L. (1983). Memory strategy instruction during adolescence: When is explicit instruction needed? In M. Pressley & J. R. Levin (Eds.), *Cognitive strategy research: Psychological Foundations* (pp. 25–49). New York: Springer-Verlag.

Pressley, M., Levin, J. R., & Delaney, H. D. (1982). The mnemonic keyword method. *Review of Educational Research 52*, 61–91.

Pressley, M., Levin, J. R., & Ghatala, E. S. (1984). Memory strategy monitoring in adults and children. *Journal of Verbal Learning and Verbal Behavior, 23*, 270–288.

Pressley, M., Levin, J. R., Kuiper, N. A., Bryant, S. L., & Michener, S. (1982). Mnemonic versus nonmnemonic vocabulary-learning strategies: Additional comparisons. *Journal of Educational Psychology, 74*, 693–707.

Pressley, M., Levin, J. R., & McCormick, C. B. (1980). Young children's learning of foreign language vocabulary: A sentence variation of the keyword method. *Contemporary Educational Psychology, 5*, 22–29.

Pressley, M., Levin, J. R., & Miller, G. E. (1981). How does the keyword method affect vocabulary comprehension and usage? *Reading Research Quarterly, 16*, 213–226.

Pressley, M., Levin, J. R., & Miller, G. E. (1982). The keyword method compared to alternative vocabulary learning strategies. *Contemporary Educational Psychology, 7*, 50–60.

Pressley, M., Ross, K. A., Levin, J. R., & Ghatala, E. S. (in press). The role of strategy utility knowledge in children's strategy decision making. *Journal of Experimental Child Psychology*.

Pressley, M., Samuel, J., Hershey, M. M., Bishop, S. L., & Dickinson, D. (1981). Use of a mnemonic technique to teach young children foreign language vocabulary. *Contemporary Educational Psychology, 6*, 110–116.

Raugh, M. R., & Atkinson, R. C. (1975). A mnemonic method for learning a second-language vocabulary. *Journal of Educational Psychology, 67*, 1–16.

Read, J. D., & Bruce, D. (1982). Longitudinal tracking of difficult memory retrievals. *Cognitive Psychology, 14*, 280–300.

Ringel, B. A., & Springer, C. J. (1980). On knowing how well one is remembering: The persistence of strategy use during transfer. *Journal of Experimental Child Psychology, 29*, 322–333.

Robinson, F. P. (1961). *Effective study* (rev. ed.). New York: Harper & Row.

Rohwer, W. D. Jr. (1973). Elaboration and learning in childhood and adolescence. In H. W. Reese (Ed.), *Advances in child development and behavior* (Vol. 8). New York: Academic Press.

Rohwer, W. D., Jr., & Bean, J. P. (1973). Sentence effects and noun-pair learning: A developmental interaction during adolescence. *Journal of Experimental Child Psychology, 15*, 521–533.

Rohwer, W. D., Jr., Rabinowitz, M., & Dronkers, N. F. (1982). Event knowledge, elaborative propensity, and the development of learning proficiency. *Journal of Experimental Child Psychology, 33*, 492–503.

Rohwer, W. D., Jr., Raines, J. M., Eoff, J., & Wagner, M. (1977). The development of elaborative propensity during adolescence. *Journal of Experimental Child Psychology, 23*, 472–492.

Rothkopf, E. Z., & Billington, M. (1975). A two-factor model of the effect of goal-descriptive directions on learning from text. *Journal of Educational Psychology, 67*, 692–704.

Rothkopf, E. Z., & Billington, M. J. (1979). Goal-guided learning from text: Inferring a descriptive processing model from inspection times and eye movements. *Journal of Educational Psychology, 71*, 310–327.

Rubin, A. (1980). A theoretical taxonomy of the differences between oral and written language. In R. J. Sprio, B. C. Bruce, & W. F. Brewer (Eds.), *Theoretical issues in reading comprehension: Perspectives from cognitive psychology, linguistics, artificial intelligence, and education* (pp. 411–438). Hillsdale, N.J.: Erlbaum.

Rumelhart, D. E. (1980). Schemata: The building blocks of cognition. In R. J. Spiro, B. C. Bruce, & W. F. Brewer (Eds.), *Theoretical issues in reading comprehension: Perspectives from cognitive psychology, linguistics, artificial intelligence and education* (pp. 33–58). Hillsdale, N.J.: Erlbaum.

Sadoski, M. (in press). An exploratory study of the relationships between reported imagery and the comprehension and recall of a story. *Reading Research Quarterly.*

Scardamalia, M., & Bereiter, C. (in press). Written composition. In M. Wittrock (Ed.), *Handbook of research on teaching* (3rd ed.).

Scardamalia, M., Bereiter, C., & Goelman, H. (1982). The role of production factors in writing ability. In M. Nystrand (Eds.), *What writers know: The language, process, and structure of written discourse.* New York: Academic Press.

Schneider, W. (in press). Developmental trends in the metamemory–memory behavior relationship: An integrative review. In D. L. Forrest-Pressley, G. E. MacKinnon, & T. G. Waller (Eds.), *Cognition, metacognition, and performance.* New York: Academic Press.

Schneider, W., & Shiffrin, R. M. (1977). Controlled and automatic human information processing: I. Direction, search, and attention. *Psychological Review 84*, 1–66.

Shatz, M. (1978). The relationship between cognitive processes and the development of communication skills. In C. B. Keasey (Ed.), *Nebraska Symposium on Motivation* (Vol. 25, pp. 1–42). Lincoln, Nebraska: University of Nebraska Press.

Shatz, M., Wellman, H. M., & Silber, S. (1983). The acquisition of mental verbs: A systematic investigation of the first reference to mental state. *Cognition, 14*, 301–321.

Shiffrin, R. M., & Schneider, W. (1977). Controlled and automatic human information processing: II. Perceptual learning, automatic attending, and a general theory. *Psychological Review, 84*, 127–190.

Shriberg, L. K., Levin, J. R., McCormick, C. B., & Pressley, M. (1982). Learning about "famous" people via the keyword method. *Journal of Educational Psychology, 74*, 238–247.

Siegler, R. S., & Shrager, J. (1984). Strategy choices in addition: How do children know what to do? In C. Sophian (Ed.), *Origins of cognitive skills*. Hillsdale, N.J.: Erlbaum.

Simon, H. A. (1979). Problem solving and education. In D. T. Tuma & F. Reif (Eds.), *Problem solving and education: Issues in teaching and research*. Hillsale, N.J.: Erlbaum.

Simon, H. A., & Hayes, J. R. (1976). The understanding process: Problem isomorphs. *Cognitive Psychology, 8*, 165–190.

Singer, H., & Donlan, D. (1982). Active comprehension: Problem-solving schema with question generation for comprehension of complex short stories. *Reading Research Quarterly, 17*, 166–186.

Smirnov, A. A. (1973). *Problems of the psychology of memory*. New York: Plenum Press.

Sommerville, S. C., & Wellman, H. M. (1979). The development of understanding as an indirect memory strategy. *Journal of Experimental Child Psychology, 27*, 71–86.

Sophian, C. (Ed.). (1984). *Origins of cognitive skills*. Hillsdale, N.J.: Erlbaum.

Thorndike, E. L. (1917). Reading as reasoning: A study of mistakes in paragraph reading. *Journal of Educational Psychology, 8*, 323–332.

Thorndike, E. L., & Woodworth, R. S. (1901) The influence of improvement in one mental function upon the efficiency of other functions. *Psychological Review, 8*, 247–261, 384–395, 553–564.

Tierney, R. J., Readence, J. E., & Dishner, E. K. (1980). *Reading strategies and practices: Guide for improving instruction*. Boston: Allyn & Bacon Inc.

Tikhomerov, O. K., & Klochko, V. E. (1981). The detection of a contradiction as the initial stage of problem formation. In J. V. Wertsch (Ed.), *The concept of activity in Soviet psychology* (pp. 341–382). Armonk, N.Y.: M. E. Sharpe.

Torgesen, J. K., & Greenstein, J. J. (1982). Why do some learning disabled children have problems remembering: Does it make a difference? *Topics in Learning and Learning Disabilities, 2*, 54–61.

Wagoner, S. A. (1983). Comprehension monitoring: What it is and what we know about it. *Reading Research Quarterly, 18*, 328–346.

Waters, H. S., & Andreassen, C. (1983). Children's use of memory strategies under instruction. In M. Pressley and J. R. Levin (Eds.), *Cognitive strategy research: Psychological foundations*. New York: Springer-Verlag.

Waters, H. S., & Waters, E. (1979). Semantic processing in children's free recall: The effects of context and meaningfulness on encoding variability. *Child Development, 50*, 735–746.

Wellman, H. M., & Johnson, C. N. (1979). Understanding of mental processes: A developmental study of *remember* and *forget*. *Child Development, 50*, 79–88.

Woodruff, E., Bereiter, C., & Scardamalia, M. (1981). On the road to computer-assisted compositions. *Journal of Educational Technology Systems, 10*, 133–148.

Yussen, S. R., Gagné, E., Gargiulo, R., & Kunen, S. (1974). The distinction between perceiving and memorizing in elementary-school children. *Child Development, 45*, 547–551.

Yussen, S. R., Kunen, S., & Buss, R. (1975). The distinction between perceiving and memorizing in the presence of category cues. *Child Development, 46*, 763–768.

2. Memory in Very Young Children

Marvin W. Daehler and Carolyn Greco

The recent flurry of research on memory in very young children has taken a long time to materialize. Numerous anecdotal descriptions detailing toddlers' "amazing" abilities to recognize scenes or to recall events occurring days, weeks, and even months earlier seem to have been met, in the past, with a twinge of curiosity and perhaps graciously phrased platitudes such as "Yes, babies and young children can do some marvelous things." Even so accomplished an observer as Charles Darwin was uncertain whether it was "worth mentioning" that his 3-year-old son recognized a picture of his grandfather whom he had not seen for 6 months. This child recalled a "whole string of events which had occurred whilst visiting him (the grandfather), and which certainly had never been mentioned in the interval" (Darwin, 1877; p. 291). Darwin's apologetic comment probably indicated uncertainty about where such an observation fit in the overall scheme of intellectual development rather than a reasoned conviction that this type of data was unimportant. In fact, precisely these kinds of observations, more systematically recorded, have yielded fresh advances in our understanding of the development of memory in very young children.

In this chapter we review work on memory development during that transitional period from infancy to preschool or between the ages of approximately 12 and 36 months. We first briefly examine the methods researchers have established to investigate memory in children this young. Previous reviews have outlined many of the limitations and strengths of these methods, especially with respect to their use with young infants (Cohen & Gelber, 1975; Olson & Sherman, 1983; Sophian, 1980), but we will stress their extension and application to the somewhat older child. We next consider what can be said about retention capacities within this age frame, eventually turning to the distinction between memory for objects, memory for location, and memory for temporal events as an organizational scheme for outlining major empirical findings. In reviewing this material, it soon becomes apparent that memory-related tasks often shed light on other aspects of intellectual growth such as the emergence of early categorization and conceptual skills and the burgeoning knowledge base. We close with a discussion of two other concerns, one related to the distinction frequently drawn between recognition and recall memory, and the other to the concept of infantile amnesia.

The Problem of Methodology

When reviewing research on memory, one fact becomes obvious. There is a glaring lack of information on the development of memory in that age period between late infancy and early childhood. This is not a new insight. In a recent monograph several other investigators repeatedly made the same point (see papers in Perlmutter, 1980). Why might this be so? One answer has been that it is difficult to find methods to use with children of this age. Toddlers lack the conceptual facility to understand complex verbal instructions, and their own expressions and other newfound competencies are often restrained and inhibited by the unfamiliar laboratory environments that routinely shelter experimental investigations of memory. Strangers' encroachments upon toddlers' home territories may also be sufficiently intimidating to hinder spontaneous, or even prompted, displays of retrieval. DeLoache (1980) pointed out two major methodological challenges: "getting the young children to understand what it is you want them to do and then, even more difficult, getting the children to *want* to do it" (p. 20).

Partly because of these difficulties, developmental researchers have left a gap in drawing a complete picture of memory development, concentrating on methodologically simpler age periods, perhaps with the expectation that any missing pieces would eventually fall into place. But recent methodological advances in research on memory with infants, and a growing realization that the toddler years comprise a period of remarkable developmental change, have dimmed such a prospect. As a consequence, researchers have finally begun to attempt to fill the void, often enlisting the help of caregivers to supplement and extend the insights of observers and experimenters trained to carry out traditional naturalistic and laboratory studies.

The impact of infant research upon these increased efforts is not difficult to evaluate; by all criteria, it must be judged enormous. Motor capacities are much further developed in the very young child compared to the infant, raising the possibility that new kinds of responses can be measured. But all researchers working with children under 3 are confronted with a common problem, that of designing tasks which capitalize upon the spontaneous willingness of subjects to participate in the testing situation. Novelty-preference procedures have been among the most successful of these.

Novelty-Preference Procedures

The majority of experiments with infants have focused on visual recognition memory. Two methodological paradigms, the habituation–dishabituation procedure and the paired-comparison procedure, dominate this research. Both of these procedures rely on a preference for novelty to reveal information about memory. Although experiments utilizing these paradigms are of fairly recent origin, the principle of an attentional preference for novel stimuli has long been evident to observers of young children. For example, Taine (1877) remarked over 100 years ago that

> ... all day long the child of whom I speak (at 12 months) touches, feels, turns round, lets drop, tastes and experiments upon everything she gets hold of; whatever it may be, ball, doll, coral, or plaything, when once it is sufficiently known she throws it aside, it is no longer new, she has nothing further to learn from it and has no further interest in it. (p. 253)

This observation illustrates why novelty-preference paradigms lend themselves so nicely to investigations of memory. Little effort is asked of subjects; they simply perform some behavior such as looking or playing that is already in their response repertoire.

Habituation–dishabituation paradigm. The habituation–dishabituation paradigm has its major roots in animal experimental psychology where researchers have been concerned primarily with understanding the nature of these processes (Groves & Thompson, 1970). Stated simply, habituation is a decrease in responding as a result of repeated exposure to a stimulus. Dishabituation is defined as the recovery of responding to prehabituation levels. It is this change in behavior, occurring over a series of trials and as a function of the organism's perception of stimuli, that constitutes evidence for memory as defined by the paradigm.

Although number and vigor of limb movements, Moro-startle reflex, non-nutritive sucking, and head turning have been used as behavioral indices with infants (Olson & Sherman, 1983), visual fixation has dominated habituation—dishabituation research and has been relied upon almost exclusively in studies with 1- and 2-year-olds. Electrophysiological measures involving the cardiac response, evoked potentials, respiration, and galvanic skin responses have also been recorded with young infants, but such measures have rarely been extended to the older infant and very young child whose increased mobility and more comprehensive appraisal of the testing environment make such procedures difficult to implement.

Paired-comparison paradigm. The other popular method of examining infant memory, and the one that has had most applicability in research with toddlers, utilizes the paired-comparison procedure. The origin of this paradigm can be traced to the beginning of this century when Marsden (1903) and Valentine (1913) reported that infants were differentially responsive to the visual world. These early pioneers presented two stimuli simultaneously to infants and measured fixation time to each. When the infants showed differential looking, preferring one stimulus over the other, their discrimination could be inferred. But it was not until the late 1950s that this method was rediscovered by Fantz (1956, 1958) and extended to investigate memory with infants. Two stimuli were presented simultaneously over a series of trials. When one (the familiar stimulus) remained the same on each trial and the other (the novel stimulus) changed on successive trials, Fantz (1964) found that infants between 2 and 6 months of age looked longer at the novel, relative to the familiar, stimulus.

Many variations of the basic paired-comparison procedure have been introduced by subsequent researchers to investigate emerging memorial skills (see Olson & Sherman, 1983 for a review of this literature). One commonly noted limitation in comparison-looking research is that recognition memory can be inferred only as long as preferential looking occurs. If no difference in looking is evidenced, then no statement about memory can be made; all that can be said is that the subject shows no preference for either of the stimuli (Sophian, 1980). But there are also many factors that can produce a preference for either the novel or familiar stimulus (e.g., interstimulus contrast, perceptual features, state; see Olson & Sherman, 1983, for a more complete description of these) and we must take them into consideration in the design of our research.

In general, of course, toddlers, just as infants, prefer attending to novel stimuli, but research with very young infants indicates that we may need to attach some qualifications to this fundamental principle. Several investigators have reported that infants less than about 2 months of age prefer familiar rather than novel stimuli (Weizmann, Cohen, & Pratt, 1971; Wetherford & Cohen, 1973). Whereas this finding may denote a developmental shift, it could be a harbinger of a more general concept that applies to every age period; a subject must have sufficient opportunity to become familiar with a stimulus in order to display a preference for another stimulus.

Hunter, Ross, and Ames (1982) found that when 12-month-olds were given a relatively long period of time to become familiar with toys, they focused upon and manipulated novel toys more than familiar toys. But when familiarization time was brief, the opposite occurred; subjects interacted with familiar toys more than novel toys. Similar results have been obtained for the visual attention of younger subjects (Caron, Caron, Minichiello, Weiss, & Friedman, 1977; Rose, Gottfried, Melloy-Carminar, & Bridger, 1982). In other words, a preference for novelty or familiarity may be exhibited by subjects at any age depending upon whether sufficient time has been allowed to encode the stimulus. This hypothesis also implies that it is possible to measure how speedily or efficiently children at different ages process information by examining rate of habituation and by manipulating length of familiarization (Fagan & Singer, 1983).

Researchers have accommodated to possible developmental and individual differences in rate of encoding information by incorporating two methodological advances in their procedures. First, stimuli are no longer generally presented for fixed durations. Instead, the length of a trial is determined by some response of the subject, most frequently by an infant looking away from the stimulus. Second, test trials have been introduced only after a subject has reached a predetermined level of habituation to the familiar stimulus. Both of these innovations have met with criticism. Determining the end of a fixation is not always an easy task (Ames, Hunter, Black, Lithgow, & Newman, 1978) and there are many different ways for arriving at a criterion for level of habituation (Cohen & Gelber, 1975).

These problems can be handled in other ways, at least with children as young as 1 year of age. Subjects can be trained to control physically their own presentation of stimuli and in our visual recognition experiments we have consistently permitted them to do so as a way of allowing very young children to encode stimuli for as long as they are interested in them. Our apparatus contains two adjacent viewing windows that are at eye level for a subject seated in a child-sized chair. Directly below, or in some cases between the windows, is some form of response device. We have found that children from 1 to 3 eagerly press a plaque and that this response quickly becomes identified with controlling presentations of the stimuli. When the child presses this plaque, a screen automatically lowers to cover the windows so that stimuli can be readied for presentation on the next trial. Occasionally, subjects perform rapid multiple responses or initiate a press before attending to the stimuli. To reduce the impact of such behavior, we have included a brief delay period of 3 or 5 sec during which the manipulandum becomes inactive at the beginning of each trial.

There are several other variables that can influence the strength of looking preferences. One is the type of stimulus that is used. We have found that objects rather than two-dimensional pictures elicit longer overall looking times on both familiarization and test trials (Daehler & O'Connor, 1980). Another factor that can be expected to influence novelty preference is the similarity between familiarization and test procedures. The data on this issue are quite limited because in most studies the procedures used on familiarization trials are also used on test trials. To do otherwise, of course, normally conflicts with the canons of good experimental design since unwanted variance is likely to be introduced. But memory in very young children may be highly context specific. For example, a change in mode of presentation of stimuli (i.e., from visual to visual-haptic or vice versa) is sufficient to counter the typical finding of a preference for novel items in children about a year of age (Gottfried, Rose, & Bridger; 1978; MacKay-Soroka, Trehub, Bull, & Corter, 1982; Ruff, 1981).

Not every change from familiarization to test has a profound effect on novelty preference. For example, some experimenters have presented a single stimulus during familiarization trials, but pairs of stimuli as in a paired-comparison procedure on test trials (e.g., Rose, Gottfried & Bridger, 1981; Ross, 1980), and have still obtained strong novelty preferences. Gottfried and Rose (1980) found on a tactual recognition test that 1-year-olds familiarized with objects in light and then tested in darkness also produced reliable novelty preferences. In our research we have used both a continuous recognition procedure in which test trials have been interspersed among the familiarization trials and alternatively, test trials grouped to follow familiarization trials (see Greco & Daehler, 1984). Robust novelty preferences have been obtained using both procedures.

Finally, it should be pointed out that by 3 years of age children are very proficient at encoding visual stimuli. Looking responses are brief and rapidly executed. Under such circumstances, and especially if subjects systematically compare differences between a familiar and novel stimulus, preferential looking may actually decline and even become nonsignificant despite excellent memory for a stimulus. Alternative measures, including vacillation rate, that is, the tendency to look back and forth between two stimuli (Kagan, Kearsely, & Zelazo, 1978), as well as traditional indices of memory (e.g., verbal recall) are likely to be more sensitive indicators of memory in older children.

Object Permanence and Object Search

Other procedures for assessing memory in infants have gained adherents in recent years. The development of object permanence has been a major topic of research in the infant literature and has usually been assessed through some form of search task. The concept of object permanence closely corresponds to the concept of memory for an object, but the former incorporates a somewhat more stringent requirement (Sophian, 1980). To demonstrate object memory, the child must indicate that he or she knows the object used to exist. To demonstrate object permanence, the child must indicate that he or she knows that the object still exists.

Because object permanence tasks typically demand both memory for objects and memory for their location, such tasks have been used to assess each of these skills directly. Infants resist initiating search when the experimenter hides "no toy" (i.e., an empty hand; see Gratch, 1975) or appears to be puzzled when an object is not found where it was expected, indicating that search behavior is governed by memory for some object (Sophian, 1980). Infants at around 9 or 10 months of age often look for a hidden object in a location where it has been found previously rather than where it has just been hidden (the $A\overline{B}$ error of stage 4 in Piaget's terminology) indicating that the infant has memory for an object even though he or she does not have a well-developed concept of its location.

The prototypical search task carried out with toddlers has two major components, an array of distinctively spaced locations such as marked or unmarked containers, and an object to be retrieved after some delay. The primary dependent measure in these studies has been percent errorless retrieval, that is, the percentage of trials on which the child searches first at the correct location. Modifications of this basic procedure have included varying the delay intervening between hiding and searching from seconds or minutes to hours or even longer (DeLoache, 1980), pretraining the hide-and-seek game (DeLoache, 1984), instructing subjects to explicitly remember the location of the object DeLoache, 1984), having subjects exhaustively consider all hiding locations before initiating search (Perlmutter, Hazen, Mitchell, Grady, Cavenaugh, & Flook, 1981), using a familiar home or nursery school environment rather than an unfamiliar laboratory setting (DeLoache, 1980, 1984; Wellman, Somerville, & Haake, 1979), and hiding several objects in multiple locations (DeLoache, 1980).

Other forms of the search task have focused on the issue of whether very young children process additional discriminative cues to aid search. These studies have typically used arrays of small containers with distinctive cues such as color and size (Daehler, Bukatko, Benson, & Myers, 1976), pictures that either match, are associatively related, or are unrelated to the target object (Perlmutter et al., 1981; Ratner & Myers, 1980), or no cues other than location (Horn & Myers, 1978).

In contrast to other research paradigms, toddlers were among the first subjects included in studies investigating memory for location (e.g., Allen, 1931; Hunter, 1917; Miller, 1934; Skalet, 1931). One major reason for the popularity of the search task is that it can be utilized with many species of animals and with human infants and children of all ages as long as they have sufficient reaching and grasping skills and a rudimentary object concept. Very young children can be introduced to the task with a minimum of instructions or pretraining. They seem to enjoy looking for things as long as the delay interval is not excessive (DeLoache, 1980; Diamond, 1983). Perhaps the biggest drawback with this procedure is that only a limited number of trials can be given within a conventional testing session, at least when longer delays are involved.

Conditioning and Imitation Paradigms

Conditioning paradigms, which have been shown to be effective even in the newborn period (e.g., Sameroff, 1971; Siqueland & Lipsitt, 1966), permit exploration of the logical relationship between learning and memory, a relationship that is not often explicitly formulated in models of memory. But studies examining the relationship between conditioning and memory in infants are scarce and toddlers are even less frequently tested in such studies.

An overreliance on novelty-preference techniques has led Rovee-Collier and Fagen (1981) to conclude that the infant's memorial abilities have been greatly underestimated. Using a paired-comparison procedure, infants at 6 months of age have been found to recognize stimuli 2 weeks later (Fagan, 1973), but Rovee-Collier, using a conditioned foot-kick response, found evidence of retention over 14 days in infants as young as 8 weeks of age (Davis & Rovee-

Collier, 1979). She and her colleagues (Rovee-Collier, Sullivan, Enright, Lucas, & Fagen, 1980; Sullivan, 1982) have reported even longer retention when infants have been given a reactivation or reminder treatment before testing. In these studies, 3-month-olds learned to activate a mobile through foot kicking. A month later they again saw the mobile, but were not permitted to activate it. Yet, 24 hours later these subjects showed retention of the foot-kicking response whereas subjects not provided the passive reminder of the stimulus did not. These data suggest that memory in some form is present long after initial training, but access to that memory is hindered by factors that are still not well understood.

Recent claims of the infant's ability to imitate facial expressions and manual gestures (Meltzoff & Moore, 1977, 1983) call attention to another possible avenue for studying infant and toddler memory. According to Piaget (1951), true imitation does not occur until an infant has the ability to represent a model, that is, until Stage 6 of the sensorimotor period or at about 18 months of age. Although precursors to this ability are found at earlier ages, it is not until the child can "invent" new behaviors through imitation that Piaget would say that true imitation has occurred.

In contrast to Piaget's findings, Meltzoff and Moore (1977; 1983) and others (Field et al., 1982) have reported that neonates will imitate some facial expressions of an adult, a response which requires a representational system far more sophisticated than Piaget would allow. Regardless of how this particular dispute becomes resolved, there is every reason to believe that imitation tasks would provide additional information about the very young child's memory. McCall, Parke, and Kavanaugh (1977) have shown that a variety of behaviors, especially single motor actions rather than vocal, social, or coordinated sequences of actions, are increasingly imitated by children from 12 to 24 months of age. These researchers also found that 26-month-olds imitated play behaviors performed by other 2-year-olds as frequently after a 24-hour delay as on an immediate test. Actually, some memory tasks can be interpreted as essentially imitation tasks (e.g., repeating a spoken list of words). That realization has probably not escaped some, but researchers have failed to take advantage of this relationship by using imitation as a point of departure for exploring memory processes with very young children.

Observational Procedures

The oldest method of studying memory, and one gaining renewed interest, relies on the natural observations of either the parent or an experimenter. In the case of recent parent observations, experimenters have provided instructions and training to increase the reliability and validity of the data collected. For example, Nelson and Ross (1980) asked parents of 2-year-olds to record occurrences of specific types of memory-related behaviors over a period as long as 3 months. Parents were asked to record the time and date, what behavior provided evidence for the memory, the circumstances and context in which it was remembered, when the object or event was last seen or experienced, whether it was a one-time or recurrent episode in the experience of the child, and whether there were any reminders of the event or object prior to its being remembered. Other parental diary studies have been conducted with babies as young as 7 months of age (Ashmead & Perlmutter, 1980). In addition, the memory demands that parents place on the child have been recorded either as part of ongoing interactions naturally occurring in the home (Ratner, 1980) or in focused environments such as during joint picture-book reading or while looking at pictures in a family album (DeLoache, 1983).

The recent emphasis on naturalistic observations of memory in very young children seems to have been prompted by two broad concerns (Perlmutter, 1980). The first of these is the virtual absence of laboratory data on long-term memory. This lack of information is especially problematic when one considers that psychologists have historically emphasized the importance of early memories for later behavior. The second concern reflects an even more important matter, the ecological validity of what we have learned about the development of memory and memory processes from conventional laboratory experiments. This criticism has been leveled at many aspects of cognitive psychology, but it is especially pertinent with respect to memory development for an age period about which we know very little in terms of either expectations or requirements in the everyday environment.

Although recent observational and diary studies have significantly increased our data base, there are many unresolved problems associated with such procedures. One problem centers on how to analyze observations. An episode can often be coded to illustrate many forms of memory and memory-related processes and there is little agreement from one investigator to another on how to classify memory behaviors. There are also substantial differences in the amount of supplementary information provided by parents and there is relatively little effort to determine the reliability of parent reports of memory. Criticisms of a more substantive nature can also be offered. Naturalistic observations have been carried out for many different kinds of memory. While that strategy has led to an awareness of the rich repertoire of knowledge remembered and expected to be remembered, it has yielded few theoretical generalizations. Wellman and Somerville (1980) have noted that such research often takes on an exploratory or pilot aura, "frequently confounded by naturally occurring covariates" (p. 47) and that it illuminates only the more obvious, descriptive aspects of memory development in toddlers. As an alternative, these investigators propose "quasi-naturalistic" approaches to studying memory development. These approaches start with naturalistic observations of memory and attempt to standardize or control them in a more systematic manner. For example, very young children are often expected to remember to carry out certain daily routines and chores such as brushing their teeth or picking up their clothes. Wellman and Somerville (1980) asked parents to observe and systematically provide prompts in the performance of established or newly requested routines so that these researchers could gain additional insights on how routines are remembered. This approach, and others like it, offer opportunities for testing fairly specific questions about the development of memory without losing the sense of the importance of such memories for children during this period of development.

The Issue of Retention

Most research on memory and its development in toddlers can be traced back to a basic concern with whether these children retain information for periods of time comparable to those reported for their older counterparts. This question is not an easy one to answer for many reasons. Continuing debates about whether memory is comprised of one, two, or more structures, each having its own unique characteristics, means that, ultimately, we may have to speak in terms of retention *abilities*. Encoding and retrieval strategies also may involve different processes and mechanisms and these can markedly influence our conceptions of retention.

Despite our recognition of these methodological and theoretical ambiguities now, the issue of retention capacity dominated the earliest attempts to organize data on the memory of infants and children and researchers continue in their efforts to piece together a picture of retention capabilities. Hurlock and Schwartz (1932) examined a large number of baby biographies published during the late 1800s and early 1900s for reports of instances of memory and memory-related behaviors. They concluded that by the end of the first year, memory is present, but short-lived with 5 or 6 days approaching the upper limit of time for which an event could be recognized. By the end of the second year, baby biographers reported recognition of objects, persons, and events over weeks. The diaries revealed considerably longer memories in the third year; length of retention was now described in terms of months. Thus, diary records provided a picture of an increasing retention capacity for several types of memory phenomena.

About the same time that Hurlock and Schwartz summarized these biographical records, more systematic experiments were being carried out investigating memory for the location of objects. Previously, Hunter (1917), using the delayed reaction task, reported that infants a year of age could withstand delays of only about 10 sec when required to search for an object in one of three locations. But delays of up to 2 or 3 days were found to be manageable by 2- and 3-year-olds (Allen, 1931; Skalet, 1931). These durations were, of course, much shorter than those recorded in diary reports, a discrepancy that may either be an artifact of the different methodologies or reflect genuine differences in memory. Nevertheless, the retention intervals were considerably longer than those claimed for most other species.

These early baby biographies and delayed reaction studies provide thought-provoking reading, but they failed to answer many questions about the development of memory and they attracted little interest for a number of decades. In fact, our current revival of interest in the memory of the toddler cannot be traced directly to these early reports, but instead to new findings concerning memory in infants and preschool children. For example, infants 6 months of age and younger were shown to recognize the recurrence of a briefly exposed stimulus after many days (Fagan, 1973; Davis & Rovee-Collier, 1979). At the other end of our age frame, Brown and others (Brown & Scott, 1971) were reporting that 3- and 4-year-olds could recognize the recurrence of tens, and possibly hundreds, of simple pictures of common objects over days, weeks, and even months.

Research by Faulkender, Wright, and Waldron (1974) and others demonstrating that preschoolers will show a visual preference for a novel stimulus after seeing a *series* of pictures paved the way for several investigations of recognition memory with toddlers in our laboratory. In one of our earliest experiments, Daehler and Bukatko (1977) presented 40 different pictures of common objects to children 19, 25, 32, and 37 months of age using a continuous presentation procedure. Each stimulus was presented only once and then reappeared paired with a novel stimulus either on the next trial or 5, 10, 25, or 50 trials after its initial appearance.

Although subjects could attend to a picture as long as they wished, mean looking times were quite brief, averaging only 3.8 sec for each stimulus during its initial presentation. Nevertheless, that was a sufficient length of time to yield memory for the pictures. Seventy-eight percent of all subjects attended to novel stimuli longer than familiar stimuli. At every age, children preferred to view the novel stimuli longer. Moreover, the preference for the novel stimuli was as great with longer lags as with shorter lags. Thus, children this young could recognize the reappearance of a large number of stimuli even after a short exposure to them and after viewing many intervening stimuli. This finding has been confirmed in subsequent studies with children as young as 12 months of age (Daehler & Greco, 1981; Daehler & O'Connor, 1981).

Even after long lags, only a few minutes passed between familiarization and test trials in these studies. In a more recent experiment, Greco and Daehler (1984) tested 24-month-olds for retention of visual information over a substantially longer period of time. Children were shown common objects from 16 different basic level categories (Rosch et al., 1976). Objects within each category appeared on four different trials in the course of the familiarization phase. Eight of the objects were then tested for recognition memory immediately following familiarization; the remaining eight stimuli were tested when subjects returned a week later. Subjects looked at each of the 16 stimuli an average of only 9.1 sec on familiarization trials. Nevertheless, a significant preference for the novel stimuli was found both on the immediate test trials and after 1 week.

These laboratory demonstrations of long-term memory for multiple, briefly exposed stimuli are impressive. But recent diary reports indicate retention of some kinds of information over much longer periods of time and confirm the observations of parents recorded nearly a century before. Nelson and Ross (1980) asked mothers to keep diaries of their 21-, 24-, or 27-month-olds' memories over a 3-month period. Mothers were instructed to provide as much background information as possible concerning each recorded memory. Most memories occurred for objects and events experienced less than 3 months before (80%). However, 8% of the recorded memories were for events that took place from 6 months to a year earlier. As might be expected, older children were more likely than younger children to remember objects and events experienced over these longer periods; in fact, memories for events occurring a year before were limited to the 27-month-olds.

Although concerned with a much shorter interval, Wellman and Somerville (1980) found no developmental differences in performance on another kind of long-term memory task. Parents frequently reported to these researchers that when charged to remind the caregiver of something, their 1- or 2-year-old would often do so, even when that reminder was to be delivered some time later. Parents were asked to test this ability more systematically, varying both the interest level of the reminder (as judged by the caregiver) and the length of time intervening between initial charge and fulfillment of the reminder obligation.

Wellman and Somerville found that 2-year-olds carried out this task as effectively as 4-year-olds regardless of whether the reminder was intended to be offered only a few minutes later, a number of hours afterwards, or even the next morning. The finding of no developmental difference was hypothesized to be a result of the caregiver's selection of tasks closely geared to each child's level of understanding and interest. When events were estimated by the caregiver to be of low interest (e.g., hanging up the wash), children provided reminders only about 20% of the time. In contrast, reminders judged to be of high interest (e.g., buying candy at the store) were remembered about 70% of the time. Finally, the difference in ability to perform this task as a function of delay was small. Subjects remembered 45% of the prompts after a short delay (1–5 min) and 35% after a delay of several hours or overnight.

Laboratory procedures probably have not come near to tapping the limits of retention capacity in toddlers. Durations more commensurate with those reported from caregivers' observations could very possibly be demonstrated using conventional experimental techniques. It may even be, as some have hinted and laboratory research has occasionally suggested, that there is not really an interesting developmental story concerning the basic memory abilities of toddlers, especially for processes associated with recognition memory (Brown, 1975; Olson, 1976; Perlmutter & Lange, 1978). But as Werner and Perlmutter (1979) have noted, such a conclusion is premature given the limited data base available at this time. Furthermore, one particularly puzzling phenomena, that of infantile amnesia, raises fundamental questions about the comparability of basic memory processes in children under about the age of 3 and those who are older. Suppose toddlers can remember events over lengthy periods of time. Then why is it so difficult to exhibit memory for those events in later childhood? We will consider that question in greater detail in a final section of this paper.

The Kinds of Information to Be Remembered

Broad questions addressed to retention capacity have given way in recent years to more specific questions focused on the kinds of information most likely to be encoded, stored, and retrieved at different ages. A number of researchers have found it convenient to distinguish memory for objects and their properties from memory for location, and these, in turn, from memory for events (e.g., Ashmead Perlmutter, 1980; Nelson & Ross, 1980; Ratner, 1980; Sophian, 1980; Wellman & Somerville, 1980). When a 2-year-old prefers to look at a novel picture or recites the names of items placed within a box, we are witnessing memory for objects. When a parent asks a 2-year-old what he or she saw at the zoo, memory for objects is again involved. Instances of memory for objects are also frequently reported in diaries and observational studies. Recognition and recall tasks typically test for this form of memory and it is frequently the properties and features of objects that serve as the major variable of interest.

Other tasks, particularly those falling under the rubric of delayed reaction experiments, have been designed to test memory for the location of objects. Here, the emphasis is not on what, but where. When a child seeks a favorite item (a potentially time consuming enterprise in the case of a misplaced security blanket) or dutifully retrieves a "borrowed" calculator in response to the admonishments of a perturbed caregiver, memory for location is being addressed. Location is a property of an object, but for most stimuli, it is not a permanent or intrinsic characteristic and it is this variability which creates new memory demands for the very young child. Finding an object typically requires remembering where it had been seen most recently, but if not there, where it might have been located at some earlier time or where it possibly could be located.

Finally, young children often display memory for events or sequences of activities or experiences. The temporally ordered nature of experience is emphasized in memory for events. A child's reenactment of the games played at a neighbor's birthday party or a visit to the grandparents' farm illustrate such memories. Narratives of this kind are reported for both unique, one-time experiences and for recurrent daily routines (Nelson & Ross, 1980).

The distinction between memory for objects, their location, and for events is not easily maintained. For example, memory for events often involves an extensive knowledge base including recognition and recall of both objects and their locations. However, the context, settings, and temporal–spatial inter-relation of these elements constitute a central aspect of the information to be retrieved in memory for events.

Memory for Objects and Their Properties

Experiments performed with infants less than a year of age have convincingly demonstrated recognition memory for visual patterns and objects (see Werner & Perlmutter, 1979; Olson & Sherman, 1983, for reviews of this literature). A related and far more challenging question concerns what conceptual properties of these entities are encoded, stored, and retrieved.

Memory for conceptual properties of stimuli. Daehler and O'Connor (1980) and Daehler and Greco (1981) tested whether both overall perceptual shape and basic conceptual information were remembered by children from 12 to 38 months of age. Perceptual similarity was defined in terms of experimenter judgments about the shape of the stimuli. A doughnut and a tire possess a number of perceptual features in common (e.g., both are round and both have holes in their centers); thus, they appear more similar than, for example, a tractor and a telephone. Conceptual similarity was defined in terms of whether two objects received the same common label from 3-year-olds and belonged to the same basic level category. For example, an orange carnation and a purple and blue violet differ perceptually in many ways, but 3-year-olds identify both as flowers (Daehler & O'Connor, 1980).

A continuous recognition procedure involving 24 different objects was used in these studies. Subjects could attend to stimuli on familiarization trials for as long as they wished, but looking times were short, as our previous research would predict. More importantly, on test trials children looked significantly longer at novel stimuli than at familiar stimuli irrespective of whether the novel member of a pair was perceptually similar (but from a different basic level category), was conceptually similar (but looked quite different perceptually), or was both perceptually and conceptually different from the familiar stimulus. However, children 18 months and older also treated stimuli in these conditions differently. Subjects preferred looking at an exemplar of a novel basic-level category more than a novel exemplar that looked quite different than its familiarized associate but which belonged to the same basic-level category. In other words, subjects demonstrated memory for both the perceptual and conceptual aspects of stimuli, but an exemplar of a novel basic-level concept elicited greater attention than just a change in the perceptual features of a basic-level concept.

The fact that conceptual information was encoded and remembered by children this young no longer seems very surprising. Many researchers have become convinced that categorization is both a necessary and common psychological activity among infants as well as older children (Bornstein, 1981; Cohen & Younger, 1983; Reznick & Kagan, 1983; Sugarman, 1983). Physical dimensions of entities such as their form, hue, or movement and feeling states may underlie the earliest categorization activity, but functional criteria soon emerge as well. Ross (1980) familiarized 12-, 18-, and 24-month-olds with one of six categories of stimuli (the letter M, the letter O, men, animals, food, or furniture). She then tested for attentional preference, pairing a novel exemplar within the familiarized category with a novel exemplar outside the familiarized category. For example, subjects were shown a number of different exemplars of food and then a new food item was presented with a piece of furniture on the test trial.

On familiarization trials subjects displayed significant habituation to those categories having the greatest perceptual similarity (Ms, Os, and men). Habituation did not occur for exemplars depicting animals, food, and furniture. Nevertheless, a significant preference for novel extracategory stimuli was found for every category at every age level. These results indicate "that 12- to 24-month-olds can not only extract the common physical features of categories whose members are perceptually alike but they can also recognize super-ordinate categories such as food and furniture in which members vary considerably in perceptual characteristics and have a related function" (Ross, 1980, p. 395).

Retention of conceptual versus perceptual information. Is there any difference in the retention of conceptual and perceptual information? Our earlier studies were not designed to test this possibility (Daehler & O'Connor, 1980; Daehler & Greco, 1981), but developmental and cognitive psychologists have been concerned with it for some time. A developmental study conducted by Scarborough (1977) sheds some light on memory for perceptual and conceptual events. He found that 4-, 8-, and 16-year-olds produced more false recognition errors of pictures that were different exemplars of the target than pictures perceptually similar to the target but depicting entirely different objects. This difference, however, occurred only at longer lags, that is, when greater numbers of trials intervened between familiarization and test. Scarborough concluded that subjects at all ages initially relied on a visual code for picture recognition, but this information was forgotten fairly rapidly so that a more enduring conceptual code became the primary source of object recognition. At the short lags both kinds of information were represented in memory, but the visual code initially "carried more weight." At the longer lags, conceptual information became a more important determinant of memory.

Support for this interpretation comes from experiments concerned with a slightly different question. Research with adults indicates that prototypic information is remembered better than specific details (e.g., Homa, Cross, Cornell, Goldman, & Schwartz, 1973; Posner & Keele, 1970; Strange, Keeney, Kessel, & Jenkins, 1970). For example, Posner and Keele (1970) presented four distortions of random dot patterns to subjects and found that immediately after learning to classify the patterns, the old exemplars were recognized better than the prototype. But after a 1-week delay, there was little evidence of forgetting of the prototypes whereas recognition of the old exemplars was much poorer. These data confirm that memory for perceptual details is considerably less durable than memory for broadly based conceptual information.

If conceptual or more generalized prototype information is retained longer, a next question might be whether the manner in which the concept is acquired has a bearing on its retention. Mervis and Pani (1980) and Hupp and Mervis (1982) suggest that basic-level category knowledge can be abstracted after exposure to only a single good exemplar of the category. However, Mervis and Pani (1980) also found that 5-year-olds display greater generalization to novel instances of a category from a single good exemplar than from a range of good, moderate, and poor exemplars. Hupp and Mervis (1982) obtained similar results with severely handicapped children and also reported more generalization to novel instances after training with three good exemplars rather than just one.

In a study for which some of the findings have already been cited, Greco and Daehler (1984) examined whether presenting only one or several basic-level category exemplars effected immediate and delayed recognition memory for the category. Twenty-four-month-olds were familiarized with either four different good exemplars of 16 basic-level categories (e.g., dogs, chairs, etc.), or with a single exemplar of each of these categories. On test trials, which occurred immediately and 1 week later, either a previously presented exemplar or an unseen exemplar of the category was paired with an instance from a novel basic-level category.

Since our previous studies revealed recognition memory after exposure to just one instance of a basic-level category, it was anticipated that on immediate test trials children would recognize an earlier exemplar, whether it occurred only once among four different exemplars or on all four familiarization trials. Of more interest was what would happen after a long delay. Perhaps only children presented varied exemplars would remember the familiarized category 1 week later. This outcome could be predicted on the assumption that (1) retention of the features of a specific exemplar is relatively poor over a long delay interval, (2) memory for basic-level category information is relatively good over a long duration, and (3) repeated presentations of the same exemplar of a category are less likely to promote abstraction of basic-level category knowledge than presentation of varied exemplars.

Greco and Daehler (1984) found that subjects attended to extracategory stimuli longer both immediately and 1 week after familiarization trials and that this attentional difference was displayed when subjects were familiarized with only one exemplar of a category or with several exemplars. Moreover, this preference was exhibited whether the member representing the familiar category had been presented on familiarization trials or had not. In other words, children 24 months of age did identify basic-level category information from only one exemplar and retained that information as well as children who had identified basic-level category information from several exemplars. The results suggest the powerful role that basic-level category information plays in the child's early knowlededge base, but further research needs to be carried out to determine whether these same findings will be obtained for superordinate and subordinate classes.

Memory for Location

The position of an object can often change and as Piaget and subsequent researchers have noted, that knowledge and the implementation of an efficient search strategy for retrieving the object is a major conceptual achievement underlying object permanence. Reason dictates that search should begin in that location where an object was last seen. But if the object is not found there, continue to search in locations where the object may have been left or found at earlier times. Infants around 9 or 10 months of age often fail to follow such a heuristic as indicated by the $A\overline{B}$ error.

Prior and current information. In a recent longitudinal study involving infants between 6 and 12 months of age, Diamond (1983) found that the $A\overline{B}$ error occurs within a very narrow delay period. When delays are short, subjects are likely to respond correctly, that is, remember where the object has been hidden most recently. But increases in delays as little as 2–3 sec beyond the narrow time span responsible for the $A\overline{B}$ error will yield random search for the hidden object. The delay necessary to obtain the $A\overline{B}$ error increases from approximately 2 sec for infants at 7 months of age to 10 sec for infants at 11 months of age.

Diamond has interpreted these results to mean that memory for the new location of an object controls behavior for a relatively short duration. However, the competing reinforced "habit" of searching at an earlier successful location is remembered somewhat longer and "wins out" when delays extend beyond the more fragile memory for its most recent location. Once the delay surpasses the duration for which any memory is present, behavior becomes random.

An equivalent kind of error is still occasionally displayed in the delayed search of toddlers and preschoolers (DeLoache & Brown, 1983; Horn & Myers, 1978; Loughlin & Daehler, 1973; Perlmutter et al., 1981; Sophian & Wellman, 1980; Webb, Massar, & Nadolny, 1972). Children in this older age range are generally quite good at retrieving objects on search tasks, but when they do make errors, search is directed to that location where an object had been retrieved on the preceding trial more frequently than would be expected by chance.

Sophian and Wellman (1983) have carried out an extensive analysis of memory for and reliance upon prior and current information by very young children. They defined memory for current information as the ability to find an object in one location before any other location was used for hiding. Memory for prior information was defined as the proportion of searches where the object was formerly found when that object was *not* seen being hidden in its new location. Both 9- and 16-month olds remembered current information and, in fact, 16-month-olds performed at nearly ceiling level on this measure. But when the object was hidden behind a screen so that subjects could only infer where it might be on the basis of prior memory, 9-month-olds showed no preference for looking in the container from which the target object had been retrieved on those earlier trials. In contrast, 16-month-olds frequently initiated search in such a location. Thus, 16-month-olds were able to use prior information to guide their search activity. Furthermore, on trials in which a child first saw an object hidden in a new location so that current and prior information were in conflict, 16-month-olds predominantly used current information to direct their search behavior. Since the 9-month-olds failed to show evidence of relying on prior memory, no adequate test of the effects of a conflict between prior and current memory was possible for this group in this study.

In a subseqent study, 2-, 2½-, and 4-year-olds were also tested for memory for prior and current information. On some trials a picture illustrating an animal or room (bedroom, kitchen, and bathroom) was placed in front of each of three containers that served as hiding locations. These pictures were introduced to test for the effects of verbal instructions on search activity. On some picture trials the subjects were informed only verbally that the target was "in the bird's box" or "in the bedroom." Performance on these trials was compared to performance when the subjects saw the object actually hidden in a box or when subjects had only prior information about where the object might be found.

Children at all three ages relied on both current and prior information in their search activity in this study. Use of current knowledge was demonstrated by the fact that at every age level, children correctly retrieved the object where it was initially hidden on more than 90% of the trials. When the object was screened while being hidden, most subjects first searched where it had been found on earlier trials, indicating that prior information could be used to guide their behavior. At all three ages, verbal instructions also served to direct search, although the performance of the 2-year-olds was significantly poorer than the performance of the older subjects in this condition. Finally, all three age groups were more likely to use current information than prior information when the two were in conflict, whether that current information was provided verbally or by observing the placement of the target. The results, then, indicate that very young children do remember prior information, will rely on it when no other information is available, but are more likely to use current information when in conflict with prior information.

Cue distinctiveness. Another issue that has received considerable attention in search tasks has been the extent to which memory for the location of an object benefits from the addition of nonspatial cues. Loughlin and Daehler (1973) found that discriminable pictures unrelated to the target object and placed in front of hiding locations failed to help children less than 3 years of age remember where the object was hidden. The addition of these pictures, however, did help 3-year-olds. Subsequent research has confirmed this developmental finding (Myers & Ratner, in press). But children less than 3 years of age can enlist discriminative cues to aid search performance under some conditions. These include (1) distinctive cues which are an intrinsic part of the hiding location, such as the color or size of a container (Daehler,

Bukatko, Benson, & Myers, 1976); (2) pictures associated with a hiding location that actually portray the target object to be retrieved (Ratner & Myers, 1980); and (3) natural or easily discriminated landmarks within the home and associated with hiding places that are otherwise not very distinctive (DeLoache & Brown, 1983). In contrast, pictures closely related to the target to be retrieved and arbitrary pictures linked to the location in which the object has been hidden, even when these discriminative pictures are singled out by verbal statements such as, "the cracker is with the _____," have not been found to be consistently helpful to subjects at 2 years of age (Horn & Myers, 1978; Ratner & Myers, 1980; but see also Blair, Perlmutter, & Myers, 1978; and Perlmutter et al., 1981 for evidence that 2-year-olds can use arbitary cues under some circumstances). At the very least, we can conclude that arbitrary pictorial cues are not an automatic aid to retrieval for 2-year-olds, while for older subjects such pictures routinely benefit performance.

Sophian and Wellman (1983) examined whether children's prior knowledge base could serve as another potential source of discriminative cues in search. As we indicated in our earlier description of their study, Sophian and Wellman added pictures of different rooms to the front of the boxes on some trials. The targets hidden in the boxes were, however, room-specific, that is, typically found in a particular room such as the bathroom (a toothbrush), bedroom (a pillow), or kitchen (a spoon). When pictures of rooms accompanied the containers, that room-specific knowledge might be used to help identify where an object was likely to be located.

Pretests revealed that the 2-year-olds could not identify pictures of the rooms as well as either 2½- or 4-year-old subjects and furthermore, that only the two oldest groups could consistently identify to which room the target item belonged (see also Ratner & Myers, 1981). As might be expected from this pretest data, the search behavior of the 2-year-olds did not benefit from the availability of room cues in front of the containers. But although the 2½-year-olds possessed room-specific knowledge, they showed no evidence of drawing upon this information. Only the 4-year-olds took advantage of prior information available in long-term memory to aid retrieval of the objects.

Our review of delayed reaction tasks reveals that with development subjects are able to capitalize upon a broad range of distinctive cues and prior information to aid memory for the location of any object. In fact, such cues become the preferred criteria for finding an object when in conflict with spatial location (Daehler et al., 1976; Horn & Ratner, 1978). The following description given by Myers and Ratner (in press) summarizes the developmental differences quite succinctly: "For those under 2 the delayed response task seemed to translate to 'remember the object is in the box located there' and they relied heavily on location cues. . . . The 3-year-olds quite obviously represented the task as 'remember the object is with that picture (or color or size),' and then spontaneously and quite consistently used arbitrary cues other than location as memory aids." This developmental change, according to DeLoache and Brown (1983), reflects more than a simple preferential difference. They have proposed that this shift reflects an increasing developmental ability to mnemonically regulate search activity. Perlmutter et al. (1981) have shown that requiring subjects to consider every possible response location before initiating search can also improve performance for 2-year-olds, perhaps another example of the role that more deliberate processes, this time during retrieval, may play in memory for location of objects. Finally, DeLoache and Brown (1984) report that children as young as 21 months of age continue to search for some time if unable to find an object and that by 2½ years of age, they search in related areas or assume that a social agent has moved the object as ways of trying to resolve the unexpected absence of a stimulus.

Memory for Events

In contrast to research on memory for objects and memory for location, no simple, standardized laboratory procedure can be singled out to illustrate memory for events. This gap may be because memory for this type of content is often tested through recall procedures which demand a relatively sophisticated level of verbal competence and a fairly complete record of the context and setting from which retrieval occurs, a record likely to be available only from eyewitness observers such as a caregiver, especially in the case of recall of unique experiences.

In her observations of the memory demands mothers place on their 30- and 42-month-olds, Ratner (1980) identified many different kinds of requests to remember activities and events. Mothers frequently asked questions such as "What are you doing?" or "What did you do?," which called for the recollection of current or very recent sequences of past activities. At other times caregivers demanded recall of events expected to take place in the future, and which had been discussed some time earlier (e.g., "Where are we going tomorrow?") or which were based on activities routinely exercised up to a year before. Ratner found that although recall of knowledge about objects or their properties was also requested, mothers, especially mothers of older children, were relatively more likely to ask questions concerned with events. In contrast, DeLoache (1983) found that 24–30-month-olds were frequently asked to name objects or people in pictures in the family photograph album, but were rarely asked to recall the events surrounding these pictures. This discrepancy may be resolved by another recent finding. Mothers do report a substantial number of memories for events or sequences of actions from their children, but the percentage of such memories dramatically increases with development: from 21% for 21-month-olds, to 35% for 24-month-olds, to 53% for 27-month-olds (Nelson & Ross, 1980). On the other hand, memories for the location of objects were less frequently reported for older children.

Wellman and Somerville (1980) describe developmental improvements in memory for another kind of event, the performance of a daily routine. Examples of such daily routines include brushing teeth, feeding a pet, and saying prayers at night. Caregivers were instructed to allow their children sufficient time to carry out one of these activities without reminders. But if the routine was not produced within the designated time, caregivers were instructed to provide increasingly direct prompts, first in the form of a visual suggestion and then in the form of a verbal prompt and eventually, a verbal instruction. Half of the 1-, 2-, and 3-year-olds who participated in this study were observed carrying out an already established routine, and the remaining half learned a new routine over the 6 days in which observations were collected.

Established routines were performed with only limited prompts, even by 1-year-olds. But there was no evidence that new routines were learned and remembered by this age group within the 6 days allowed in this study. Two- and three-year-olds, on the other hand, displayed increasing evidence of memory for new routines, and for the oldest subjects, both previously established and new routines were completed nearly perfectly by the end of the observations. In a similar study carried out with 2- and 4-year-olds in a nursery school, it was found that younger subjects continued to need both more prompts and more specific prompts to remember the routines.

Nelson (1983) has recently described another procedure for gaining information about the very young child's memory for events. She recorded the verbal conversations of a 21-month-old as the child was about to go to sleep in her crib. The data were collected two or three times per week over a period of 5 months. The monologues frequently included references to events that had transpired during the day or just prior to bedtime and also reflected memory for events that she had been told were about to happen in the future.

Utterances such as these could provide a rich source of information about the very young child's memory and how it is integrated with planning and problem solving. For example, Nelson noted that the child she studied did not appear to distinguish between memories for specific events and memories for more general knowledge. As a result, Nelson concluded that for children this age "personal episodic memory does not exist in the same way that it does for the adult" (Nelson, 1983). DeLoache (1983) also reported that mothers of 24- to 30-month-olds seldom asked their children to detail specific events surrounding a picture in the family photograph album, although they did interrogate their children concerning general knowledge of objects and events represented in the pictures. As DeLoache points out, these data confirm Nelson's hypothesis (Nelson & Gruendel, 1981) that the earliest recall of events is in the form of generalized scripts rather than specific personal experiences.

Some Lingering Concerns

We close our discussion of memory in very young children by first considering the distinction between recognition and recall, a distinction frequently made but one which we have not found very useful. It has been known for some time that various kinds of memory tasks differ in encoding and retrieval requirements. In recognition tasks, cues presented at encoding are re-presented at retrieval. Recognition tasks may vary in the numbers and kinds of distractors that are included on test trials, but "correct" cues match those occurring during encoding of the information. In contrast, the information to be retrieved is absent at testing in free recall tasks and, thus, the subject must produce or generate some representation which denotes his or her memory for the object, location, or event. Item matching is sufficient for accurate performance on recognition tasks, but at least one additional processing step, that is, some form of item generation, is required on recall tasks.

Because of the added processing required in recall tasks, researchers have frequently concluded that recognition and recall are two qualitatively distinct forms of memory, each with its own developmental history. For example, Piaget (Piaget & Inhelder, 1973) proposed that recognition is a basic process found in lower vertebrates as well as human infants and very young children. Since it is closely aligned to perception, recognition memory arises early both phylogenetically and ontogenetically. In fact, evidence for recognition memory has been reported in human infants only days after their birth (Friedman, 1972) and is routinely displayed by infants between 3 and 6 months of age. But since recall memory demands the production of a symbol to represent information to be remembered, it, according to Piaget and others, will not be found in infants until about a year of age when more cognitively advanced representational capacities emerge.

Although researchers have often tried to map the onset and development of both recognition and recall memory, we believe that continued efforts should be directed to reflect the fact that memory tasks fall on a continuum from those in which encoding and retrieval conditions are highly comparable to those in which encoding and retrieval conditions are enormously disparate in both the cues that are available and the responses that are demanded from the subject. The distinction between recognition and recall is especially problematic in assessing occurrences of memory in naturalistic settings but no less difficult to apply when evaluating laboratory tasks. For example, Piaget described an intermediate kind of memory, reconstruction, to account for the ability to remember the order or organization of an array of stimuli. In tasks assessing reconstruction memory, items "match" those seen earlier, thus incorporating a form of recognition. But the information to be remembered also requires generation of some kind of symbol or model to represent the organization of the items and that activity is more closely aligned to the demands of a recall task. Search behaviors are another case in point. Some researchers have described them as more like recognition tasks (Perlmutter et al., 1981), others as more like recall tasks (Olson & Sherman, 1983). Aspects of the search situation such as the physical location of the hiding places or any supplementary discriminative cues matching those present at encoding may be processed much as in visual recognition tasks (Sophian, 1980). But there is also the requirement of generating the object to be retrieved, remembering that something is actually in one of the hiding places.

Other tasks such as those involving cued recall may not include retrieval cues that "match" those provided during initial encoding of information, at least cues presented by the experimenter. But it is virtually impossible to rule out other contextual or self-generated cues that subjects might associate with the experimenter-provided cues and these may comprise a key aspect of a matching process which facilitates memory during retrieval.

Our proposition is that a gradient of identity between cues at encoding and cues at retrieval helps determine the efficiency and accuracy with which information is retrieved. We additionally hypothesize that as the disparity between encoding and test conditions becomes greater, the difficulty of retrieving information increases and that this difficulty is disproportionately greater for very young children than for older children because they are less likely to encode or create cues that can be matched to retrieval cues. This hypothesis bears similarity to some other theories of memory. Tulving and Thompson's (1973) principle of encoding specificity states that the nature of what is perceived and stored by the subject will determine which cues are maximally effective for retrieval of the information. Extraexperimental cues, such as superordinate category names provided in a cued-recall task, may be effective because during the initial presentation of category members, that category relationship was encoded. Conversely, retrieval cues fail when they do not match or are not related to what was encoded. Goodnow (1971) makes a similar point with respect to performance on cross-modal matching tasks. Lack of overlap in cues sampled at encoding and retrieval by different modalities or a modality that is not effectively used may contribute to memory differences associated with cross-modal matching between auditory, visual, and tactual information processing systems. Spear (1978) presents a model of animal memory that also considers the role of cues at encoding and retrieval. In his model, however, since "lower animals are especially dependent on contextual stimuli to identify what must be remembered" (p. 49), the cues are more likely to be the environmental cues (internal and external) present during conditioning. He concludes that the effectiveness of memory retrieval is contingent upon the similarity of the cues present and noticed at testing and those that are represented in memory.

We suggest that further research be carried out to examine how similarities between encoding and retrieval conditions influence memory in infants and very young children. Experiments in our laboratory and by others have varied the physical and conceptual similarity of stimuli presented on familiarization and test trials to determine their effects on attentional preferences (Greco & Daehler, 1984). The stimuli have differed in circumscribed, limited ways from encoding to test, but response demands remained the same. Relatively little evidence of a difference in memory emerged in this study. But it is possible that as retrieval cues move from either identity matches or closely associated cues to more abstract cues, for example, from basic-level conceptual exemplars to superordinate members of a category (Mervis & Crisafi, 1982), that younger children's performance will be markedly affected. In contrast, because perceptual features overlap so greatly for subordinate categories, memory may actually be quite good for stimuli related in this fashion.

A cue identity gradient helps to explain some other findings with respect to the effects of context on memory. Ruff (1981) and Mackay-Soroka, Trehub, Bull, and Corter (1982) have demonstrated that 8- and 9-month-olds show preferences for novel objects only when the conditions at familiarization and testing are the same. When infants were permitted to inspect stimuli visually, they revealed novelty preferences but only when the recognition test was in the visual modality. When the infants were permitted haptic as well as visual inspection of the stimuli, novelty preferences were revealed only when haptic and visual inspection was available on test trials. If the infant experienced a modality change from familiarization to test, then preference scores were not significantly different from chance.

We cannot at this time rule out another possible explanation for the findings obtained by Ruff (1981) and Mackay-Soroka et al. (1982). It may be that a familiar stimulus is recognized but its occurrence in a changed setting is in itself novel and results in greater attention to it. This point simply reinforces the notion that preferences may be governed by factors other than stimulus novelty and that alternative methods for testing the gradient hypothesis are urgently needed. Nevertheless, it may be precisely because the memory of infants and very young children is more limited to the perceptual context in which events are encoded that a stimulus in a new context is less likely to be remembered. If others are like us, we suspect that one favored trick of older children as well as adults for improving recollection of some object or event is to try to reproduce, either physically or imaginatively, the setting or context in which that object or event was initially encoded. The ability to *detect* matching cues may be a major factor contributing to developmental differences in memory very early in childhood; the ability to *generate* those matching cues through various mnemonic techniques certainly is a major factor contributing to developmental differences in later childhood (see, for example, Pressley, 1982).

The concern with ability to remember details over great lengths of time has led to another related issue, that of infantile amnesia. Campbell and Spear (1972) have written at length on the enigma created by psychology's common assumption that early experience has significant and long-lasting effects upon behavior, and the fact that memories for specific events during early periods of development are seldom, if ever, able to be reported. In contrast, information from later preschool and elementary years often provides a significant source of nostalgia for adults.

The reason for the discontinuity is unclear and a number of motivational, social, physiological and cognitive hypotheses have been proposed (see White & Pillemer, 1979). The possibility that significant information is never or seldom stored below the preschool age period cannot be viably entertained. For example, Nelson and Ross (1980) indicated that 2-year-olds remember information for as long as a year, even an event that occurred only once. The legion of research concerned with infant memory also weighs heavily against this possibility.

Nelson and Ross (1980) offer a two-pronged explanation for infantile amnesia. First, specific instances are generally difficult for young children to retrieve. Whereas mothers report some instances of memory for particular experiences among 2-year-olds, children are more likely to report events in general terms rather than in specific terms. Second, because specific events experienced by the young child often have much in common, they fuse so that individual memories lose their unique and salient aspects. Research findings on infantile amnesia in lower organisms such as rats provide some support for this idea. Berk, Vigorito, and Miller (1979) trained weanling pups and adult rats on a conditioned fear task and animals were tested 2, 8, 16, 32, and 64 days later. Pups showed retention equivalent to adults after 2 days but not after the longer intervals. When given nonreinforced exposures to the fear-provoking stimulus in the testing chamber or in other contexts 24 hours prior to the 2-day retention test, pups showed little or no fear, whereas adults continued to display fear responses even after as many as 16 nonreinforced trials. In addition, pups generalized extinction to stimuli other than the one used to invoke fear during the original training. The authors concluded that immature rats were more likely than adult rats to generalize from stimuli within the task to extraexperimental stimuli present in the retention environment, thereby making pups more susceptible to forgetting than their adult counterparts.

There are other interpretations of infantile amnesia and some of these of course, are compatible with the ideas presented by Nelson and Ross. Information may be organized and encoded in some developmentally different, perhaps, immature form, a form that becomes inaccessible as new sensory, neurological, or cognitive organizations emerge (Neisser, 1967; White & Pillemer, 1979). For example, it is possible that information is not initially encoded in verbal form and therefore cannot be easily retrieved. Nelson and Ross present one observation, however, indicating that verbal encoding is not necessary for information to be recalled several months later. A toddler, who had moved away 2½ months earlier, started naming a friend when he came into sight of that friend's house again. But the friend's name had been learned after the toddler had moved away. What is interesting about this observation is not the fact that a verbal response could serve to indicate memory, but rather, how important specific cues present at both encoding and retrieval may be for eliciting evidence of that memory.

Perhaps the cues encoded in early development are not "seen" in memory tasks given at much later periods of development because different attributes are salient at retrieval and these differences are unlikely to elicit memory for an early childhood event (Campbell & Spear, 1972). Based on Pascual-Leone's (1970) theory of cognitive development, White and Pillemer (1979) have elaborated a theory of infantile amnesia which states that because early memories are not formed and attended to by conscious mental efforts, they are not easily addressed by conventional retrieval methods. Instead, early memories are brief and fragmentary and are only "attached to situations" so that "if a situation is repeated, it tends to bring back the memory" (p. 60). In other words, the context at retrieval must closely conform to the context at encoding if evidence of memory is to be obtained from early periods of development.

White and Pillemer propose that events encoded by children less than 5 years of age are especially likely to be fragmentary and context dependent since mental processing is severely constrained before this age. Three- and four-year-olds have great difficulty retrieving events to general questions such as "What did you do at school?" but are much more responsive to specific questions such as "Can you tell me one funny thing that happened at your school?" (Todd & Perlmutter, 1980). Thus, young children do need more particular and detailed cues if they are to retrieve anything of substance. But in every study of infantile amnesia with which we are familiar, subjects have been asked to retrieve long-term memories with vaguely expressed instructions or with highly limited, supporting contextual cues. If children fail to carry out active mental processing (White & Pillemer, 1979) or fail to generate mnemonic cues at the time of encoding, cues substantially more similar to the encoding context may be required to obtain evidence for memory. Thus, some type of retrieval task having a format more similar to recognition memory may be more appropriate for obtaining evidence for very-long-term memory from the earliest periods of childhood. While such tasks may not be easy to design, they could provide new insights concerning infantile amnesia and memory development in very young children.

References

Allen, C. N. (1931). Individual differences in the delayed reaction of infants. *Archives of Psychology, 19* (Whole No. 127).

Ames, E. W., Hunter, M. A., Black, A., Lithgow, P. A., & Newman, F. M. (1978). Problems of observer agreement in the infant control procedure. *Developmental Psychology, 14*, 507–511.

Ashmead, D. H., & Perlmutter, M. (1980). Infant memory in everyday life. In M. Perlmutter (Ed.), *New directions for child development: Children's memory*, No. 10. San Francisco: Jossey-Bass.

Berk, A. M., Vigorito, M., & Miller, R. R. (1979). Retroactive stimulus interference with conditioned emotional response retention in infant and adult rats: Implications for infantile amnesia. *Journal of Experimental Psychology: Animal Behavior Processes, 5*, 284–299.

Blair, R., Perlmutter, M., & Myers, N. A. (1978). The effects of unlabeled and labeled picture cues on very young children's memory for location. *Bulletin of the Psychonomic Society, 11*, 46–48.

Bornstein, M. H. (1981). Psychological studies of color perception in human infants. In L. P. Lipsitt & C. K. Rovee-Collier (Eds.), *Advances in infancy research* (Vol. 1). Norwood, NJ: Ablex.

Brown, A. L. (1975). The development of memory: Knowing about knowing and knowing how to know. In H. W. Reese (Ed.), *Advances in child development and behavior* (Vol. 10). New York: Academic Press.

Brown, A. L., & Scott, M. S. (1971). Recognition memory for pictures in preschool children. *Journal of Experimental Child Psychology, 11,* 401–412.

Campbell, B. A., & Spear, N. E. (1972). Ontogeny of memory. *Psychological Review, 79,* 215–236.

Caron, A. J., Caron, R. F., Minichiello, M. D., Weiss, S. J., & Friedman, S. L. (1977). Constraints on the use of the familiarization-novelty method in the assessment of infant discrimination. *Child Development, 48,* 747–762.

Carter, P., & Strauss, M. S. (1981). Commentary: Habituation is not enough, but it's not a bad start—a reply to Sophian. *Merrill-Palmer Quarterly, 27,* 333–337.

Cohen, L. B., & Gelber, E. R. (1975). Infant visual memory. In L. B. Cohen & P. Salapatek (Eds.), *Infant perception: From sensation to cognition* (Vol. 1) .New York: Academic Press.

Cohen, L. B., & Younger, B. A. (1983). Perceptual categorization in the infant. In E. K. Scholnick (Ed.), *New trends in conceptual representation: Challenges to Piaget's theory?* Hillsdale, N.J.: Erlbaum.

Daehler, M. W., & Bukatko, D. (1977). Recognition memory for pictures in very young children: Evidence from attentional preferences using a continuous presentation procedure. *Child Development, 48,* 693–696.

Daehler, M. W., Bukatko, D., Benson, K., & Myers, N. (1976). The effects of size and color cues on the delayed response of very young children. *Bulletin of the Psychonomic Society, 7,* 65–68.

Daehler, M. W., & Greco, C. (1981). The effects of lag and category membership on recognition memory in very young children. *Bulletin of the Psychonomic Society, 18,* 301–304.

Daehler, M. W., & O'Connor, M. P. (1980). Recognition memory for objects in very young children: The effect of shape and label similarity on preference for novel stimuli. *Journal of Experimental Child Psychology, 29,* 306–321.

Darwin, C. (1877). A biographical sketch of an infant mind. *Mind, 2,* 285–294.

Davis, J., & Rovee-Collier, C. K. (1979). A conditioning analysis of long-term memory in 8-week-old infants. Paper presented at the meetings of the Eastern Psychological Association, Philadelphia.

DeLoache, J. S. (1980). Naturalistic studies of memory for object location in very young children. *New directions for child development: Children's memory,* No. 10. San Francisco: Jossey-Bass.

DeLoache, J. S. (1983). Joint picture book reading as memory training for toddlers. Paper presented at Semi-Annual Meetings of the Society for Research in Child Development, Detroit.

DeLoache, J. S. (1984). Oh where, oh where: Memory-based searching by very young children. In C. Sophian(Ed.), *Origins of cognitive skills.* Hillsdale, N.J.: Erlbaum.

DeLoache, J. S., & Brown, A. L. (1983). Very young children's memory for the location of objects in a large scale environment. *Child Development, 54,* 888–897.

DeLoache, J. S., & Brown, A. L. (1984). Where do I go next? Intelligent searching by very young children. *Developmental Psychology, 20,* 37–44.

Diamond, A. (1983). Development of recall memory in the infant as indicated by performance on the AB̄ Stage IV object permanence task. Paper presented at the Society for Research in Child Development, Detroit.

Fagan, J. F., III. (1973). Infants' delayed recognition memory and forgetting. *Journal of Experimental Child Psychology, 16*, 424–450.

Fagan, J. F., III, & Singer, L. T. (1983). Infant recognition memory as a measure of intelligence. In L. P. Lipsitt & C. K. Rovee-Collier (Eds.), *Advances in infancy research* (Vol. 1). Norwood, N.J.: Ablex.

Fantz, R. L. (1956). A method for studying early visual development. *Perceptual and Motor Skills, 6*, 13–15.

Fantz, R. L. (1958). Pattern vision in young infants. *The Psychological Record, 8*, 43–47.

Fantz, R. L. (1964). Visual experience in infants: Decreased attention to familiar patterns relative to novel ones. *Science, 146*, 668–670.

Faulkender, P. J., Wright, J. C., & Waldron, A. (1974). Generalized habituation of concept stimuli in toddlers. *Child Development, 45*, 1002–1010.

Field, J. M., Woodson, R., Greenberg, R., & Cohen, D. (1982). Discrimination and imitation of facial expressions by neonates. *Science, 218*, 179–181.

Friedman, S. (1972). Habituation and recovery of visual response in the alert human newborn. *Journal of Experimental Child Psychology, 13*, 339–349.

Goodnow, J. J. (1971). The role of modalities in perceptual and cognitive development. In J. Hill (Ed.), *Minnesota symposium on child psychology* (Vol. 5). Minneapolis: University of Minnesota Press.

Gottfried, A. W., & Rose, S. A. (1980). Tactual recognition memory in infants. *Child Development, 51*, 69–74.

Gottfried, A. W., Rose, S. A., & Bridger, W. H. (1978). Effects of visual, haptic, and manipulatory experiences on infants' visual recognition memory for objects. *Developmental Psychology, 14*, 305–312.

Gratch, G. (1975). Recent studies based on Piaget's view of object concept development. In L. B. Cohen and P. Salapatek (Eds.), *Infant perception: From sensation to cognition* (Vol. 2). New York: Academic Press.

Greco, C., & Daehler, M. W. (1984). Immediate and delayed recognition memory for basic level categories in two-year-olds. Unpublished manuscript.

Groves, P. M., & Thompson, R. F. (1970). Habituation: A dual-process theory. *Psychological Review, 77*, 419–450.

Homa, D., Cross, J., Cornell, D., Goldman, D., & Schwartz, S. (1973). Prototype abstraction and classification of new instances as a function of number of instances defining the prototype. *Journal of Experimental Psychology, 101*, 116–122.

Horn, H., & Myers, N. A. (1978). Memory for location and picture cues at ages two and three. *Child Development, 49*, 845–856.

Hunter, M. A., Ross, H. S., & Ames, E. W. (1982). Preferences for familiar or novel toys: Effects of familiarization time in 1-year-olds. *Developmental Psychology, 18*, 519–529.

Hunter, W. S. (1917). The delayed reaction in a child. *Psychological Review, 24*, 74–87.

Hupp, S. C., & Mervis, C. B. (1982). Acquisition of basic object categories by severely handicapped children. *Child Development, 53*, 760–767.

Hurlock, E. B., & Schwartz, R. (1932). Biographical records of memory in preschool children. *Child Development, 3*, 230–239.

Kagan, J., Kearsley, R., & Zelazo, P. (1978). *Infancy: Its place in human development.* Cambridge, MA: Harvard University Press.

Loughlin, K. A., & Daehler, M. W. (1973). The effects of distraction and added perceptual cues on the delayed reaction of very young children. *Child Development, 44*, 384–388.

MacKay-Soroka, S., Trehub, S. E., Bull, D. H., & Corter, C. M. (1982). Effects of encoding and retrieval conditions on infants' recognition memory. *Child Development, 53*, 815–818.

Marsden, R. E. (1903). Discussion and apparatus: A study of the early color sense. *Psychological Review, 10*, 37–47.

McCall, R. B., Parke, R. D., & Kavenaugh, R. D. (1977). Imitation of live and televised models by children one to three years of age. *Monographs of the Society for Research in Child Development, 42* (Serial No. 173).

Meltzoff, A. N., & Moore, M. K. (1977). Imitation of facial and manual gestures by human neonates. *Science, 198*, 75–78.

Meltzoff, A. N., & Moore, M. K. (1983). Newborn infants imitate adult facial gestures. *Child Development, 54*, 702–709.

Mervis, C. B., & Crisafi, M. A. (1982). Order of acquisition of subordinate-, basic-, and superordinate-level categories. *Child Development, 53*, 258–266.

Mervis, C. B., & Pani, J. R. (1980). Acquisition of basic object categories. *Cognitive Psychology, 12*, 496–522.

Miller, N. E. (1934). The perception of children: A genetic study employing the critical choice of delayed reaction. *Journal of Genetic Psychology, 44*, 321–339.

Myers, N. A., & Ratner, H. H. (in press). Memory of very young children in delayed response tasks. In J. Sidowski (Ed.), *Cognition, conditioning, and methodology: Contemporary issues in experimental psychology*. Hillsdale, N.J.: Erlbaum.

Neisser, V. (1967). *Cognitive psychology*. Englewood Cliffs, N.J.: Prentice-Hall.

Nelson, K. (1983). Memories in the crib. Paper presented at the biennial meetings of the Society for Research in Child Development, Detroit.

Nelson, K., & Gruendel, J. (1981). Generalized event representations: Basic building blocks of cognitive development. In M. Lamb & A. Brown (Eds.), *Advances in developmental psychology* (Vol. 1). Hillsdale, N.J.: Erlbaum.

Nelson, K., & Ross, G. (1980). The generalities and specifics of long-term memory in infants and young children. In M. Perlmutter (Ed.), *New directions for child development: Children's memory*. San Francisco: Jossey-Bass.

Olson, G. M. (1976). An information processing analysis of visual memory and habituation in infants. In T. J. Tighe & N. Leaton (Eds.), *Habituation: Perspectives from child development, animal behavior, and neurophysiology*. Hillsdale, N.J.: Erlbaum.

Olson, G. M., & Sherman, T. (1983). Attention, learning and memory in infants. In M. Haith & J. Campos (Eds.), *Manual of child psychology: Vol. 2. Infancy and the biology of development*. New York: Wiley.

Pascual-Leone, J. (1970). A mathematical model for the transition rule in Piaget's developmental stages. *Acta Psychologica, 63*, 301–345.

Perlmutter, M. (Ed.). (1980). *New directions for child development: Children's memory*, No. 10. San Francisco: Jossey-Bass.

Perlmutter, M., Hazen, N., Mitchell, D. B., Grady, J. C., Cavanaugh, J. C., & Flook, J. P. (1981). Picture cues and exhaustive search facilitate very young children's memory for location. *Developmental Psychology, 17*, 104–110.

Perlmutter, M., & Lange, G. (1978). A developmental analysis of recall-recognition distinctions. In P. A. Ornstein (Ed.), *Memory development in children*. Hillsdale, N.J.: Erlbaum.

Piaget, J. (1951). *Play, dreams, and imitation in childhood.* New York: Norton.

Piaget, J., & Inhelder, B. (1973). *Memory and intelligence.* New York: Basic Books.

Posner, M. I., & Keele, S. W. (1970). Retention of abstract ideas. *Journal of Experimental Psychology, 83,* 304–308.

Pressley, M. (1982). Elaboration and memory development. *Child Development, 53,* 296–309.

Ratner, H. H. (1980). The role of social context in memory development. In M. Perlmutter (Ed.), *New directions for child development: Children's memory,* No. 10. San Francisco: Jossey-Bass.

Ratner, H. H., & Myers, N. A. (1980). Related picture cues and memory for hidden-object location at age two. *Child Development, 51,* 561–564.

Ratner, H. H., & Myers, N. A. (1981). Long-term memory and retrieval at ages 2, 3, 4. *Journal of Experimental Child Psychology, 31,* 365–386.

Reznick, J. S., & Kagan, J. (1983). Category detection in infancy. In L. P. Lipsitt & C. K. Rovee-Collier (Eds.), *Advances in infant research* (Vol. II). Norwood, N.J.: Ablex.

Rosch, E. H., Mervis, C. B., Gray, W., Johnson, D. M., & Boyes-Braem, P. (1976). Basic objects in natural categories. *Cognitive Psychology, 8,* 382–439.

Rose, S. A., Gottfried, A. W., & Bridger, W. H. (1981). Cross-modal transfer and information processing by the sense of touch in infancy. *Developmental Psychology, 17,* 90–97.

Rose, S. A., Gottfried, A. W., Melloy-Carminar, P., & Bridger, W. H. (1982). Familiarity and novelty preferences in infant recognition memory: Implications for information processing. *Developmental Psychology, 18,* 704–713.

Ross, G. S. (1980). Categorization in 1- to 2-year-olds. *Developmental Psychology, 16,* 391–396.

Rovee-Collier, C. K., & Fagen, J. W. (1981). The retrieval of memory in early infancy. In L. P. Lipsitt (Ed.), *Advances in infancy research* (Vol. 1). Norwood, N.J.: Ablex.

Rovee-Collier, C. K., Sullivan, M. W., Enright, M., Lucas, D., & Fagen, J. W. (1980). Reactivation of infant memory. *Science, 208,* 1159–1161.

Ruff, H. A. (1981). The effect of context on infants' responses to novel objects. *Developmental Psychology, 17,* 87–89.

Sameroff, A. J. (1971). Can conditioned responses be established in the newborn infant? *Developmental psychology, 5,* 1–12.

Scarborough, H. S. (1977). Development of visual name and conceptual memory codes for pictures. *Journal of Experimental Child Psychology, 24,* 260–278.

Siqueland, E. R., & Lipsitt, L. P. (1966). Conditioned head-turning behavior in newborns. *Journal of Experimental Child Psychology, 3,* 356–376.

Skalet, M. (1931). The significance of delayed reactions in young children. *Comparative Psychology Monographs, 7*(4), 1–81.

Sophian, C. (1980). Habituation is not enough: Novelty preferences, search, and memory in infancy. *Merrill-Palmer Quarterly, 25,* 239–257.

Sophian, C., & Wellman, H. M. (1980). Selective information use in the development of search behavior. *Developmental Psychology, 16,* 323–331.

Sophian, C., & Wellman, H. M. (1983). Selective information use and perseveration in the search behavior of infants and young children. *Journal of Experimental Child Psychology, 35,* 369–390.

Spear, N. E. (1978). *The processing of memories: Forgetting and retention*. Hillsdale, N.J.: Erlbaum.

Strange, W., Keeney, T., Kessel, F., & Jenkins, J. (1970). Abstraction over time of prototypes from distortions of random dot patterns. *Journal of Experimental Psychology, 83*, 508–510.

Sugarman, S. (1983). *Children's early thought: Developments in classification*. Cambridge: Cambridge University Press.

Sullivan, M. W. (1982). Reactivation: Priming forgotten memories in human infants. *Child Development, 53*, 516–523.

Taine, M. (1877). On the acquisition of language by children. *Mind, 2*, 252–259.

Todd, C. M., & Perlmutter, M. (1980). Reality recalled by preschool children. In M. Perlmutter (Ed.), *New directions for child development: Children's memory*, No. 10. San Francisco: Jossey-Bass.

Tulving, E., & Thomson, D. M. (1973). Encoding specificity and retrieval processes in episodic memory. *Psychological Review, 80*, 352–373.

Valentine, C. W. (1913–1914). The colour perception and colour preferences of an infant during its fourth and eighth months. *British Journal of Psychology, 6*, 363–386.

Webb, R. A., Massar, B., & Nadolny, T. (1972). Information and strategy in the young child's search for hidden objects. *Child Development, 43*, 91–104.

Weizmann, F., Cohen, L. B., & Pratt, J. (1971). Novelty, familiarity and the development of infant attention. *Developmental Psychology, 4*, 149–154.

Wellman, H. M., & Somerville, S. C. (1980). Quasi-naturalistic tasks in the study of cognition: The memory-related skills of toddlers. In M. Perlmutter (Ed.), *New directions for child development: Children's memory*, No. 10. San Francisco: Jossey-Bass.

Wellman, H. M., Somerville, S. C., & Haake, R. J. (1979). Development of search procedures in real-life spatial environments. *Developmental Psychology, 15*, 530–542.

Werner, J. S., & Perlmutter, M. (1979). Development of visual memory in infants. In H. W. Reese & L. P. Lipsitt (Eds.), *Advances in child development and behavior* (Vol. 14). New York: Academic Press.

Wetherford, M. J., & Cohen, L. B. (1973). Developmental changes in infant visual preferences for novelty and familiarity. *Child Development, 44*, 416–424.

White, S. H., & Pillemer, D. B. (1979). Childhood amnesia and the development of a socially accessible memory system. In J. F. Kihlstrom & F. J. Evans (Eds.), *Functional disorders of memory*. Hillsdale, N.J.: Erlbaum.

3. Social Contexts and Functions of Children's Remembering

Scott G. Paris, Richard S. Newman, and Janis E. Jacobs

It has been remarked that the very essence of civilization consists of purposely building monuments so as not to forget. In both the knot and the monument we have manifestations of the most fundamental and characteristic feature distinguishing human from animal memory. (Vygotsky, 1978, p. 51)

Whether we examine histories of societies or lives of individuals, we can review ample evidence of the cues that are erected to prevent forgetting. Statues, notes, and even knots can help to remind us of particular events in the past or to cue us to perform designated actions in the future. Vygotsky was interested in the *socialized construction* of these cultural artifacts and personal signs as mental cues that serve parallel functions in sociohistory and memory development. The "essence" in both is "purposely building" "so as not to forget." The intentional selection of cues and mnemonic tactics to aid remembering is a developmental accomplishment that is part of higher mental functions according to Vygotsky (1978). Remembering, planning, and other forms of directed reasoning extend basic psychological processes through the use of signs and tools in the broadest sense of cognitive instruments.

In this chapter we discuss how people construct, share, and teach various tactics for remembering. Our chief concern is to understand how children learn to remember strategically and effectively in everyday situations such as searching for lost objects or studying for future recall. We are guided in this analysis by Vygotsky's (1978, pp. 56–57) three principles of internalized cognitive processes:

1. An operation that initially represents an external activity is reconstructed and begins to occur internally.

2. An interpersonal process is transformed into an intrapersonal process.
3. The transformation of an interpersonal process into an intrapersonal one is the result of a long series of developmental events.

In the beginning of this chapter we try to show how Vygotsky's perspective can enlarge and complement traditional views about the development of mnemonic strategies. In the next section we review research that illustrates how children's strategic remembering depends on the context of the activity, the social guidance provided, and cultural practices such as schooling. In the final section we postulate several psychological concepts that children learn about remembering that seem vital to self-directed use of mnemonic strategies as well as to subsequent maintenance and transfer of effective techniques for remembering. These developing notions of agency, purpose, and instrumentality add details to Vygotsky's framework by focusing on the psychological principles of self-directed learning that children come to understand.

Prevailing Accounts of Memory Development

During the past 15 years, the study of children's memories has been a cornerstone of research on cognitive development. The popularity of the field has been fueled by advances in cognitive science, implications of memory research for education, and, most especially, by the richness of the field of inquiry. Quite simply, there are many interesting questions to ask about children's memories and countless experimental paradigms to use. Many of these studies have been *descriptive*; that is, they report how children of different ages or abilities remember a stimulus array. The ages may vary from infancy to adolescence; the tasks may require recognition, reconstruction, or recall; and the stimuli might include visual patterns, digits, words, or prose. A second group of memory studies are *instructional* because the emphasis is on teaching children to remember under various conditions or with different types of mnemonic aids (e.g., Belmont & Butterfield, 1977; Pressley, Heisel, McCormick, & Nakamura, 1983). These studies have shown that children can be taught through instructions, modeling, and reinforcement to use some simple strategies that they ordinarily do not produce spontaneously (Brown, 1975; Flavell, 1970; Kail & Hagen, 1982). A third group of research studies could be regarded as *naturalistic* because researchers have investigated how children remember common tasks and events in everyday settings (e.g., remembering to brush one's teeth, Wellman & Somerville, 1980). These studies have been relatively rare compared to the preponderance of descriptive and instructional studies. As a consequence, much of what we know about memory development is derived from laboratory tasks and the skills required to solve them instead of the rich diversity of everyday tasks and social situations.

Researchers from all three orientations have emphasized similar developmental accomplishments that underlie improved memory performance. First, remembering becomes more automatic with age. Children can recognize previously seen stimuli more quickly and they can use similar mental operations to store and retrieve more items (Case, 1978; Kail & Bisanz, 1983). Improvements in automaticity, speed, and capacity reflect the consequences of both practice and maturation in what Vygotsky would refer to as "elementary psychological functions" or basic memory processes. A second factor that influences memory development is the accumulation of children's knowledge about the world (Chi, 1978; Naus & Ornstein, 1983). Familiarity with words, objects, and events permit subjects to fit new information into available schemas or scripts (Anderson, 1978). Piaget and Inhelder (1973) also conducted a number of studies in an attempt to show that children's developing knowledge serves to organize information for recall.

Basic processes and knowledge have been recognized as important factors in memory performance since the early studies of Binet, Ebbinghaus, and Bartlett. With the advent of information processing models of thinking came a new emphasis on cognitive strategies and executive functions. Ann Brown (1975) summarized these two developmental accomplishments as "knowing how to know" and "knowing about knowing." Developmental improvements in remembering, especially on laboratory types of memory tasks, are associated with children's use of strategies of rehearsal, organization, and elaboration to facilitate encoding and retrieval (Hagen, Jongeward, & Kail, 1975; Paris & Lindauer, 1977; Pressley, 1982). Finally children between 4 and 12 years of age become progressively more aware of the person, task, and strategy variables that influence remembering as they become increasingly able to adjust their behavior to situation memory demands (Cavanaugh & Perlmutter, 1982; Flavell & Wellman, 1977).

In order to see how these variables operate in concert, imagine a standard memory task presented to a 6-year-old and a 16-year-old. Suppose that 24 pictures were spread out on a table and the children were told to study them for 5 minutes and then to recall as many as possible. The pictures included six examples from four semantic categories such as vehicles, fruits, animals, and toys. A typical 6-year-old might name the pictures but would most likely limit studying to repeated visual inspection of one item at a time. A typical 16-year-old, though, would probably label and rehearse related blocks of items as she rearranged the pictures into categorical groups. The child's knowledge of the underlying concepts and her awareness of appropriate strategies would facilitate rapid and efficient studying. By 16 years of age, children usually exhibit self-controlled, flexible strategies for remembering. Thus, basic processes, knowledge, strategies, and awareness all contribute to more effective remembering by older children.

This is where most chapters on memory development end. However, we would like to start at this point by acknowledging the importance of these four developmental accomplishments and by supplementing the usual novice-to-expert description. It seems to us that researchers have concentrated so much on the processes of remembering that they have ignored the purposes and contexts of memory as well as the social and motivational dynamics that contribute to children's learning how to remember strategically. This may be due in part to the prevalence of adult information processing models in cognitive psychology that have guided research on memory development. Research on control processes that influence memory reveals how rehearsal, organization, and other mnemonic techniques alter the speed, accuracy, and efficiency with which information is accessed. This type of research helps us to identify parameters that affect the operation of "the system" but it does not necessarily lead us to confront critical developmental issues regarding the importance of the mnemonic techniques, their natural occurrence, nor their courses of acquisition. We know that world knowledge, cognitive strategies, and metacognition can affect how quickly, how accurately, and how much adults remember but we do not have adequate descriptions of the developmental, social, and cognitive principles that guide children to remember better with age.

The Nature of Strategies for Remembering

Our attempt to understand how children control and improve remembering is tied to cognitive strategies so we need to discuss the nature of strategies at the outset. It seems to us that the package of correlated cognitive accomplishments documented by memory researchers includes both "basic" and "higher" mental functions. These need to be unpacked because the basic processes seem to be influenced little by social instruction or cognitive construction of mnemonic techniques. Recognition memory, judgments of recency, incidental memory, and memory of frequency-of-occurrence information are examples of remembering that are neither directed nor intentional (e.g., Hasher & Zacks, 1979).

Children's remembering on other kinds of tasks, though, seems greatly influenced by knowledge, strategies, awareness, and other people. These include episodic tasks such as remembering rhymes and songs, lists of items, series of events, and text information. Indeed, these memory tasks are often transmitted and practiced in homes and schools with social guidance. We can also include planful attempts to retrieve information, to prepare for future recall, or to monitor one's current memory state as self-controlled, higher functions. Thus, some tasks permit or require cognitive strategies more than others. Certainly a great deal of children's remembering is unintentional, nonstrategic, and not very susceptible to control by the individual or other people. Such basic memory processes are not the focus of this chapter. Instead, we examine "higher" aspects of children's remembering that can be controlled and directed to serve functions such as learning and problem solving.

The distinction between "basic" processes that reflect largely maturational changes and "higher" processes that depend on deliberate and self-controlled reasoning rests on the notion of *strategy*. It is fair to say that the construct has been used in widely different ways that are often confusing and contradictory.

Strategy is often used synonymously with process, technique, or skill which obscures the motivated, intentional, goal-directed nature of strategic actions. Nickerson, Salter, Shepard, and Herrnstein (1984) define strategies as "selected means to ends, consciously chosen approaches to tasks." They emphasize that strategies can only be defined and evaluated in relation to the goal which they are designed to achieve. Repeating a list of words mindlessly for no purpose is echolalia, not mnemonic rehearsal. The pitfall of some cognitive models is that the behavior or operation has been defined as strategic without reference to the subject's goal, purpose, or perception of the activity. Thus, strategies can be defined mistakenly by the *forms* of behavior rather than by the *functions* that they serve in the individual's ongoing activity.

A definition of cognitive strategy that emphasizes selected means to particular goals requires a specification of the individual's motivated purpose on a task within a context. Anything less is an incomplete description that includes assumptions about the generality of the behavior across tasks, people, or contexts—assumptions that are unnecessary and potentially dangerous because they attribute motivational effects and cognitive utility normatively without regard to the individual's intent or purpose. We prefer to define a cognitive strategy as a selected action performed for the purpose of achieving a particular goal. The action must be chosen or constructed by the individual or else the person is mindlessly complying with directions. Most importantly, the subject must perceive a causal link between performing the action and attaining a goal. The goal, however, can be either self-selected or designated by someone else. Effectiveness is a criterion that can be used to judge strategies but it is not a defining characteristic. A child who puts a book under his pillow at night in order to remember the contents better is using a mnemonic strategy; it is just not helpful.

This kind of definition of a strategy as a motivated, goal-directed action is unlike mechanical subroutines that operate normatively to promote memory (cf. Chi & Rees, 1983; Trabasso, 1983). The definition implies that we should measure more than (a) the likelihood that these subroutines will be accessed and (b) the effectiveness with which they are applied. Considerably more information about children's personalized strategies could be obtained by measuring children's perceived goals in memory tasks and their perceptions of the utility and significance of the mnemonic techniques that they are directed to perform (or that they invent or select). Attention to the contexts of remembering can inform us about children's interpretations of the task and their own performance goals. For example, there may be wide differences in children's motivations and choices of strategy if they perceive the goal of a memory task as satisfying extrinsic purposes such as obedience or reward instead of intrinsic goals of task mastery (Lepper & Greene, 1975; Maehr, 1983; Nicholls, 1983).

In this chapter we would like to avoid extended discussions of how strategy and skills differ, whether strategies are general or task-specific, and how multiple goals are connected within networks or hierarchies of strategies. Paris, Lipson, and Wixson (1983) and Nickerson et al. (1984) discuss these issues and we believe that they merit extensive discussion. For the present purposes, though, we want to call attention to the socialized and temporalized nature of strategies. We do not believe that all cognitive strategies arise from explicit tuition nor that direct instruction is necessarily required or desirable all the time. Children undoubtedly construct personalized strategies for learning and remembering without help; some of the strategies may be idiosyncratic and some conventional. Yet experience with tasks does not insure that children will understand the need to recruit cognitive strategies nor that they will understand the required effort and utility of the actions. Young children and students with learning impairments have particular difficulty in acquiring and using appropriate strategies (Brown, Bransford, Ferrara, & Campione, 1983).

We need to understand how and when other people facilitate children's acquisition of strategies by providing opportunities for discovery, by modeling effective behavior, and by increasing demands for self-controlled use of strategies. The difference in performance between what children can do alone and what they can do with assistance is referred to as "the zone of proximal development" by Vygotsky (1978). We need to analyze these zones in order to understand how parents, teachers, and peers guide children to acquire mnemonic strategies and how they transfer the responsibility for selecting appropriate means and goals to children (Day, 1983). The issue here is to identify how social guidance prompts the personal construction of strategies that employ cognitive signs and tools to accomplish mnemonic purposes.

Finally, we want to note that strategies may be important not as ends in themselves but as resources for remembering when automatic skills fail or are unavailable. We would not expect a young or naive learner to use strategies, and it may be more effective for experts to use strategies only when trouble arises in the application of habitual skills. Strategies may be most important at times when the requirements for successful performance are explicit. These occasions might arise when children recognize that they need a plan to correct or insure their memories. Or someone else might evaluate the individual's performance and provide advice. Events that precipitate consideration of one's mnemonic states and processes foster "strategic episodes" in which people, individually or interactively, can appraise their own memory-related means and goals. These episodes are probably brief, recurrent experiences that are primarily evident in early stages of learning, explicit instructional interactions, and self-initiated troubleshooting. In this view, mnemonic strategies are important and observable only at some points in learning and performance; they are not necessarily customary behavior nor more effective than automatic skills. Indeed, we think that cognitive strategies are localized in learning and development of fluent skills and they should not be regarded as the uniform mediators of remembering across tasks or ages.

As a foreground to our discussion we have tried to show how cognitive strategies must be viewed as personalized, contextualized, socialized, and temporalized in order to be understood fully. Conceptual frameworks and data that embrace these dimensions of children's remembering can help to identify principles of learning that promote effective, self-controlled memory skills. But how do children learn to remember deliberately and flexibly? How do they learn what to do, when to do it, and why it helps memory? We think that much of this information and the motivation to employ it are learned through repeated social guidance. This includes informal interactions between adults and children as well as more explicit tutoring and instruction in social contexts. A theoretical view of memory development that emphasizes social interactions was proposed by Soviet researchers such as Vygotsky (1962, 1978) and Yendovitskaya (1971). (Meacham [1977] and Wertsch [1979] provide excellent summaries of this view.) The underlying tenet is that social supports and purposes for remembering exert great influence on children's recall. According to Vygotsky (1978), mental strategies for remembering must be constructed by children from their social interactions. Vygotsky called this a shift from an *inter*psychological plane of functioning to an *intra*psychological plane. But it is not just imitation of others or transferral from adult to child of step-by-step plans for remembering. Children need to be motivated to remember, they need to know how to promote memory, and they need to know how to adjust their behavior to new goals and tasks. In Soviet terminology, *activities* are social interactions such as play and work that supply motives for behavior. *Actions* include particular goals (such as remembering) to which behavior is directed. *Operations* are specific means or strategies that are used under various conditions to accomplish goals.

The Soviet approach to memory emphasizes social modeling of behavior and active participation of the learner so that the actions and operations can be internalized. Thus, mothers provide practice and social examples of memory aids when they play games with young children, when they ask children the identity or location of objects, when they give cues for memory, when they show children how to remember, and when they give corrective feedback. The Soviets emphasize a developmental trend from involuntary to voluntary memory behavior in children that coincides with the American emphasis on the acquisition of mnemonic strategies. The trend toward deliberate remembering by school-aged children is fostered by the increasing complexity engineered into the tasks as well as by the shifts in responsibility from parents to children. The zone of proximal development represents a degree of task difficulty in which guided learning and tutoring are needed for success until children can internalize adults' roles and solve the tasks independently. Thus Vygotsky's approach treats learning through social guidance and motivation as central to an account of memory development.

From these views on children's memory, we can extract several common themes. First, as children progress from infancy to teenagers they learn to act intentionally and to assume greater responsibility for directing their own learning. Second, children's remembering is influenced by the nature of the task including the purpose of the activity as well as knowledge about the stimuli. Third, children acquire techniques for processing information that can be instrumental as mnemonic strategies to aid recall. We shall refer to these principles as agency, purpose, and instrumentality. We believe that children learn these concepts from social interactions that involve tangible aspects of remembering such as games, question answering, and problem solving. That is why the social context and purposes are so important to children's acquisition of natural, functional skills for remembering. In the following section we illustrate how these concepts develop progressively with informed social guidance and how they underlie flexible, motivated, self-directed memory skills. We examine research on children's memory skills in the home and as a consequence of schooling and other cultural experiences.

Social Contexts of Memory Development

Traditional studies of children's memory skills have used laboratory tasks adapted from research with adults or animals. Typical experiments involve brief sessions with school-aged children in unfamiliar rooms with unfamiliar adults who ask children to remember arrays of pictures, words, objects, or stories. Although laboratory studies achieve control over many extraneous variables, the situations appear vastly different from young children's usual demands on memory such as recalling summer vacations, bedtime stories, or the route to a friend's home. At the outset it is important to recognize that laboratory and everyday memory tasks may provide quite different demands and supports for remembering. Wellman and Somerville (1982) point out that success on laboratory memory tasks requires verbal sophistication, speedy responses, focused attention, cooperation with strangers, and an ability to apply cognitive processes to novel tasks removed from common experiences. Preschoolers and young children do not excel in these behaviors and, thus, their memory skills appear quite limited on traditional laboratory tasks. Yet we know from observation that preschoolers remember a huge amount of information, and more than one parent has been surprised to discover what a 3–4-year-old can recall. Perhaps this is because children have more interest and personal involvement in events that occur in their everyday surroundings. Or it may be that familiar contexts and people provide structure to the activities so that social purposes and appropriate behaviors are more readily discerned (Istomina, 1975).

The context provided by home and family is usually meaningful, familiar, and comfortable for most children and, thus, may facilitate early remembering. Several researchers have conducted observational studies of infants in their homes but a more efficient method has been to enlist the aid of parents as observers. Ashmead and Perlmutter (1980), for example, asked the mothers of 11 infants to record instances of memory behavior that they observed in the home. The infants were 7, 9, and 11 months old at the beginning of the 6-week study. Parents were visited by the experimenters who explained how to record various types of evidence in the diaries. Families recorded an average of 27 memory episodes such as the following:

My husband called from work and I let him talk to Rob. He looked puzzled for a while and then he turned to look at the door. Rob thought of the only time he hears his dad's voice when he knows dad isn't home is when his dad just got home. He heard his dad's voice and based on past experiences, he reasoned that his dad must be home, so he looked at the door. (Ashmead & Perlmutter, 1980, p. 4)

The episodes in this study were classified into different kinds of memory based on (1) perceptual attributes, (2) functional attributes, (3) locations of objects or people, (4) initiative social interactions by infants, or (5) responsive social interactions. Infants at all ages exhibited all types of memory, although 7-month-olds tended to show fewer episodes based on initiated than responsive social interactions. Some of the earliest memories of infants reasonably focus on the characteristics of people and objects in their immediate environments. Spatial locations were particularly well remembered by older infants. Ashmead and Perlmutter (1980) also found that infants appear to recall social interactions and to identify people as causal agents quite readily.

In a similar study, Nelson and Ross (1980) asked 19 mothers to record evidence of their children's memory behavior. The children were older, however, and ranged from 21 to 27 months of age at the start of the 3-month study. Mothers reported an average of only six memory episodes per child which points up the scarcity of specific memory examples as well as differences in reported frequencies with the Ashmead and Perlmutter study. Variability among parents and different instruction by experimenters may contribute to these differences. However, the kinds of memory episodes observed in both studies were similar. Forty percent of all memories reported in the Nelson and Ross (1980) study were related to specific events such as birthday parties or dance classes. Overall, older children recalled more episodes than younger children. However, 21-month-olds remembered object locations more often than 27-month-olds. They also note that locations of objects or people cued memories most frequently and especially for the youngest toddlers. Most of the recalled episodes were verbal (rather than actions or gestures) and 80% had occurred within the past 3 months. However, there were several reports of memory for episodes occurring 6–12 months earlier.

Research by Todd and Perlmutter (1980) supports some of the developmental trends discussed so far. They tape-recorded children during individual play sessions with an experimenter who asked various questions to elicit their memories. Six 2- and 3-year-olds and six 3- and 4-year-olds were observed. Throughout 2 hours of observation, children related information about an average of 25 past events that included specific details as well as general comments. Forty percent of the events were routine activities such as playing with toys and 42% involved novel experiences involving, for example, a mouse, holiday, or visit to a zoo. Approximately half of the episodes were recalled spontaneously by children, mostly routine events, while the other half were elicited by the experimenter's questions. About half of the recalled episodes had taken place more than 6 months earlier. As expected, older children had longer memories than younger children but the long-term retention of all these preschoolers is truly remarkable. Finally, Todd and Perlmutter (1980) asked parents about the details and accuracy of children's reported episodes. Parents substantiated nearly 90% of the recalled events which indicates excellent accuracy by children of only 2–4 years of age. A similar study was conducted by Galotti and Neisser (1982) to investigate 26–59-month-olds' memories of Christmas day. They found that all children were able to recall at least one present and one incident from Christmas day, but that younger children have less control over the recall process than older children. When they have trouble answering, they remain silent or say the first thing that comes into their heads. In contrast, older children appear to be able to think back to the day in question at the experimenter's request and are better able to monitor their recall attempts.

These studies of infants and toddlers reveal good memory for specific episodes over long time intervals. Recall with external cues is gradually replaced by spontaneous recall without cues by 3–4-year-olds. Perceptual and functional attributes, particularly spatial locations, appear to be important components of young children's memories. With repeated experience and language development, 3–4-year-olds can report general events as well as specific autobiographical memories in great detail. It is clear that some routines of everyday life with family members are especially meaningful to toddlers and easy to remember.

Perhaps the best example of the roots of memory skills used in familiar contexts can be found in young children's searching behavior for hidden objects (see Wellman & Somerville, 1982). Piaget noted that 1-year-olds can remove blankets, covers, and barriers to expose hidden objects. These skills clearly involve mental representation and memory. Searching for objects, though, as in hide-and-seek games or Easter egg hunts involves more sophisticated, intentional skills. DeLoache and Brown (1979) reported a hide-and-seek study in which 1, 2, and 3-year-olds displayed surprisingly good memories and searching skills. The task was presented as a hide-and-seek game to children, in which they were told that a stuffed animal (Big Bird or Mickey Mouse) would be hidden and they were to watch so that they could find it later. The parent was instructed to hide the toy in a natural hiding place in the home such as behind a pillow or inside a cupboard and to set a kitchen timer. Children could search for the toy when the timer rang. The toy was hidden in a different location each time. In the basic task young children did very well. Children who were 25–30 months old averaged 84% correct trials over four studies; 18–24-month-olds averaged 59% correct. A variation of this task had mothers hide Big Bird for longer periods (varying from 30 minutes to overnight). Children were still correct on 77% of the overnight trials.

The high levels of performance on this task may be due to several things. Certainly interest level and personal meaningfulness are important. According to reports by parents and experimenters, children found the "Big Bird game" very enjoyable. Children may be more motivated to remember in an activity of interest to them because they understand the rules of hide-and-seek and attach personal significance to finding the toy. Involvement in tasks with activities and objects that have personal meaning may facilitate memory for those tasks (cf. Lindberg, 1980).

A second factor may have been the familiarity of the hiding places. Children may be better able to use contextual cues within a familiar environment to help them remember. To test this, DeLoache (1980) tested 2-year-old children on the same task, but varied the contextual familiarity. Children were all tested in their own homes on a hide-and-seek task and on a delayed response task. Four metal boxes were the hiding locations for the delayed response task. The top of each box was decorated with a bright picture that children were asked to name at the beginning of the session. A toy was hidden in one of the boxes and children waited until a timer rang to find the toy. The hide-and-seek task was the same, except that the toy was hidden in a natural hiding place in the room. Performance was significantly better on the hide-and-seek task. Young children appear to have significantly better memory in a naturalistic setting, perhaps because the environment facilitated the use of contextual cues to trigger memory.

Interest, personal significance, and familiarity may all underlie the intentional effort to remember that enhances young children's memory abilities in naturalistic settings. In the Big Bird study, the children were instructed to remember where Big Bird was hiding in order to find him when the bell rang. The child's ability to remember may have been enhanced because of the familiar environment, salience of the hiding place, or meaning of the game. Intentionality may surface in young children when the goal is explicitly recognized and task demands are lowered so that the research situation is more similar to everyday memory tasks that children encounter.

Interpersonal Guidance in Remembering

Natural contexts can facilitate young children's remembering by providing opportunities to remember common routines and objects. Adults help to structure children's attempts to remember within these contexts and the salient activities of homelife. Adults guide children's learning and problem solving by linking familiar behavior to new problems. Both formal and informal instruction occur during social interactions that can increase children's understanding of strategies required for successful remembering.

As noted earlier, Soviet psychologists believe that cognition and memory develop within the context of social interactions (Vygotsky, 1978). The child's memory is thought to be initially controlled by the structure of external social interactions, but through daily activities and the guidance of adults the structure is internalized, and remembering becomes a goal to the child. Reliance on external memory aids is replaced by reliance on internal mechanisms. For example, at first the child may only remember to wear a sweater outside when his mother reminds him. Then Mom may suggest placing the sweater by the door to remember, gradually withdrawing her aid. Eventually, the child will internalize the need to remember to wear a sweater when going outside. Wertsch and Stone (1978) have called the process by which a child produces a simple aspect of a task while being directed by the adult "proleptic instruction" because the adult anticipates the child's responses and potential problems. The adult integrates explanation and demonstration with an emphasis on the learner's participation. The goal is the child's internalization and personalization of the instructional principles.

Even young toddlers seem able to accept partial responsibility for remembering high-interest activities at home. Wellman and Somerville (1980) investigated this by asking parents to record their 1–3-year-olds' memories for familiar routines such as saying a prayer at bedtime or brushing teeth. Some routines were old and some newly introduced (such as reading a bedtime story). Parents were instructed to see if children would remember the routines without prompting (which, by the way, is difficult because parents supply so many reminders to brush teeth, wash hands, and put away clothes). The researchers found that old routines were recalled more easily than new ones and that 3-year-olds remembered more than younger children. They also found a learning effect showing that children improved their recall of new and old routines more often as parents withheld the prompts and expected them to remember on their own. This is a compelling demonstration of the shift from external parental responsibility to the child's intentional remembering at a young age.

A second study (Somerville, Wellman, & Cultice, 1983) investigated 2-, 3-, and 4-year-olds' intentional attempts to remember by involving them in reminding tasks. Parents asked children to remind them to do something at a specified time in the future. The tasks were either of high or low interest to children (i.e., buy candy for the child at the supermarket vs. take the laundry out of the dryer). Tasks also varied on the amount of time between being told to remind and the specified time to do the task. Each child was asked to carry out reminding tasks eight times over a 2-week period. At the appointed time to remember, children were given 5–10 minutes to remember, then given nonverbal hints, and finally asked, "Wasn't there something you were supposed to remind me of?" if they still did not remember. The results showed that high-interest tasks were performed correctly more often than low interest, and that children performed better after short delays than long delays. There were no age differences on the high-interest tasks. Even 2-year-olds performed correctly 80% of the time. From these examples, it can be seen that children as young as 2 have developed the ability to remember deliberately in a meaningful situation. Although the focus of these studies was not the parent's actions, it is clear that expecting children to remember routines and prompting them for memory facilitated children's recall of information.

In order to study social interactions beween mothers and children during memory tasks, several investigators have studied mothers in naturalistic settings. Rogoff (1982) conducted a study in which mothers were asked to prepare their children for a memory test in a room resembling a kitchen. The task was to put groceries away on shelves. The groceries were to be put onto particular shelves according to categories and mothers were to help children remember the arrangement so that children could duplicate it when mothers were not present.

The mother–child pairs were videotaped during this task and a second task resembling a school activity. The school activity involved sorting pictures of common objects into a divided tray. In both cases, mothers were provided with a list of where the groceries or pictures belonged. Transcripts of the videotapes were analyzed in several different ways but Rogoff and Gardner (1984) have provided excerpts from a transcript of a mother and her 8-year-old son that are informative for our purposes.

MOTHER	CHILD
This should be fun (looks in grocery bag containing items).	
Okay, we just got home from the store, okay?	
	Yeah.
And we want to have everything in a certain place, so everyone knows where it goes.	
Okay first of all, lets start with this one (points to shelf 1).	
Okay, let's pretend we're going on a picnic (points to shelf 1) and we'll think: what do we need for a picnic? (Looks into grocery bag of items.) So let's look through here (pulls out can of olives). Uh . . . olives are good for a picnic. So we'll keep the picnic things here, okay? (Places olives on shelf 1.)	
	(Follows mother to shelf 1.)
Continues with dill pickles, etc., finishes shelf 1.	
All right, we're through with that (gestures to shelf 1) okay? You just glance at that.	
	Turns and looks at shelf 1.
If I brought all of these things and I wasn't home, then you'd just put them right back there. Okay? So there's olives, pickles, and ketchup just for picnics.	

In the excerpt the mother began by establishing the context (home from grocery shopping). She also tried to add some motivation (this should be fun) for the child. She focused the child's attention on shelf 1 and established a familiar script for the child (picnics). Throughout the discourse, the mother attempted to involve the child and make sure he understood (okay?). Near the end, she began to prepare him for the test, but she did it within the context of the "pretend" situation. In this study, it is easy to see that adults convey many types of information relevant for remembering. The interactions contain specific instructions for using mnemonic strategies (categorization), intentionality, task meaning, and motivation. Parents use such interactions in daily dialogues to transmit memory information to their children, although it is not always so explicit.

Another illustration from the same study describes the negotiation of a child's readiness to accept more responsibility for the task. This illustrates the beginning of the transition from external control to internal control.

MOTHER	CHILD
(Picks out margaine, hands to child.) This goes on bread.	
	(Studies item.)
Where do you put that? (Touching margarine, practically pushing it in correct direction.)	
	Ah (unintelligible comment). (Places margarine appropriately and returns to mother.)
(Picks out ketchup, holds toward child.) What is this?	
	Ketchup (moves to place it on incorrect shelf).
No.	
	(Pauses in midstep.)
Where does it go? Think.	
	(Backs up to center of room, appears to "think.")
Ok. (Looks at appropriate shelf.)	
	(No move.)
(Points at correct shelf.) It goes over here with the pickles and the olives.	
	(Nods, places item on correct shelf.)

In this example, the mother and her 7-year-old daughter were each adapting to the other to establish the appropriate level of responsibility. The mother clearly felt that the child should be able to remember with only the help of minor cues. The daughter signalled that she was not ready to take that responsiblity yet. Such research on the instructional interaction of mothers and their children illustrates the important role of joint participation and negotiation in the act of transferring cognitive information.

Wood, Bruner, and Ross (1976) characterized the transmission of knowledge from expert to novice (mother to child) as a "scaffolded" situation where the expert creates a structure or scaffold in which the novice can extend current skills and knowledge to reach a higher level of expertise (not unlike proleptic instruction). As illustrated in the grocery shopping study, scaffolding might include open-ended questions, nonverbal instructions, greater involvement of the child, and more time spent reviewing. Similar investigations have been conducted that focus on mother–child interactions in various problem-solving tasks (Wertsch, McNamee, McLane, & Budwig, 1980; Wood & Middleton, 1975). It has been shown that mothers regulate children's problem-solving behavior by attending to children's performance, aiming instructions at particular levels, and responding by shifting levels when children succeed or fail. This interaction leads to a transition from what may be termed "other-regulation" to "self-regulation."

Price, Hess, and Dickson (1981) measured mothers' encouragement of child-generated verbalizations while they taught children a block-sorting task. This longitudinal study spanned the ages of 3–6 years for 66 preschoolers and the researchers found that encouragement to verbalize resulted in enhanced memory of parent-taught information. While mothers are still available to help and correct, they urge children to accept responsibility for the task by encouraging verbalizations about the blocks. Children's remarks also allow mothers to monitor and respond to children's actual performance. In a later study of mother's instruction of lower-case letters, Price (1984) found that children's ability to remember letters depends on the amount of support for child-generated verbal responses provided by mothers in conjunction with the parent's emphasis on learning particular letters. Price (1984) describes the preschool years as a period of "mnemonic dependence" during which children benefit from mnemonic activities but require ongoing support from adults. This is an example of one of the ways that interactions between parents and children can promote self-regulated remembering. Eventually, responsibility for the memory task shifts to children who use deliberate strategies to accomplish the task.

A critical aspect of such instructional interactions between adults and children is each participant's view of the task. Wertsch (1984) points out that it is important to recognize that although the adult and child may be interacting on the same task, their goals and understanding of the task may be very different. He emphasizes the need to consider the adult's and the child's intrapsychological definitions of the situation and the negotiated intersubjective situation definition. The negotiated definition will depend on the accuracy of the adult's perceptions of the child's needs and will influence the choice of instructional style and methods. Ninio (1983) has provided evidence of the importance of mother–child interaction by describing mother–infant dyads jointly involved in "reading" picture books. Mothers of 17–22-month-olds were quite sensitive to signals of word knowledge, or lack of it, by their children. If children showed comprehension of a word, mothers attempted, on subsequent appearances of the same word, to elicit labeling (production) or pointing (recognition) from their children. If they appeared not to know the word, mothers followed with simple labeling of the same referent on its next appearance. The mother's choice of verbal format seemed to demonstrate sensitivity to the child's level, resulting in monitoring and fine-tuning of her teaching style. For example, Rogoff, Ellis, and Gardner (1984) found that mother–child instruction on their classification task varied, both quantitatively and qualitatively, as a function of age of the child and the mother's perception of the task difficulty for the child. The school version of the classification task was seen as more difficult than the home, grocery version for 6-year-olds, but not 8-year-olds. Accordingly, the mothers gave more instruction (i.e., more directives, open-ended questions, and nonverbal instructions) to the younger children on the school task than to the younger children on the home. Both younger groups received more help than either group of older children. If younger and older children had identical learning experiences, the younger ones would have been expected to do more poorly. But because mothers adjusted their instruction flexibly, younger children did better on the school than the home task and both groups remembered as well as the older children.

A recent study by Saxe, Gearhart, and Guberman (1984) investigated young children's understanding of the goals of a counting task and the level and amount of assistance they received from their mothers to accomplish the task. Mothers were asked to teach their 2½–5-year-old children a game that involved putting the same number of pennies in a cup as there were pictures of "Cookie Monster" on a model board. They found that young children did not understand the goal of using the model to complete the task. Their mothers provided assistance by direct modeling or directing very low-level subgoals which were consistent with the child's understanding of the task. Older children understood that the goal was to use the number of "Cookie Monsters" as a guide for obtaining the required number of pennies; therefore their mothers provided directives that supported the child's construction of the goal. Mothers of both high- and low-ability children continually adjusted the goal structure during the activity depending on the child's success on each subgoal. This study clearly illustrates the importance of the adult's ability to adjust instructions based on the perceived level of the child and the child's ability to communicate current understanding of the task.

Siegler and Shrager (in press) have recently proposed a memory-based model of how 4- and 5-year-olds choose among various strategies to do simple addition problems (e.g., $4 + 3 = ?$). Critical to the model are the associative strengths of the various addition facts in the children's long-term memory. Interestingly, it appears that parental influence is an important determiner in the development of these associative strengths. Parents were asked to give their children addition problems, as they might at home. They were much more likely to present problems that their children, in fact, had an easy time with (e.g., $4 + 1 = ?$) than ones that were difficult (e.g., $1 + 4 = ?$). It is not clear whether the parents were well attuned to their children's present level of mastery or had accurate intuitions about learnability. In either case, practice with parents is seen to provide an important influence on children's learning and remembering. An important component of this practice is awareness of the children's abilities and their readiness for the shift from "other regulation" to "self-regulation."

The family thus plays an important role in helping children take responsibility for meeting memory demands. Children internalize not only strategies, but the *need* to remember as well. The scaffolding created by parents includes beliefs, values, motives, and societal expectations. Wertsch, Minick, and Arns (1984) provide an interesting assessment of how societal expectations (at the *activity* level) can influence psychological behavior (at the *operational* level). Their study also provides some evidence of contrasting roles of teachers and parents. They observed 12 adult–child Brazilian dyads in the process of constructing a copy of a model puzzle. Children were 5–6-years-old, and adults were either elementary school teachers (with their students) or rural mothers (with their own children). Observation of the dyads focused on children's independent work at reproducing the models and the amount of help that was given by adults. It was found that there were significant differences in the adult's and the child's level of responsibility, according to whether the adult was a teacher or a mother. On the level of *operational* analysis, it was clear that the teachers fostered more independent behavior in the children than the mothers did. On the level of *action* analysis there were no differences: both groups of dyads were guided by the same goal, to make copies of the models. Both groups achieved the goal, but it is at the *activity* level of analysis that Wertsch et al. draw inferences that perhaps explain the operational differences.

The two groups of adults had different levels of exposure to formal school: the mothers had less than 4 years of schooling and the teachers had all come to within at least 1 year of finishing high school. Wertsch et al. argue that differences in how the dyads divided up their joint tasks are related to the amount of adults' formal schooling. Teachers' governing motive of their activity was the learning process. Children were encouraged to carry out all aspects of the copying task from the beginning, even if this meant using a trial-and-error approach. Efficient task completion was of secondary interest. The mothers, on the other hand, seemed to be governed by a motive of correct and efficient completion of the specific task at hand; they delegated little independence and chance for failure to their children. Perhaps their motives were their children's achievement and success, prevention of their children's frustration, and minimization of the loss of economic resources (i.e., time and material).

Although speculative, this type of analysis is potentially important in explaining long-term effects of socialization on children's thinking. Learning in a setting where the activity is not overpowered by short-term motives (e.g., minimizing the risk of economic loss) might be associated with relative freedom to experiment with trial-and-error learning. In turn, this might facilitate the development of a general tendency to transfer skills from one domain to another, i.e., have multiple access to knowledge (see Greenfield & Lave, 1982).

Analogous to this teacher–mother difference in the fostering of independent behavior among Brazilian children are the results of another study by Rogoff and her colleagues. Ellis and Rogoff (1982) contrasted tutoring situations in which adults and 9-year-olds instructed 7-year-olds. Again, the task involved classification skills. Adult teachers gave much more verbal instruction, especially concerning categories, than did the 9-year-old teachers. However, there was no difference in nonverbal instruction. The child tutors simply placed items in categories for their young pupils, as opposed to taking a higher-level rule approach coupled with allowing them to participate in the task. The children taught by adults did much better on the classification task. The contrast between mature and immature teachers illustrates the importance of children's active participation in their own learning during social interactions. We might add an additional inference from these findings about the need for instruction to be sensitive to the specific needs of the child so that scaffolding can be added and removed as needed, during that social interaction.

The Ellis and Rogoff (1982) study reminds us that social guidance does not occur only in adult–child interactions. Children also interact with one another and potentially construct a group dynamic of involvement for the purpose of remembering. Lomov (1978) presents an account of the joint recall of a dyad of older school children and how this differs from their individual recall. The study is preliminary and nondevelopmental, yet it illustrates how remembering in an interpersonal context might influence an individual's remembering at a later time. Lomov asked individuals to recall the text of a fairly well-known poem and later asked dyads made up of the same individuals to recall the same material. Observations showed that with joint recall there was mutual correction, hypothesis testing and discussion of forgotten words, use of recalled words as cues for further recall, more active and emotionally laden search, and greater accuracy and confidence in the correctness of recall. Overall, the dyads had greater recall than the sum of each individual's recall. Thus, remembering was mediated effectively by social guidance and motivation provided by dyadic interaction. It supports Vygotsky's claim about the importance of inter-psychological functioning and eventual transfer to the individual's plane of intrapsychological functioning.

Thus, within familiar contexts that provide interest and personal significance to children, social interactions involving a variety of different "players" facilitate the development of deliberate remembering. We have provided evidence that interactions between parents and children promote self-regulated remembering. Research on child–child cognitive interactions is just beginning (e.g., Doise & Mugny, 1979) but promises to inform us further about the socialization of memory skills.

Cultural Practices

Besides the home and family, perhaps the greatest influence on children's development is provided by schools and teachers. Schooling presents challenging tasks to students that require literacy, calculation, and memorization. We have seen how teachers can adjust task difficulty for students of various abilities and provide encouragement and instruction accordingly. The school context is thus a catalyst for developing memory skills. A variety of cross-cultural research indicates the benefits of schooling for memory development

(Laboratory of Comparative Human Cognition, 1983) and provides a useful comparison of differences in environmental demands independent of age.

Although memory skills may not be taught directly in some schools, formal schooling appears to influence the acquisition of mnemonic strategies. Sharp, Cole, & Lave (1979) observed that Mexican adolescents and adults who attended school could remember unrelated word pairs and could cluster words according to semantic categories better than unschooled subjects. In parallel research in Morocco and Mexico, Wagner (1974, 1978) found that children and adolescents with more schooling engaged in verbal rehearsal strategies more often than people with little schooling. Cole, Gay, Glick, and Sharp (1971) observed better free recall and clustering of items among schooled than unschooled Kpelle people of Liberia. All of these researchers speculated that classroom instruction may provide an advantage to schooled subjects for deliberate remembering of isolated bits of information because of their familiarity with verbal tasks. Scribner and Cole (1981) subsequently reported that African Vai people who were literate in the Vai script but who had little formal schooling had better memory abilities than illiterate, unschooled Vai.

It is important to note, however, that memory performance of schooled and unschooled groups can sometimes be alike. Scribner (1974) allowed West African subjects to sort items to be remembered into piles reflecting their own personal organization of the stimuli. All subjects used their own groups (e.g., concrete-functional catgories, such as putting a knife and orange together because "the knife cuts the orange") to cluster and recall items equally well, but abstract-semantic categories (e.g., foods in one pile, tools in another, etc.) were used more often by subjects with more schooling. When the task structure is familiar and meaningful to subjects, memory differences due to age (Waddell & Rogoff, 1981), schooling (Sharp, Cole, & Lave, 1979), and culture (Mandler, Scribner, Cole, & DeForest, 1980; Rogoff & Waddell, 1982) are reduced. Still, literacy and schooling familiarize children with many of the demands of tasks requiring deliberate learning and memory. Rogoff (1981) summarizes the effects of schooling on memory cogently:

> From a large number of studies using memory tests, it appears that nonschooled subjects generally have less success than do schooled subjects on these tasks and are unlikely to engage spontaneously in strategies that provide greater organization for unrelated items. However, under conditions in which an appropriate organizational strategy is made explicit, nonschooled subjects are able to make use of it. Since differences do not generally appear until the schooled sample has received several years of schooling, it seems that some experience at school influences learning of organizational strategies. The lack of facility of nonschooled people in actively constructing connections between unrelated items should perhaps not be regarded as a difference in memory, but rather as a difference in a particular problem-solving skill that may seldom be necessary for subjects who do not have to learn to remember lists of initially unrelated items (as in school). Although nonschooled subjects take longer to learn associations between words, once learning is achieved, retention in memory is equal for subjects with different amounts of schooling. (Rogoff, 1981, p. 245)

Remembering lists of items, stories, pictures, and similar sets of novel stimuli are common school activities that may help to make memory goals and strategies more evident to children familiar with formalized learning contexts. Indeed, several investigators have suggested that informal learning in everyday contexts is considerably different than the artificial learning of scientific concepts in school (Greenfield & Bruner, 1969; Rogoff, 1981; Vygotsky, 1962). Schooling provides repeated practice on classifying, organizing, generalizing, and explaining information out of the context of functional production. Some people regard this as "decontextualized knowledge," solely for the purpose of learning and remembering the information. However, repeated practice in school with memory goals and mnemonic strategies may provide children an understanding about the general need for intentional actions as well as the differential utility of various cognitive strategies.

Schooling provides specific mnemonic "tools" that can aid remembering. For example, finger spelling and mime representations are used as memory strategies by deaf children (Liben & Drury, 1977). Specialized techniques for learning and memory often accompany beginning instruction on spelling, reading, and writing. Islamic students recite the Quran in chanted verses (Wagner & Lofti, 1980) and American children often recite multiplication tables or the Pledge of Allegiance. Perhaps the most common tool used by schools is note taking and record keeping. Underlining passages, taking notes, and writing summaries are external strategies that accompany repeated tests of recall in classroom learning (Brown, Campione, & Day, 1982). Many of these skills are modelled directly for students and encouraged through instruction and feedback. It is in this sense that mnemonic strategies are socially constructed, shared, and taught as systems of signs or overt tools that can help to mediate memory.

In this view, social institutions, contexts, and agents provide mediated activities for higher mental functions (Vygotsky, 1978) that help individuals adapt to the cognitive demands of everyday tasks. Thus, schools provide special memory demands and require the acquisition of literacy, test-taking skills, and memory strategies to meet those challenges. Individuals in other cultures or nonschool contexts may confront different demands on their memories and hence develop different tools to adapt to them. The use of notched sticks and knots are used as memory aids by some cultural groups. History and cultural contexts shape the activities of people and the utility of diverse tools, both physical and cognitive, that fulfill specific goals. These tools indicate an extension beyond natural memory, to culturally elaborated organization for knowledge and behavior.

The cultural influence on cognitive skills is illustrated well by recent research on the abacus. The abacus has been used for centuries in the Orient as a tool for counting and calculation. Today in the era of the electronic calculator, the abacus is still used routinely in China and Japan. Children are introduced to it at an early age, and the cultures promote its use through special abacus training schools and school-sponsored contests among children. The abacus expert is highly revered in Chinese and Japanese societies. Perhaps the most interesting finding about abacus experts is the mental representation of numbers that they develop (Stigler, 1984). Through continual practice in motoric skill, experts apparently represent the abacus mentally to the point of using an "internal abacus" for calculations. Reaction time analyses have shown that experts' mental calculations with the internal abacus actually involve faster processing than the use of the physical abacus. Thus, the abacus is an example of a culturally defined tool that plays an important role in children's working memory.

How pervasive in the thought of the child is this role of a simple, age-old tool? Hatano and Osawa (1983) have demonstrated that practice in computing large numbers with the abacus is associated not only with improved performance in mental arithmetic, but also with enhanced short-term memory for digits in general. Transfer to verbal stimuli (e.g., letters of the alphabet and names of fruits) is not found, however. So, while there is generalization of training from the use of the abacus, the effect is still constrained to a specific domain or mode of processing. Research by Stigler (1984) and Hatano and Osawa (1983) provides an illustration of the power of cultural practices on children's cognitive development. Memory performance and mental representation clearly reflect the impact of cultural values, practices, and tools.

Cultural practices that facilitate memory development are also present in nonschool contexts. An excellent example is the way in which Kpelle children of Liberia come to learn and understand traditional proverbs of their elders. Kulah (1973) has described verbal games of riddles and storytelling played by two teams of children of varying ages. Embedded within the riddles and stories are parts of the proverbs. In a paired-associates fashion, the two teams line up and challenge each other, exchanging phrases of the riddles. The oldest child of the first team challenges the oldest child of the second team and so on until the final turns of the game are taken by the two youngest children. The team that remembers the most parts of the pairs of riddles is the winner. Remembering serves the function of cultural transmission of the proverbs, and at the same time, the form of the game facilitates remembering. With increasing age, children become more challenged in the game because their turns come earlier; younger children benefit from personal observation before taking their turns. The outcome of this ritualistic game is that older children become better able to organize the various riddles and stories according to their meanings and to interpret them as important proverbs of their community.

Thus, schooling and educational experiences can facilitate memory development. It should be noted that the superior memory abilities of schooled subjects are not due simply to various artifactual reasons, such as family background differences or selection bias in who attends school (Rogoff, 1981). The acquisition of academic and literacy skills appear to foster particular strategies suited to goals of deliberate remembering.

Cognitive Consequences of Everyday Remembering

We began this chapter by noting that laboratory studies of children's memory often focus on children's emerging knowledge and strategies but neglect the socialized, motivated aspects of the contexts and activities of memory development. Recent evidence, though, has provided a richer description of the ways in which parents, teachers, and peers help children to remember ordinary events. We have noted how children as young as 1 and 3 years of age begin to act intentionally to facilitate recall. By age 4 or 5, children have begun to distinguish purposes and means for remembering. We believe that children learn several general principles about remembering from their repeated, practical attempts to negotiate their daily activities. We have labeled these principles agency, purpose, and instrumentality. We would like to elaborate on their developmental significance because they may provide insight about the concepts transferred and learned within zones of proximal development. It is important to recognize that these principles are constructed by children first as externally mediated and then as internally mediated activities. The psychological principles permit individual variations in style, effort, and effectiveness of remembering because they do not rest on assumptions about cognitive universality of knowledge organization or the uniform benefits of some mnemonic techniques.

Agency

The first concept is the recognition that memory can be enhanced by an active agent. Children discover that memory is not always automatic, easy, or accidental; it can be promoted by self-directed actions. As Brown (1978) and Flavell (1978) have pointed out, children acquire a sensitivity to the need to act in order to remember. Social agents such as parents typically assume this role for children when they remind or prompt them to remember, indicate to children that they should or can remember some information, and tell or show them explicitly how to remember. Social agents *participate* in remembering with young children, provide models and practice, and give encouragement to attend, remember, and try hard. The need to allocate effort toward remembering is thus apparent first in a social interaction and later internalized as self-agency. This may promote feelings of self-efficacy for remembering (cf. Bandura, 1982).

Human agency includes at least three critical dimensions: *intentionality, responsiblity*, and *criticism*. Intent underlies the need to act and the coordination of means–end relations. Even 1- and 2-year-olds can show longing or wanting as intentional behavior. Searching for lost objects and manipulating others' behavior can also be early instances of intention. Intention presupposes a goal or outcome to which behavior is directed but even good intentions are not realized easily by young children (Wellman, 1977). At least three things hamper children's intentional remembering. First, cognitive goals as ends in themselves are difficult to pursue although they can be accomplished as part of a larger meaningful activity. Second, children may have few cognitive or behavioral means available for acting on their intentions. Ignorance in this instance may breed frustration or trial and error. Third, children may have appropriate behavior available but through lack of experience they do not regard the behavior as instrumental for cognitive goals. Naivete yields a "production deficiency" in this case (Flavell, 1970).

Intention to act is coupled with a developing notion of responsibility, that is, the retrospective, reflective attribution of an outcome to one's own behavior. We think that it is important for young children to realize that their behavior causes successful or unsuccessful recall. Parents often provide these attributions with praise and information as feedback. They also can provide models for children to observe the relation between memory and particular actions for encoding or retrieval. Todd and Perlmutter (1980) note that toddlers develop causal notions of people as responsible agents and several researchers point out that adults shift responsibility from tutors to learners through instruction (Pearson & Gallagher, 1983; Rogoff, in press).

Remembering involves more than prospective plans and retrospective attributions. It also includes self-appraisal and criticism as one tries to remember. Adults usually serve as critics to young children by eliciting and rewarding effort and by suggesting specific actions as memory aids. As adults expect better memory from children, they give them more responsibility for recalling information without cues or guidance. Knowledge about memory that is often regarded as metamemory is exactly the kind of information that is supplied initially by adults. Estimates of (a) personal memory abilities, (b) what is known or not known, (c) task difficulty, and (d) mnemonic aids can be learned from experience and other people so that they become internalized, reflective knowledge. These evaluations and cues are apportioned according to the difficulty of the task and the child's past level of performance so that criticism is delivered in a variable manner that is fair to the child in the situation. Parents serve as good models for self-appraisal and progressively demand from children greater degrees of self-management for remembering. The overt practice and later internalization of self-criticism is evident in the Soviet emphasis on verbal mediation (Vygotsky, 1978), research on self-control (Mischel & Patterson, 1978), cognitive behavior modification (Meichenbaum & Asarnow, 1978), and metacognition (Brown, Bransford, Ferrara, & Campione, 1983).

Purposes of Remembering

A second concept that children acquire about remembering concerns goals. Adults set memory objectives for infants and toddlers and evoke imitation and recall for a variety of gestures, sounds, and words. Social games and interactive learning predominate as memory goals but gradually are supplanted by task-mastery goals. Remembering is often a vehicle for everyday social exchanges and exploration of the physical world for young children. However, it later becomes a cognitive goal in its own right (Smirnov & Zinchenko, 1969). Only rarely before school age are children required to remember objects or events solely for the sake of memorization. By age 6–7, though, we expect children purposefully to remember phone numbers, addresses, spelling, and a variety of facts.

Children also learn that the goals of remembering vary greatly in different contexts. At home children may need to recall their daily routines and the location of objects. At school, they may be required to remember lists of facts. Indeed, many children around the world need to remember practical aspects of work such as weaving, cooking, or tending animals. These complicated activities can demand a great deal of effort and particular mnemonic actions from young children. As we have seen, these everyday activities afford rich opportunities for socially guided learning and remembering.

Instrumental Actions

A third conceptual understanding that children acquire is that certain actions can aid recall. Even 3-year-olds understand that staring at an object or touching it helps them recall which object is concealing a toy (Wellman, Ritter, & Flavell, 1975). They quickly learn that there are external, physical aids to recall, such as tying a string around one's finger, as well as internal, cognitive actions such as rehearsal (Kreutzer, Leonard, & Flavell, 1975). But children learn more than a discrete set of procedures for remembering. They learn that actions vary in effectiveness, effort, and payoff.

The concept of instrumentality is the critical link between means and goals (Paris, 1978) and between agency and purpose. There are at least two important aspects of this concept: utility and economy. Utility refers to the relative effectiveness of different mnemonic actions. Young children often close their eyes and "think hard" but the action is usually less helpful than imagery, rehearsal, elaboration, or other techniques. Children often judge the utility of techniques from repeated practice but it is important to distinguish between situations in which children choose to remember strategically from those situations in which children use the same actions only in compliance with adults' directions. Understanding the instrumental utility of mnemonic actions can be promoted by modeling and feedback (Borkowski, Levers, & Gruenen-felder, 1976; Kennedy & Miller, 1976). Informed instruction about the utility of mnemonic techniques also can facilitate children's use of strategies. For example, Paris, Newman, & McVey (1982) provided 6- and 7-year-olds with five successive days of memory tests for categorizable pictures. After two days of practice, all children were shown how to use categorization, labeling, rehearsal, self-testing, and blocked recall to aid memory. Yet only half of the subjects were informed *why* these strategies were useful and instrumental for remembering. On subsequent days only children in the elaborated instruction group continued to use the strategies. All children had used them immediately following instruction but only those children who showed awareness of the utility of the actions used them spontaneously as self-directed strategies. Children were aware of the differential utility: some strategies were seen by the children as more effective than others (e.g., categorization), and these strategies were in fact used more often than the others. The children who demonstrated this awareness of strategy utility also remembered significantly more items than the other children.

Instrumental economy reflects children's understanding of the effort required and the benefits derived from implementing various actions. It would seem that children learn to be naive economists in the sense of weighing the pros and cons of investing effort in order to obtain a payoff with a certain value. Children consider costs in relation to the personal meaningfulness of task success. If actions are cumbersome or time consuming, children may choose not to use them at all. In a similar manner, some mnemonic techniques may be regarded as having potential utility and not being time consuming, but have no salience, significance, or personal value for the individual. In these instances the burden falls on the instructor or adult to persuade children that the extra effort is warranted and that the mnemonic actions are meaningful and worthwhile. If children are not convinced of the utility and economy of mnemonic actions, it seems unlikely that they will use them spontaneously as strategies. Instead, they might only be invoked under duress, for some extrinsic reward, or as a sign of obedience. Self-directed and enthusiastic learning seem unlikely under such conditions.

Conclusions

Throughout this chapter we have reviewed studies of children remembering familiar events at home and school. The collective presentation of research on "ordinary memory" complements the large body of laboratory studies on how children remember lists of words, series of pictures, and information presented in text or discourse. It also reveals the importance of social guidance and context for the acquisition of techniques that foster remembering. We believe that these factors enlarge our understanding of how children learn to control and regulate their efforts to remember because they focus on interpersonal dynamics of instruction in familiar settings over periods of time and practice. Our emphasis is decidedly on learning how to remember in a deliberate fashion and how such learning fits into children's general development. The theoretical and methodological implications of a social–cognitive–developmental approach to children's remembering can be clarified with reference to four dimensions of children's cognitive strategies and higher mental functions.

First, we have tried to describe the *personalized* nature of children's remembering. Early memories are rooted in daily interactions with caregivers in familiar surroundings. The events, objectives, and routines that are remembered are personally significant and relevant. More importantly, the techniques acquired to enhance memory often reflect individual differences because they are signs and tools constructed within social interactions and task involvement. Clearly, parents and cultures prescribe widely different cues for remembering including knots, rehearsal, and a mental abacus. But the shared use of such devices as memory aids should not mislead us to assume that mnemonic techniques are either universal or normative. Individuals recruit and employ cognitive strategies as goal-directed actions based on their perceptions of the utility and economy of the actions. This instrumental function is personalized and does not always lead to consensus about good strategies. Indeed, the hallmark of strategic behavior is adjusting one's actions to changing task demands and conditions—not perseverating blindly with a technique denoted as a strategy by someone else.

What are the implications of an approach that emphasizes personal construction and motivated use of cognitive strategies? On a theoretical level we need to avoid ipso facto definitions of a cluster of behaviors (e.g., rehearsal, imagery, semantic grouping, elaboration) as cognitive strategies. Whether or not these actions are strategic is an empirical question that can only be answered by assessing the individual's goals, motives, and understanding. These kinds of data also need to be collected with various tasks and conditions in order to distinguish habitual from strategic actions. Children's beliefs about sensible and appropriate actions to follow help determine their spontaneously recruited strategies. Without evidence of children's motives and beliefs, it is not possible to determine if they perform a given action by accident, for extrinsic reward, as social obedience, or for cognitive mastery (Maehr, 1983; Paris & Cross, 1983). Thus, we advocate methods that investigate subject's metacognitions, attributions, and motivations so that their subjective perceptions of the task and actions can be related to their behavior. These kinds of data can be gathered over time and practice so that we can chart changes due to learning and development also. If learning how to use strategies to control and foster memory depends on personal evaluations and understanding, then our theories and methods of studying memory development should incorporate children's subjective orientations to mnemonic means and goals (cf. Paris, 1978).

A second dimension of memory development that is emphasized in the chapter is *context*. The people and situations surrounding children's activities in which they remember provide context and direction for their reasoning. It is not just the availability, frequency, and familiarity of objectives and people at home that influence remembering. It is the cultural selection of activities and the social construction of contexts for interaction that shape the cognitive experiences of children. There have been several noteworthy attempts to embed development in contextualistic frameworks such as Rogoff, Gauvain, and Ellis (1984) and the Laboratory of Comparative Human Cognition (1983). The latter paper proposes a model of distributed processing in which cognitive processes are context-specific and socially dependent. Michael Cole and his colleagues contrast this model with a traditional central-process model in which experiences provide general increments to the knowledge of the system. The dichotomy highlights the role of context in a theoretical alternative to the central-processor model that predominates in Piagetian and information-processing accounts of cognitive development. The strong implications for research are to evaluate the settings of children's remembering activities in the same ways that ethologists and ethnographers chart contexts of behavior. Experimental researchers could also vary systematically the contextual characteristics surrounding children's efforts to remember in order to assess their relative influence on cognition.

We also drew attention in this chapter to *social interactions* that support children's remembering at home and school. This fundamental dimension of learning to remember has been neglected in most research on memory development. Typical laboratory studies provide social interactions, of course, but these interactions with unfamiliar adults are usually devoid of the warmth and reciprocity that we observe among parents or teachers helping children master new tasks. Indeed, the social dynamics and personal motivation of the laboratory context may be dissimilar to remembering in everyday settings. Memory researchers could investigate remembering in different circumstances with varying degrees of social support but they rarely do. That is why the reseach by Rogoff, Wertsch, Brown, Cole, and others on cooperative learning and how adults help children to remember is so important. The emphasis in these studies is on reciprocal interactions that facilitate a transfer of knowledge and responsibility for self-regulation. The learning and coaching that occur in these episodes is quite different from laboratory assessment of how well children recruit or apply task-appropriate strategies. The theory and method of the former is designed to reveal the development of learning how to remember while the latter is designed to measure static features of the availability or accessibility of information.

The fourth characteristic that we emphasized is the *temporalized* aspect of cognitive strategies. Strategies that promote memory are not acquired quickly or easily by young children, yet there has been a paucity of longitudinal research on memory development. Our theories need to be expanded to trace the rudimentary forms of intentional remembering from toddlers (Wellman, 1977) to continued refinement of strategies by adults (Pressley, Levin, & Bryant, 1983). We also need to clarify the temporal locus of strategies within skill development. Voluntary memory according to Vygotsky (1978) is only a phase between undirected "natural memory" of preschoolers and the automatic, involuntary forms of remembering observed among adolescents. It seems to us that strategies, metacognition, and other kinds of rationality included in executive processing models have been elevated to high status in cognitive models and used perhaps erroneously as end points of cognitive development. Cognitive strategies are useful during initial learning and troubleshooting but they seem less efficient and desirable than automatic skills that accomplish the same functions. Longitudinal research is required to reveal the course of strategy acquisition and automation.

Toward a Theory of Functional Remembering

In summary, we believe that children's remembering is personalized, contextualized, socialized, and temporalized. In order to understand any given episode of memory as well as the ontogeny of remembering, researchers will need to attend to these dimensions. That means the collection of additional data across time and settings as well as enlarged theories to account for individual differences in remembering. We are not advocating a simple contrast between memory observed in the laboratory and remembering in "natural" contexts. Instead we are trying to draw attention to the repeated, social, motivated interactions that are the catalysts for children's learning about voluntary memory because these dimensions of memory development may be critical for understanding acquisition, training, and remediation of mnemonic strategies. These practical and educational objectives require theories that specify how to improve remembering in addition to providing developmental descriptions of memory performance.

We think that children learn about agency, purpose, and instrumentality from repeated interactions from socially guided remembering. Mnemonic tools and signs (e.g., notes and imagery) are provided to children with informative instruction and graduated practice just as good coaches teach novices to play tennis or use calculators. These principles are often made explicit during coaching and direct instruction and they include precisely the kinds of strategy specific knowledge that facilitate generalization, transfer, and self-regulation (Pressley, Borkowski, & O'Sullivan, 1984). In fact, we have used direct instruction in the classroom to improve reading skills by informing children about the necessity of specific effort (agency), the goals of reading (purpose), and the utility of various strategies under different conditions (instrumentality) (Paris, Cross, & Lipson, in press; Paris & Jacobs, in press). These principles are learned within the zones of proximal development during guided practice and instruction and are at the heart of what is transferred from the inter- to the intrapsychological plane of functioning.

The importance of social contexts and purposes for children's remembering reveals that remembering and memory development are both *relativistic* and *functional*. Neither of these characteristics is captured well in current accounts of children's remembering and we hope that this chapter offers a heuristic and complementary perspective. By relativity we mean that children's remembering varies not only by the task difficulty and age of the subject but that significant individual variations in remembering occur due to social guidance, cultural practices, self-perceptions, beliefs, and motivation. Rather than treating these factors as extraneous sources of variance to control, researchers should examine the relative influence of these variables on children's remembering because, as we have seen, they contribute significantly to the manner and degree to which information is recalled.

Children learn to remember in the context of meaningful activities so that there is purpose for their efforts; remembering is functional. This does not mean simply that children are motivated or that they seek rewards for memorizing. The views of Vygotsky and other Soviet researchers call attention to the larger activities in which remembering occurs for young children. They tried to distinguish cognitive and social purposes for different mnemonic actions and that is partly why we tied our analyses to Vygotsky's work. The pragmatic aspects of motivated remembering are ignored in almost all other accounts of memory. There is no reason that our theories and methods cannot be expanded to consider the functions served by cognitive activities.

Children learn from everyday memory tasks that remembering can be fun and socially enjoyable. After all, pat-a-cake and other games of gestures and rhymes are appealing because of their social interactions, not their didactic value. Children also learn that effective remembering can insure proper behavior such as remembering to straighten one's room or to brush one's teeth. Remembering is functional as well as fun. Although researchers have only begun to investigate such mundane demands on memory as remembering to brush one's teeth, these kinds of repetitive events may provide the foundation for memory development. These episodes are embedded in ongoing activities and are therefore meaningful and functional. Even toddlers understand the necessity of remembering to stop at a red traffic light or to look both ways before crossing a street.

The early functionalists such as Dewey and Angell espoused views that were strikingly similar to those of Vygotsky. They believed that mental processes had utility and helped people adapt to their environments. Feeling, thinking, and willing were interwoven in the same manner that people collectively influenced individual behavior. There was not a separation of mind–body into physical and psychological stimuli nor was consciousness ephemeral. Heidbreder (1933) noted that, "the problem of functionalism may be defined as that of discovering the fundamental utilities of conscious activities" (p. 216). She also provided this capsule summary of her views:

> . . . functionalism was interested primarily in activities—in mental processes not merely as contents but as operations. Furthermore, it was interested in studying them in their natural setting and from the standpoint of their utility. . . . It had about it, too, an air of common sense, unabashed by academic taboos. In examining mental processes, it asked the questions of the practical man: "What are they for?" "What difference do they make?" "How do they work?" Obviously such questions cannot be answered by studying mental processes in and by themselves. . . . To answer that question, it is necessary to go beyond the process itself and consider the connections it makes: to investigate both its antecedents and its consequences, to discover what difference it makes to the organism, and to take into account its whole complex setting in the complex world in which it appears. (p. 202)

It seems to us that our understanding of children's remembering would be enriched considerably if developmental theories and methods were predicated on such fundamental principles.

Acknowledgment. We are very grateful to Jim Wertsch for providing thoughtful and constructive criticisms of earlier versions of this paper.

References

Anderson, R. C. (1978). Schema-directed processes in language comprehension. In A. Lesgold, J. Pellegrino, S. Fokkema, & R. Glaser (Eds.), *Cognitive psychology and instruction*. New York: Plenum.

Ashmead, D. H., & Perlmutter, M. (1980). Infant memory in everyday life. In M. Perlmutter (Ed.), *Children's memory: Vol. 10. New directions for child development*. San Francisco: Jossey-Bass.

Bandura, A. (1982). Self-efficacy mechanism in human agency. *American Psychologist, 37*, 122–147.

Belmont, J. M., & Butterfield, E. C. (1977). The instructional approach to developmental cognitive research. In R. V. Kail & J. W. Hagen (Eds.), *Perspectives on the development of memory and cognition*. Hillsdale, N.J.: Erlbaum.

Borkowski, J. G., Levers, S. R., & Gruenenfelder, T. A. (1976). Transfer of mediational strategies in children: The role of activity and awareness during strategy acquisition. *Child Development, 47*, 779–786.

Brown, A. L. (1975). The development of memory: Knowing, knowing about knowing, and knowing how to know. In H. W. Reese (Ed.), *Advances in child development and behavior* (Vol. 10). New York: Academic Press.

Brown, A. L. (1978). Knowing when, where, and how to remember: A problem of metacognition. In R. Glaser (Ed.), *Advances in instructional psychology*. Hillsdale, N.J.: Erlbaum.

Brown, A. L., Bransford, J. D., Ferrara, R. R. A., & Campione, J. C. (1983). Learning, remembering, and understanding. In J. H. Flavell & E. M. Markman (Eds.), *Handbook of child psychology: Cognitive development* (Vol. 3). New York: Wiley.

Brown, A. L., Campione, J. C., & Day, J. D. (1982). Learning to learn: On training students to learn from text. *Educational Researcher, 10*, 14–23.

Case, R. (1978). Intellectual development from birth to adulthood: A neo-Piagetian perspective. In R. S. Siegler (Ed.), *Children's thinking: What develops?* Hillsdale, N.J.: Erlbaum.

Cavanaugh, J. C., & Perlmutter, M. (1982). Metamemory: A critical examination. *Child Development, 53*, 11–28.

Chi, M. T. H. (1978). Knowledge structure and memory development. In R. S. Siegler (Ed.), *Children's thinking: What develops?* Hillsdale, N.J.: Erlbaum.

Chi, M. T., H., & Reese, E. T. (1983). A learning framework for development. In M. T. H. Chi (Ed.), *Trends in memory development research: Contributions to human development* (Vol. 9). Basel: Karger.

Cole, M., Gay, J. A., Glick, J. A., & Sharp, D. W. (1971). *The cultural context of learning and thinking*. New York: Basic Books.

Day, J. O. (1983). The zone of proximal development. In M. Pressley & J. R. Levin (Eds.), *Cognitive strategy research*. New York: Springer-Verlag.

DeLoache, J. S. (1980). Naturalistic studies of memory for object location in very young children. In M. Perlmutter (Ed.), *Children's memory: Vol. 10. New directions for child development*. San Francisco: Jossey-Bass.

DeLoache, J. S., & Brown, A. L. (1979). Looking for Big Bird: Studies of memory in very young children. *The Quarterly Newsletter of the Laboratory of Comparative Human Cognition, 1*, 53–57.

Doise, W., & Mugny, G. (1979). Individual and collective conflicts of centrations in cognitive development. *European Journal of Social Psychology, 9*, 105–108.

Ellis, S., & Rogoff, B. (1982). The strategies and efficacy of child versus adult teachers. *Child Development, 53*, 730–735.

Flavell, J. H. (1970). Developmental studies of mediated memory. In H. W. Reese, & L. P. Lipsitt (Eds.), *Advances in child development and behavior* (Vol. 5). New York: Academic Press.

Flavell, J. H. (1978). Metacognitive development. In J. M. Scandura & C. J. Brainerd (Eds.), *Structural/process theories of complex human behavior*. The Netherlands: Sijthoff & Noordoff.

Flavell, H. H., & Wellman, H. M. (1977). Metamemory. In R. V. Kail & J. W. Hagen (Eds.), *Perspectives on the development of memory and cognition*. Hillsdale, N.J.: Erlbaum.

Galotti, K. M., & Neisser, U. (1982). Young children's recall of Christmas. *The Quarterly Newsletter of the Laboratory of Comparative Human Cognition, 4*(4), 72–74.

Greenfield, P. M., & Bruner, J. (1969). Culture and cognitive growth. In D. A. Goslin (Ed.), *Handbook of socialization theory and research*. New York: Rand McNally.

Greenfield, P. M., & Lave, J. (1982). Cognitive aspects of informal education. In D. A. Wagner & H. W. Stevenson (Eds.), *Cultural perspectives on child development*. San Francisco: Freeman.

Hagen, H. W., Jongeward, R. H., & Kail, R. V. (1975). Cognitive perspectives on the development of memory. In H. W. Reese (Ed.), *Advances in child development and behavior* (Vol. 10). New York: Academic Press.

Hasher, L., & Zacks, R. T. (1979). Automatic and effortful processes in memory. *Journal of Experimental Psychology: General, 108*, 356–388.

Hatano, G., & Osawa, K. (1983). Digit memory of grand experts in abacus-derived mental calculation. *Cognition, 15*, 95–110.

Heidbreder, E. (1933). *Seven psychologies*. New York: Appleton-Century-Crofts.

Istomina, Z. M. (1975). The development of voluntary memory in preschool-age children. *Soviet Psychology, 13*, 5–64.

Kail, R. V., & Bisanz, J. (1983). Information processing and cognitive development. In H. W. Reese (Ed.), *Advances in child development and behavior* (Vol. 17). New York: Academic Press.

Kail, R. V., & Hagen, J. W. (1982). Memory in childhood. In B. Wolman (Ed.), *Handbook of developmental psychology*. Englewood Cliffs, N.J.: Prentice-Hall.

Kennedy, B. A., & Miller, D. J. (1976). Persistent use of verbal rehearsal as a function of information about its value. *Child Development, 47*, 566–569.

Kreutzer, M. A., Leonard, C., & Flavell, J. H. (1975). An interview study of children's knowledge about memory. *Monographs of the Society for Research in Child Development, 40* (1, Serial No. 159).

Kulah, A. A. (1973). The organization and learning of proverbs among the Kpelle of Liberia. Unpublished doctoral dissertation, University of California, Irvine.

Laboratory of Comparative Human Cognition. (1983). Culture and cognitive development. In W. Kessen (Ed.), *Handbook of child psychology: History, theory, and methods* (Vol. I). New York: Wiley.

Lepper, M. R., & Greene, D. (1975). Turning play into work: Effect of adult surveillance and extrinsic rewards on children's intrinsic motivation. *Journal of Personality and Social Psychology, 31*, 479–486.

Liben, L., & Drury, A. (1977). Short-term memory in deaf and hearing children in relation to stimulus characteristics. *Journal of Experimental Child Psychology, 24*, 60–73.

Lindberg, M. A. (1980). Is knowledge-base development a necessary and sufficient condition for memory development? *Journal of Experimental Child Psychology, 30*, 401–410.

Lomov, B. F. (1978). Psychological processes and communication. *Soviet Psychology, 17*, 3–22.

Maehr, M. (1983). On doing well in science: Why Johnny no longer excels; Why Sara never did. In S. Paris, G. Olson, & H. Stevenson (Eds.), *Learning and motivation in the classroom*. Hillsdale, N.J.: Erlbaum.

Mandler, J., Scribner, S., Cole, M., & DeForest, M. (1980). Cross-cultural invariance in story recall. *Child Development, 51*, 19–26.

Meacham, J. A. (1977). Soviet investigations of memory development. In R. V. Kail & J. W. Hagen (Eds.), *Perspectives on the development of memory and cognition*. Hillsdale, N.J.: Erlbaum.

Meichenbaum, D., & Asarnow, J. (1978). Cognitive behavior modification and metacognitive development: Implications for the classroom. In P. Kendall & S. Hollon (Eds.), *Cognitive-behavioral interventions: Theory, research, and procedures*. New York: Academic Press.

Mischel, W., & Patterson, C. J. (1978). Effective plans for self-control in children. In W. A. Collins (Ed.), *Minnesota symposium on child psychology* (Vol. 11). Hillsdale, N.J.: Erlbaum.

Naus, M. J., & Ornstein, P. A. (1983). The development of memory strategies: Analysis, questions, and issues. In M. T. H. Chi (Ed.), *Trends in memory development research* (Vol. 9). Basel: S. Karger.

Nelson, K., & Ross, G. (1980). The generalities and specifics of long-term memory in infants and young children. In M. Perlmutter (Ed.), *Children's memory: Vol. 10. New directions for child development*. San Francisco: Jossey-Bass.

Nicholls, J. G. (1983). Conceptions of ability and achievement motivation: A theory and its implications for education. In S. Paris, G. Olson, & H. Stevenson (Eds.), *Learning and motivation in the classroom*. Hillsdale, N.J.: Erlbaum.

Nickerson, R. S., Salter, W., Shepard, S. & Herrnstein, J. (1984). The teaching of learning strategies (Report 5578). Bolt Beranek & Newman, Inc.

Nino, A. (1983). Joint book reading as a multiple vocabulary acquisition device. *Developmental Psychology, 19*, 445–451.

Palinscar, A. S., & Brown, A. L. (1984). Reciprocal teaching of comprehension-fostering and monitoring activities. *Cognition and Instruction, 1*, 117–175.

Paris, S. G. (1978). Coordination of means and goals in the development of mnemonic skills. In P. A. Ornstein (Ed.), *Memory development in children*. Hillsdale, N.J.: Erlbaum.

Paris, S. G., & Cross, D. R. (1983). Ordinary learning: Pragmatic connections among children's beliefs, motives, and actions. In J. Bisanz, G. Bisanz, & R. Kail (Eds.), *Learning in children*. New York: Springer-Verlag.

Paris, S. G., Cross, D. R., & Lipson, M. Y. (in press). Informed Strategies for Learning: A program to improve children's reading awareness and comprehension. *Journal of Educational Psychology*.

Paris, S. G., & Jacobs, J. E. (in press). The benefit of informed instruction for children's reading awareness and comprehension skills. *Child Development*.

Paris, S. G., & Lindauer, B. K. (1982). The development of cognitive skills during childhood. In B. Wolman (Ed.), *Handbook of developmental psychology*. Englewood Cliffs, N.J.: Prentice-Hall.

Paris, S. G., & Lindauer, B. K. (1977). Constructive aspects of children's comprehension and memory. In R. V. Kail & J. W. Hagen (Eds.), *Perspectives on the development of memory and cognition*. Hillsdale, N.J.: Erlbaum.

Paris, S. G., Lipson, M. Y., & Wixson, K. K. (1983). Becoming a strategic reader. *Contemporary Educational Psychology, 8*, 293–316.

Paris, S. G., Newman, R. S., & McVey, K. A. (1982). Learning the functional significance of mnemonic actions: A microgenetic study of strategy acquisition. *Journal of Experimental Child Psychology, 34*, 490–509.

Pearson, P. D., & Gallagher, M. C. (1983). The instruction of reading comprehension. *Contemporary Educational Psychology, 8*, 317–344.

Piaget, J., & Inhelder, B. (1973). *Memory and intelligence*. New York: Basic Books.

Pressley, M. (1982). Elaboration and memory development. *Child Development, 53*, 396–309.

Pressley, M., Borkowski, J. G., & O'Sullivan, J. T. (1984). Memory strategy instruction is made of this: Metamemory and durable strategy use. *Educational Psychology, 19*, 94–107.

Pressley, M., Heisel, B. E., McCormick, C. G., & Nakamura, G. V. (1983). Memory strategy instruction with children. In C. J. Brainerd & M. Pressley (Eds.), *Progress in cognitive development research: Vol. 2. Verbal processes in children*. New York: Springer-Verlag.

Pressley, M., Levin, J. R., & Bryant, S. L. (1983). Memory strategy instruction during adolescence: When is explicit instruction needed? In M. Pressley & J. R. Levin (Eds.), *Cognitive strategy research*. New York: Springer-Verlag.

Price, G. G. (1984). Mnemonic support and curriculum selection in teaching by mothers: A conjoint effect. *Child Development, 55*, 659–668.

Price, G. G., Hess, R. D., & Dickson, W. P. (1981). Processes by which verbal-educational abilities are affected when mothers encourage preschool children to verbalize. *Developmental Psychology, 17*, 554–564.

Rogoff, B. (1981). Schooling and the development of cognitive skills. In H. C. Triandis & A. Heron (Eds.), *Handbook of cross-cultural psychology* (Vol. 4). Boston: Allyn & Bacon.

Rogoff, B. (1982). Integrating context and cognitive development. In M. E. Lamb & A. L. Brown (Eds.), *Advances in developmental psychology* (Vol. 2). Hillsdale, N.J.: Erlbaum.

Rogoff, B. (in press). Social guidance of cognitive development. In E. Gollin (Ed.), *Colorado symposium on human socialization: Social context and human development*. New York: Academic Press.

Rogoff, B., Ellis, S., & Gardner, W. (1984). The adjustment of adult–child instruction according to child's age and task. *Developmental Psychology, 20*, 193–199.

Rogoff, B., & Gardner, W. (1984). Guidance in cognitive development: An examination of mother–child instruction. In B. Rogoff & J. Lave (Eds.), *Everyday cognition: Its development in social context*. Cambridge: MA: Harvard University Press.

Rogoff, B., & Waddell, K. J. (1982). Memory for information organized in a scene by children from two cultures. *Child Development, 53*, 1224–1228.

Saxe, G. B., Gearhart, M., & Guberman, S. R. (1984). The social organization of early number development. In B. Rogoff and J. V. Wertsch (Eds.), *Children's learning in the "zone of proximal development": Vol. 23. New directions for child development*. San Francisco: Jossey-Bass.

Scribner, S. (1974). Developmental aspects of categorized recall in a West African society. *Cognitive Psychology, 6*, 475–494.

Scribner, S., & Cole, M. (1981). *The psychology of literacy*. Cambridge, MA: Harvard University Press.

Sharp, D., Cole, M., Lave, C. (1979). Education and cognitive development: The evidence from experimental research. *Monographs of the Society for Research in Child Development, 44*.

Siegler, R. S., & Shrager, J. (in press). Strategy choices in addition: How do children know what to do? In C. Sophian (Ed.), *Origins of cognitive skills*. Hillsdale, N.J.: Erlbaum.

Smirnov, A. A., & Zinchenko, P. I. (1969). Problems in the psychology of memory. In M. Cole & I. Maltzman (Eds.), *A handbook of contemporary Soviet psychology*. New York: Basic Books.

Somerville, S. C., Wellman, H. M., & Cultice, J. C. (1983). Young children's deliberate reminding. *Journal of Genetic Psychology, 143*, 87–96.

Stigler, J. W. (1984). "Mental abacus": The effect of abacus training on Chinese children's mental calculation. *Cognitive Psychology*.

Todd, C. M., & Perlmutter, M. (1980). Reality recalled by preschool children. In M. Perlmutter (Ed.), *Children's memory: Vol. 10. New directions for child development*. San Francisco: Jossey-Bass.

Trabasso, T. (1983). Discussion: What is memory development to be the development of? In M. T. H. Chi (Ed.), *Trends in memory development research: Contributions to human development* (Vol. 9). Basel: Karger.

Vygotsky, L. S. (1962). *Thought and language*. Cambridge, Mass.: MIT Press.

Vygotsky, L. S. (1978). *Mind in society*. Cambridge, MA.: Harvard Press.

Waddell, K. J., & Rogoff, B. (1981). Effect of contextual organization on spatial memory of middle-aged and older women. *Developmental Psychology, 17*, 878–885.

Wagner, D. A. (1974). The development of short-term and incidental memory: A cross-cultural study. *Child Development, 54*, 389–396.

Wagner, D. A. (1978). Quranic pedagogy in modern Morocco. In L. Adler (Ed.), *Issues in cross-cultural research*. New York: Academic Press.

Wagner, D. A., & Lotfi, A. (1980). Traditional Islamic education in Morroco: Sociohistorical and psychological perspectives. *Comparative Education Review, 24*, 238–251.

Wellman, H. M. (1977). The early development of intentional memory behavior. *Human Development, 22*, 86–101.

Wellman, H. M., Ritter, K., & Flavell, J. H. (1975). Deliberate memory behavior in the delayed reactions of very young children. *Developmental Psychology, 11*, 780–787.

Wellman, H. M., & Somerville, S. C. (1980). Quasi-naturalistic tasks in the study of cognition: The memory related skills of toddlers. In M. Perlmutter (Ed.), *Children's memory: Vol. 10. New directions for child development*. San Francisco: Jossey-Bass.

Wellman, H. M., & Somerville, S. C. (1982). The development of human search ability. In M. Lamb & A. Brown (Eds.), *Advances in developmental psychology* (Vol. 2). Hillsdale, N.J.: Erlbaum.

Wertsch, J. V. (1979). The social interactional origins of metacognition. Paper presented at the biennial meeting of the Society for Research in Child Development, San Francisco.

Wertsch, J. V. (1984). The zone of proximal development: Some conceptual issues. In B. Rogoff and J. V. Wertsch (Eds.), *Children's learning in the "zone of proximal development": Vol. 23. New directions for child development*, San Francisco: Jossey-Bass.

Wertsch, J. V., Minick, N., & Arns, F. J. (1984). The creation of context in joint problem solving action: A cross-cultural study. In B. Rogoff & J. Lave (Eds.), *Everyday cognition: Its development in a social context*. Cambridge, MA: Harvard University Press.

Wertsch, J., McNamee, G. D., McLane, J., & Budwig, N. A. (1980). The adult–child dyad as a problem-solving system. *Child Development, 51*, 1215–1221.

Wertsch, J. V., & Stone, C. A. (1978). Microgenesis as a tool for developmental analysis. *Quarterly Newsletter of the Laboratory of Comparative Human Cognition, 1*, 8–10.

Wood, D., Bruner, J. S., & Ross, G. (1976). The role of tutoring in problem solving. *Journal of Child Psychology and Psychiatry, 17*, 19–100.

Wood, D., & Middleton, D. (1975). A study of assisted problem solving. *British Journal of Psychology 66*, 181–191.

Yendovitskaya, T. V. (1971). Development of memory. In A. V. Zaporozhets & D. B. Elkonin (Eds.), *The psychology of preschool children*. Cambridge: M.I.T. Press.

4. Memory Development in Cultural Context

Barbara Rogoff and Jayanthi Mistry

Introduction

This chapter describes perspectives on memory development provided by cross-cultural research and theory. We argue that the development of memory skill is closely tied to familiar tasks which children and adults practice and to the purpose for remembering the material. Furthermore, memory development is broadly situated in the social contexts and cultural institutions in which memory skills are practiced. Our perspective is that remembering serves practical goals (in memory tests and naturalistic memory activities alike) which organize, constrain, and support the individual's performance through features of the task, its purpose, and the social and cultural contexts of remembering.

The majority of cross-cultural psychological studies of memory and memory development have used procedures derived from U.S. laboratory studies to examine whether people in other cultures perform in a similar manner. Such studies have been motivated by interest in testing U.S. theories for their universality or variability across cultures, and by attempts to separate variables which can vary simultaneously in the U.S. but are separable in other cultures (e.g., attempting to separate the role of formal schooling from that of age in understanding developmental progressions in memory skills).

In much of this cross-cultural research, the relation of culture and memory has been examined using a model in which culture serves as an independent variable and memory serves as the dependent variable or outcome of variation in cultural variables. We will argue that this approach oversimplifies the relation between culture and memory, in that culture and memory are conceived as separate variables rather than mutually embedded aspects of cultural and individual systems. The influence of culture on the individual is frequently studied by comparing the memory performance of individuals from two (or sometimes more) different cultures. Some studies provide a closer comparison to "unpackage" (Whiting, 1976) the influential aspects of culture (e.g., schooling, urbanization) and the crucial aspects of memory performance (e.g., the process and content tested and the familiarity of the materials).

In this chapter we begin by summarizing research comparing memory performance in different cultures, treating culture as an independent variable. We examine research attempting to unpackage the culture variable as well as attempts to make traditional laboratory memory tasks more culturally relevant. This leads to a consideration of how remembering is related to the culture in which individuals are embedded. Following discussion of research showing that memory development occurs in culturally organized activities, we elaborate the theme that memory development is channeled by the oppportunities individuals have to learn particular skills in the organization of everyday activities practiced in their culture. We take the perspective that culture is meshed with (rather than separate from) individual memory development and is practiced in the context of routine activities. To understand memory performance, or to compare performances of individuals from different cultures, it is essential to place the memory performance in the context of the subject group's interpretation of the task to be accomplished, the goal in performing the activity, and the broader social context of such activities in their experience. We contrast this concept of development that integrates culture and memory with concepts of development that treat memory performance and cultural background separately.

Research Treating Memory and Culture as Separate Variables

On tasks resembling those used in Western research, non-Western subjects are widely observed to perform more poorly than subjects from the culture where the tests originated (see influential reviews by Cole & Scribner, 1977, and Wagner, 1981). Some of the most commonly used tasks derived from U.S. research have been serial recall of lists of words or series of pictures, and free recall of lists of words or pictures. The usual finding has been that non-Western subjects do not perform as well as Western subjects.

Some investigators have attempted a closer examination of *how* culture may relate to memory. In the following sections we discuss research that focuses on how specific aspects of background experience varying cross-culturally relate to memory performance (to unpackage the culture variable), and research that examines how variation in the memory tests used relates to cultural differences (to unpackage the memory variable).

Variations in Memory Performance on the Basis of
Background Experience

In the attempt to determine how culture influences memory performance, cross-cultural researchers have examined characteristics which commonly vary with non-Western versus Western groups, such as amount of formal schooling (or literacy), degree of modernization, and urban versus rural residence.

Studies comparing memory performance of rural versus urban subjects have not been extensive, so it is premature to draw general conclusions. However, two studies find better performance by rural compared to urban subjects. Moroccan rural subjects recognize more pictures of rugs than their urban counterparts, perhaps due to greater familiarity with rugs and rug patterns (Wagner, 1981). Rural children in Kenya outperform urban children in digit recall, perhaps due to their greater compliance and deference to the experimenter, behavior which Weisner (1976) expects to improve performance on digit recall and other rote memory tasks.

A few other studies that attempt to unpackage cultural differences in cognitive performance, for example by examining the connection between memory and maternal teaching styles or children's self-directedness, can be found in an excellent review by Nerlove and Snipper (1981). The intervening variable which has received the most attention and produced consistent results is literacy or the amount of formal Western-style schooling (Rogoff, 1981).

Schooling. Cross-cultural comparisons of memory performance by individuals varying in schooling experience allow consideration of whether the changes in memory performance observed across childhood in the U.S. might be due to experience with school rather than maturation. Western children enter school at about age 5, and there is high correlation beween age and grade in school thereafter until adulthood. Hence there is a danger that "cognitive-developmental research in the United States has been measuring *years of schooling*, using *age* as its proxy variable" (Laboratory of Comparative Human Cognition, 1979, p. 830). In many nontechnological societies, formal schooling is not yet universal, so the relative independence of age and amount of schooling provides investigators with a natural laboratory for investigating the effects of age and schooling separately.

Results show a powerful effect of schooling on performance on the memory tasks that have been used. Nonschooled subjects generally have less success than do schooled subjects on tasks such as paired associate learning (Hall, 1972), free recall (Cole, Gay, Glick, & Sharp; 1971; Sharp, Cole, & Lave, 1979), and serial recall (Fahrmeier, 1975; Stevenson, Parker, Wilkinson, Bonnevaux, & Gonzalez, 1978).

Schooling appears to influence the use of organizational strategies. Non-schooled subjects are unlikely to engage spontaneously in strategies that provide greater organization to help remember the unrelated items that are presented in such tasks. But if an appropriate organizational strategy is made explicit, nonschooled subjects are able to make use of it. For example, in paired associate learning, if there is an explicit relationship between the items in the pairs (such as bull–sheep, from the same semantic category), there is less effect of schooling than when there is little relationship between items (e.g., bull–root; Sharp, Cole, & Lave, 1979).

Similarly, in free recall tasks, recall and clustering by nonliterate subjects increase when the category organization of the items is more clear. The category structure of lists of items is used more by nonliterate subjects when the categories are marked simply by sorting items and holding all those from the same category over a specific chair, compared to holding the items randomly over different chairs (Cole et al., 1971). Free recall and clustering also improve when nonliterate subjects are told the category names at the time of presentation of the list, and at the time of recall are asked to remember all the items from one category, then given the name of another category and asked to recall those items, and so on. Interestingly, when such cuing is discontinued, recall and clustering remain high (Cole et al., 1971). If a personally meaningful organization of free-recall items is made available by having subjects sort items into piles until a stable organization is reached, nonliterate subjects make use of their personal organization in structuring later free recall (Scribner, 1974).

Since differences between schooled and nonschooled groups do not generally appear until the schooled sample has received several years of schooling (Cole et al., 1971), it seems that some experience at school influences learning of organizational strategies. Actively constructing connections between unrelated items may seldom be necessary for subjects who do not have to learn to remember lists of initially unrelated items (as in school). School is one of the few situations in which a person has to remember information deliberately, as a goal in itself, and make initially meaningless, unrelated pieces of information fit together sensibly. Many of the strategies used in memory test performance (which shares those task demands) may be taught or encouraged by schooling. As evidence that the correlation beween schooling and test performance may be a tautology, Cole, Sharp, and Lave (1976) point out that versions of many of the memory tests used in cross-cultural research can be found in Binet's early work searching for behavior that predicted performance in school. It should not be surprising that greater schooling predicts performance on tests designed to discriminate children's school performance.

In addition to considering background experiences which relate to memory performance, cross-cultural research has investigated cultural differences in memory performance as a function of the nature of the tests given. Of course, some of the variations based on the nature of the test relate to variation in the subjects' background experience, especially schooling.

Variations in Memory Performance According to the Nature of the Tests

Research aimed at determining how cultural differences in memory vary as a function of the test focuses on three topics: What memory processes are used (recognition or recall processes; control processes vs. structural features of memory), how memory compares in different modalities (verbal vs. spatial tasks), and how familiarity of the materials used in the test relates to performance.

Patterns of performance on memory tests tapping different processes. The notion that cultural differences vary as a function of the process of memory being tested has received some attention (Cole & Scribner, 1977; Rogoff, 1981; Wagner, 1981). The general hypothesis is that on memory tasks requiring the deliberate use of mnemonic strategies, cultural differences would be heightened, whereas in tests that rely less on such strategies the cultural differences would be less. However, studies that compare performance on recognition tasks (which are assumed to require less use of strategies than recall tests) in different cultures show an inconsistent pattern that does not support the idea that cultural differences are minimized on such tests. Three chapters that review cross-cultural studies of recognition memory each point to the inconclusiveness of data on cultural differences in recognition: Cole and Scribner state that "under some conditions, for some response measures, recognition of unacculturated peoples can exceed that of their educated counterparts" (1977, p. 254); Wagner (1981) calls for more research to untangle the findings; and Rogoff (1981) suggests that familiarity with the response demands of recognition tests may underlie the occasionally better performance of schooled than nonschooled subjects. Thus research on recognition memory is not sufficiently consistent to test the idea that cultural differences are less on these tasks presumed to require less deliberate use of mnemonic strategies.

Other studies addressing cultural variations in the use of strategies employ probed serial recall tasks to examine the use of control processes (deliberate strategies) versus structural features of memory (e.g., sensory memory store). Such tasks involve showing the subject a series of cards with pictures and then turning them face down in linear order. The subject is then shown a "probe card" with a picture corresponding to one of the face-down cards and asked to point to the location of its mate. With United States subjects, heightened recall for the first items shown ("primacy effect") has been explained in terms of the use of rehearsal as a recall strategy. Heightened performance on the last item(s) shown ("recency effect") has been attributed to use of the sensory memory store, considered a structural feature of memory.

Several studies using the probed serial recall task support the idea that cultural differences reside more in the use of strategies than in structural aspects of memory. Wagner (1974) found greater recall and a greater primacy effect for Yucatan subjects with more schooling than for those with less schooling. Schooling differences in the recency effect, while significant, were not as striking as differences in the primacy effect. In a later study with Moroccan males, Wagner (1978) found that schooled subjects at older ages (over 13 years) showed greater recall, much greater primacy, and only slightly greater recency than nonschooled subjects. He concluded that control processes (e.g., rehearsal) are much more subject to environmental influences than are structural features of memory (e.g., sensory store, as inferred from minimal differences in recency effect).

Patterns of performance according to modality of materials. While the bulk of memory studies have involved verbal materials (usually lists of words), there is some interest in whether the usual pattern of poorer performance by non-Western as compared to Western subjects occurs with spatial materials. Intriguing anecdotes credit some non-Western people with impressive skills in finding their way in large-scale space: Eskimos and Australian aborigines are reputed to be very skilled in remembering their way through local terrain; Polynesian sailors similarly impress Western observers with their skill in remembering the lay of the ocean in complex navigation from island to island (Gladwin, 1970; Levy-Bruhl, 1926; Lewis, 1976).

Empirical work on cultural differences in spatial memory is rather sparse, but there are several findings of superior or equivalent spatial memory performance by non-Western populations compared to Western groups. Kleinfeld (1971) found better recall for drawn designs among Eskimo children than urban Caucasian children. Kearins (1981) found better recall for spatial arrangement of objects by aborigines dwelling in the Western Desert of Australia than by suburban white Australian youth. The suburban adolescents' performance was especially poor for arrays of objects that were not easily labeled (sets of different rocks or different bottles). Drinkwater (1976) showed that nontribal aborigine youth equated in schooling with a white suburban sample performed the same on a spatial array as the white suburban subjects. These findings of Eskimo and Aborigine superiority on spatial tests have been interpreted in terms of the needs of Eskimo and desert Aborigine people to develop good spatial memory to find their way in environments which appear to the Western eye to be bleak and short of landmarks, changing with the wind and storms.

However, studies with non-Western populations in less extreme environments also show enhanced memory for location and spatial arrangement contrasting with the more usual performance decrement of non-Western subjects. Rural Guatemalan ladino children demonstrated better recall for location of objects than for the identity of objects, while children in Buffalo showed equal recall for location and identity (Meacham, 1975). Massachusetts children recognized inventory information (identity of objects) more accurately than spatial arrangements, while Guatemalan Indian children recognized spatial rearrangements as well as they did the inventory of the photograph (Newcombe, Rogoff, & Kagan, 1977). Das, Manos, and Kanungo (1975) found no differences between Canadian Indians, whites, and blacks in recall for designs, and they found very little difference between populations on a visual short-term memory task requiring recall of the spatial arrangement of digits in a grid. Rogoff and Waddell (1982) found slightly (nonsignificantly) better performance by Guatemalan Indian children compared to U.S. children on reconstruction of the placement of objects in a model panorama. Together, these results suggest that non-Western people perform equally or better on spatial material than Western people.

What aspect of spatial memory tasks encourages good performance by non-Western people? One interpretation, consistent with Hasher and Zachs' (1979) notions on automaticity, is that spatial information requires little deliberate effort to be encoded, and thus people who have difficulty implementing deliberate strategies do not have difficulties with spatial tasks. We do not favor this hypothesis, largely because spatial tasks involve a variety of processes which should be examined in greater depth. In a later section we argue that cultural differences may disappear when the task employs a meaningful context organizing the items, which subjects may use to aid their recall. Such contextual support is present in some spatial tasks, and contrasts with the absence of organizing links in the usual lists of verbal materials. The presence of organizing context may account for some of the findings of excellent performance by non-Western people in spatial tasks. Other factors, including perhaps the lesser need for deliberate strategies, probably also come into play.

Patterns of performance as a function of familiarity of materials. Cross-cultural researchers who supplement their "experimental" measures of performance with ethnographic observations of everyday activities are struck by the difficulty that people have with particular skills in the laboratory while spontaneously using the skills of interest in their everyday activities (see discussion in Cole, Hood, & McDermott, 1978; Laboratory of Comparative Human Cognition, 1979; Rogoff, 1981). For example, Micronesian navigators who show extraordinary skills in memory, inference, and calculation in sailing between islands perform abominably on standard tests of intellectual functioning (Gladwin, 1970).

As a first attempt to make laboratory tasks more culturally appropriate to the population tested, researchers have used task materials selected from the indigenous environment. Much of the work comparing cognitive processing using familiar versus unfamiliar materials has been done in the domain of classification (Price-Williams, 1962). For example, nonliterate Liberian adults are more successful in classifying bowls of rice than geometric stimuli (both differing in color, shape, and number), and U.S. undergraduates respond to requests to sort bowls of rice with the same hesitance and bewilderment shown by Liberian nonliterates asked to sort cards decorated with squares and triangles (Irwin & McLaughlin, 1970; Irwin, Schafer, & Feiden, 1974). Both groups, when tested with unfamiliar materials, sorted in a manner considered less advanced.

Studies of memory have also attempted to use familiar materials to enhance the ecological validity of the work. A few studies have directly compared performance on memory tests when familiar materials versus unfamiliar materials are used. For example, a comparison of the dialect used for testing with United States children revealed that recall of stories was equal for white children tested in Standard English and black children tested in Black English vernacular, though white children recalled more than black children when they were tested in Standard English and black children did better than white when they were tested in Black English vernacular (Hall, Reder, & Cole, 1975). Similarly, Hawaiian dialect speakers recalled more information from stories presented in dialect than in standard English, while Standard English speakers from Hawaii recalled more from stories presented in Standard English than in Hawaiian dialect (Ciborowski & Choy, 1974). And historical shifts in frequency of word usage accounted for differences in the free recall of young and elderly U.S. adults: Elderly adults recalled words that were commonly used in their youth better than those that were frequent in contemporary usage (Worden & Sherman-Brown, 1983).

In free-recall tasks, the use of indigenous categories available for clustering words appears to benefit recall. Black adolescents recalled more words and clustered to a greater extent than white adolescents in a task using categories elicited from the black subjects (Franklin, 1978). While the white subjects were familiar with the words on the list, their lack of familiarity with the categorization scheme put them at a disadvantage.

Similarly, the availability of familiar schemas for stories seems to aid recall of stories (Bartlett, 1932). In culturally foreign stories, recall shows importations or distortions from familiar schemas. For example, Americans distort stories in recall to avoid ending a story on a negative note or with unresolved problems (Rice, 1980). U.S. college students recall more from stories whose schemas are familiar than from stories taken from other cultural groups (Kintsch & Greene, 1978). Thus memory performance is related to the familiarity subjects have with the materials to be remembered. Familiarity involves both experience with the specific materials and experience with how they are used. In the next section we argue that considerations of familiarity of use lead researchers to examine the integration of memory tasks and cultural background.

Research Integrating Memory Tasks in Cultural Context

As mentioned earlier, use of indigenous materials in memory tests has derived from attempts to make research culturally appropriate. However, even if the materials used and the memory processes tested are familiar, if they are not integrated into an activity which resembles some activity practiced by the subjects, the task is likely to be perceived as foreign. This perspective is involved in several lines of research which relate the memory test to memory activities practiced in routine cultural contexts.

In this section we discuss (a) research examining memory performance when a culturally meaningful context provides structure for the material to be remembered, (b) research in which a meaningful purpose integrates the memory task in an appropriate cultural activity, and (c) research that utilizes memory tasks related to the usual practices of the cultural groups as well as research that takes into account not just the cultural appropriateness of the task materials and goal but also the social interactional context of the task.

Meaningfully Organized Context Relating the Materials

The memory tests commonly used in cross-cultural research present isolated bits of information upon which organization must be imposed (through rehearsing, clustering by category, or elaborating the associations between items) in order to relate the items to each other in the service of remembering. Cross-cultural differences appear most commonly in memory tasks in which the structure of the material is not made explicit (Cole & Scribner, 1977). The presentation of isolated bits of information serves the psychologist's purpose of simplifying the units to be recalled and limiting the amount of previous experience brought to the particular associations to be remembered. However, this simplicity is likely to be an illusion, as Bartlett pointed out in his critique of the nonsense syllable:

> Uniformity and simplicity of structure of stimuli are no guarantee whatever of uniformity and simplicity of structure in organic response . . . isolation [of response] is not to be secured by simplifying situations or stimuli and leaving as complex an organism as ever to make the response. What we do then is simply to force this organism to mobilise all its resources and make up, or discover, a new complex reaction on the spot. (1932, pp. 3–6)

The processes required to invent connections between isolated bits of information may be quite unrelated to everyday memory where the information is interrelated by meaningful context rather than requiring imposed organization.

Western literate people have special demands and opportunities to develop the use of memory aids appropriate for remembering lists of isolated pieces of information, especially through their experience with school. Goody (1977) points out that with psychological tests involving lists of decontextualized words, facility stems from familiarity with lists and the classification systems that lists promote (e.g., alphabetic, categorical). Goody suggests that making and remembering lists is a product of literacy. Remembering lists of unrelated material unorganized by meaningful schemas may be an unusual experience outside of school, where pupils frequently have to use strategies to ensure recall of material they have not understood.

While non-Western people may have less practice than Westerners in creating order for isolated bits of information as required in standard list memory tasks, non-Westerners may have as much environmental press to remember information which is embedded in a structured context and to use strategies incorporating the existing organization, using meaningful relationships among items as an aid to recall. Subjects can use schemata representing their knowledge of usual relationships among objects and events to organize their memory for items appearing in a meaningful context. With contextually organized materials, non-Western subjects may remember information as well as their Western counterparts, since the majority of the memory problems faced by modern and traditional people alike involve material which is organized in a complex and meaningful fashion, rather than lists of items which have been stripped of organization. For example, in remembering the arrangement of the top of a desk, a serial listing of items is generally insufficient, since items are spatially arranged in three dimensions and items overlap and bear multiple relationships with each other. Despite outward appearances, there is usually some conceptual order to the array which helps the user of the desk to locate an object.

To determine whether memory for contextually organized materials follows a different cross-cultural pattern than that observed in standard list-memory tasks, Rogoff and Waddell (1982) examined the performance of Mayan and U.S. children on the reconstruction of contextually organized three-dimensional miniature scenes. Each child watched as a local experimenter placed 20 miniature objects such as cars, animals, furniture, people, and household items into a panorama model of a town, containing a mountain, lake, road, houses, and some trees. All objects were pretested for familiarity to both groups of children. The 20 objects were removed from the panorama and reintegrated into the pool of 80 objects from which they were drawn, and after a delay of minutes, the child reconstructed the scene.

The Mayan sample had shown striking decrements in list memory performance in a previous study (Kagan, Klein, Finley, Rogoff, & Nolan, 1979), but they were expected to perform as well as the U.S. children on the test using contextually organized materials. The Mayan children performed slightly, but not significantly, better than the U.S. children. This supports the idea that when information to be remembered is organized in a meaningful manner, cultural differences usually found with lists of unrelated items do not appear.

The slight advantage of the Mayan children seemed to be due to the attempts by some U.S. children to apply a strategy useful for remembering unorganized lists—rehearsal. About a third of the 30 U.S. children, but only 1 of the 30 Mayan children, rehearsed the names of the objects in the panorama as they studied. This is an effective strategy for remembering lists of decontextualized items immediately after presentation, but may be inappropriate for remembering contextually organized material. It is likely that rehearsal of object names would help only minimally in reconstruction, since the objects are present in the pool at the time of the delayed test, and a major task is remembering their locations. A child who has learned strategies for remembering lists of words may indiscriminately apply those strategies to inherently organized material, without regard for the relevance of such strategies to the particular task. Kearins (1981) suggests that successful reconstruction of spatial arrays is accompanied by remembering the "look" of the arrangement, rather than by the use of verbal strategies as in standard list-memory tasks.

The unusual finding of equivalent performance cross-culturally may be due to the ubiquity of having to remember things in everyday life using the contextual organization of the material as a recall aid. All people have to remember such information as to how to get to an acquaintance's house, where to find things in the kitchen, and what occurrences led to an important event. In contrast to lists of items whose interrelationships have been minimized for research purposes, such information is organized in a complex but coherent fashion. List-memory tests may have led us to overlook cognitive processes occurring in memory for contextually organized materials which are important in the everyday memory activities of all people.

Further support for the notion that the organization of materials is a factor in population differences in memory performance is available in a comparison of aged and middle-aged U.S. adults who were asked to reconstruct a contextually organized panorama versus an array of the same objects with the contextual organization removed (Waddell & Rogoff, 1981). Aged adults have shown similar memory decrements on standard list-memory tests as have non-Western subjects, but when reconstructing the panorama with information organized by the familiar scene, age differences in memory performance disappeared. The usual poor performance by the aged subjects (compared to the middle-aged subjects) occurred when they reconstructed the array in which the objects were placed in a bank of cubicles containing buildings and landscape objects identical to those used in the panorama, but not organized in a meaningful scene. While both age groups replaced objects in the panorama in an order indicating that they used the organization of the scene to guide reconstruction, only the middle-aged subjects replaced objects in the cubicles in an order indicating that they made use of the layout. (Use of spatial organization correlated positively with correct object placement.) The aged subjects instead seemed to attempt to reproduce the order in which the objects were placed in the cubicles by the experimenter, a strategy which correlated negatively with correct object placement.

The common cross-cultural and age differences in memory performance may thus be somewhat limited in that the tests given require structuring of unrelated items. Memory for contextually organized material seems to function somewhat independently of and involve different skills than memory for noncontextually organized materials. This interpretation may account for some of the findings of excellent performance by non-Western subjects on spatial tasks.

But this effect is unlikely to be limited to spatial relationships. Some research involving contextually organized verbal information, such as recall of stories, has found superior or equivalent performance by non-Western compared to Western subjects (Dube, 1982; Mandler, Scribner, Cole, & DeForest, 1980; Ross & Millsom, 1970). Exceptional memory for narrative material by nonliterate bards has been noted in some provocative cases (Cole & Scribner, 1977; Hunter, 1979; Lord, 1965; Neisser, 1982). And traditional navigators may use complex story mnemonics to organize their memory for the layout of the ocean and the stars (Price-Williams, 1981). Tasks that allow the contextual organization of the material to be used as a recall aid may reduce the differences found in cross-cultural memory test performance.

Meaningful Purpose to the Memory Activity

In many of the cases noting outstanding memory performance by non-Western people, the memory feat is accomplished in the service of a culturally important nonmnemonic goal. Remembering is a means rather than the goal of the activity. This is true for remembering spatial information to avoid getting lost while navigating, and for remembering verbal material in narrating stories to entertain, discussed earlier. It is also the case for the preservation of oral history by specialists in Africa (D'Azevedo, 1982) and for memory of battles and raids by Arabian shaykhs (Mack, 1976).

Memory research has concentrated on situations in which memory is a goal in itself, rather than a means to a practical goal such as remembering an important appointment (Brown, 1975; Smirnov & Zinchenko, 1969). Without a purpose for remembering material, thousands of trials of exposure may still not ensure remembering, as was the case with Professor Sanford's morning prayer, read daily over 25 years, but not learned (Sanford, 1917, reprinted 1982). Remembering in everyday life is usually in the service of accomplishing some other goal rather than being itself the end for the activity. When preschool children are asked to remember a list of items in order to bring them back from a toy store, their free recall is much better than in standard free-recall tasks where the purpose for remembering is to expose one's memory to an experimenter (Istomina, 1977).

Subjects who are unfamiliar with performing solely for the evaluation of a teacher or an experimenter (such as young or nonschooled children) are likely to find the purpose of remembering items in a memory test obscure. This too may give Western children a performance advantage when compared with non-Western, especially nonschooled, children. For schooled children, tests may not be a comfortable situation, but at least the children are familiar with what is expected of them and they have had some practice exercising their memories for no other practical purpose. They have background knowledge in the social script for participating in a test which the nonschooled subjects lack. Memory situations in experiments as well as in practical thinking are given structure and meaning by the "dominant social tendencies" (Bartlett, 1932) that organize the activity. Subjects who do not share such expectations or purposes are likely to approach the memory task differently.

The Organization of Memory in Social and Cultural Practice

Research discussed so far has dealt with memory tasks incorporating some aspect of the broader sociocultural milieu in which it is embedded by considering meaningful contexts which structure the memory activity or give it purpose. Especially when one considers the integration of familiarity of materials and memory processes with background experience, it becomes clear that memory performance is highly tied to the ways people have practiced using their memory skills.

This section presents cross-cultural research demonstrating that the social context affects cognitive development at both an institutional/material level and at an interpersonal level, consistent with Vygotsky's (1978) sociocultural theory. At the institutional level, cultural history provides organizations and tools useful to cognitive activity (through institutions such as school and inventions such as literacy) and it provides practices facilitating socially appropriate solutions to problems (e.g., scripts for events; common mnemonic devices). In this view, the results reviewed in previous sections on the role of familiarity of materials, their integration in meaningfully organized contexts, and the meaningfulness of the goal are all interpretable as aspects of the broader social context of the activity.

The role of institutional and cultural practices. The relation between cultural conventions for handling intellectual problems and individual memory performance has been explored with regard to the role of literacy, classification systems, mathematical tools, and the institution of formal schooling. Such cultural practices appear to organize the ways individuals remember, in a functional relationship.

To examine the functional relationship between the practice of literacy and memory skills, Scribner and Cole (1981) designed a memory task resembling the incremental method of learning the Quran practiced by subjects literate in Arabic (i.e., learning a string of words in order and adding one word to the series on each attempt). They compared the performance of Vai people who vary in the use of several types of literacy: Arabic literacy gained in study of the religious script in traditional Quranic schools, literacy in the indigenous Vai script learned for practical correspondence through informal instruction, literacy in English for official purposes learned in Western-style schools, and lack of literacy at all. The Arabic literates had a great advantage over the other groups on recall of words when the preservation of word order was required, consistent with memory practices used in learning the Quran. Regression analyses indicated that the amount of time spent studying the Quran predicted performance on memory tests incorporating serialization. This contrasts with a lack of literacy group differences on recall of words irrespective of order, and on recall of folk stories. Scribner and Cole conclude that learning to be literate in the Quran influences recall only when the format and sequencing of the to-be-remembered material models previous learning habits.

The relation between memory and cultural practices for organizing objects conceptually was examined by Lancy and Strathern (1981). They compared clustering in free recall by children from two societies in Papua, New Guinea that varied in the complexity of the folk taxonomies employed in their language (i.e., classification of objects). Ponam folk classification uses taxonomic categories similar to those common in Western societies. In contrast, Melpa folk classification has a paucity of suprageneric terms; instead of relying on taxonomic classification with its superordinate–subordinate relations, Melpa people use an alternate strategy which they call "making twos" or grouping by pairs. Melpa phrases expressing "group" or "together" all contain the word "two" or "partner." For example, in Melpa classification, plant, animal, and color terms are ordered in pairs of polar opposites, for example, planted versus wild, and light (or red) versus dark (or black). Ponam children exhibited greater recall as well as more clustering of items (with amount of clustering and free-recall scores correlated) than Melpa children. The authors argue that taxonomic classification, common among the Ponam as well as Western groups, is only one mode of organizing discrete elements, and may have been elevated to an artifically high status as *the* mode of organization to use. Consistent with this suggestion, Super and Harkness (in press) note that on free-recall lists designed to reflect taxonomic categories, U.S. adults cluster more than Kenyan adults, while on comparable lists designed for clustering on the basis of function, Kenyan adults cluster more.

Cultural tools for mathematical operations also hold a specific functional role for remembering information related to their use. Japanese abacus experts use interiorized representations of the abacus which allow them to mentally calculate without an abacus as accurately as with one, and often faster (Hatano, 1982). Their mental abacus is of extended size and can represent a number of many digits. While abacus experts can recall a series of 15 digits either forward or backward, their memory span for the Roman alphabet and for fruit names is not different from the usual 7 ± 2 units found for most adults in memory span tasks. The special processes involved in their impressive mental abacus operations are tailored to the activities in which they were practiced.

For understanding memory development, the most important cultural institution may be Western schooling, which structures cognitive activity by providing norms and strategies for effective performance on memory tests. That is, Western schooling inculcates students with culturally based definitions of cleverness and acceptable means for solving problems. It provides an emphasis on fast performance as in timed tests that may be unusual outside of school in many cultures. Differences between cultural groups may be ascribable largely to interpretation of what problem is being solved in the task and to different values regarding "proper" methods of solution (e.g., speed, reaching a solution with a minimum of moves, mentally solving problems rather than physically manipulating materials, and working independently rather than collaboratively; Goodnow, 1976). Schooling may provide practice in specific approaches to memory problems, such as emphasis on word-for-word recall and the imposition of organization on arbitrary items, and it may even provide training in the use of mnemonic strategies as used in memory experiments. In addition, the cultural tools and techniques used in school involve conventions and formats which are also used in memory studies, such as organizing a list by taxonomy rather than function, representing a sequence by placing items in a left-to-right array, or restricting choice alternatives in a multiple-choice format.

The social interactional context of memory practice. Operating concurrently with the institutional and cultural practices which organize memory development, but at a different grain of analysis, is the immediate social interactional context of learning and using memory skills. Both the social interactions at the time of a particular performance and those with which subjects are familiar in their usual practice of memory are important for understanding memory performance. Social interaction structures individual activity, especially as information regarding tools and practices is transmitted through interaction with more experienced members of society during development. Particular patterns of interpersonal relations are organized by institutional conventions and the availability of particular cultural tools.

Social aspects of experimental situations are unfamiliar to some groups. For example, the relationship between Experimenter and Subject may be rapidly grasped by Western children familiar with testing in school, but may be highly discrepant from familiar adult–child interactions for non-Western children and adults. Schooled people are more familiar with an interview or testing situation in which a high-status adult, who already knows the answer to the question, requests information of a lower-status person, such as a child (Irvine, 1978). It is not uncommon in traditional societies for the interaction between adults and children to be characterized by commands from the adult and compliance by the child, rather than any interest in children's opinions (Blount, 1972; Harkness & Super, 1977). The practice of testing school children at an arbitrary point in the learning process, before the material has been fully mastered, may be unusual in cultures where learners begin to participate in an activity when they feel competent at the skill being learned (Cazden & John, 1971). In traditional society a year of school dramatically increases children's ability to finish an experiment—regardless of correctness of answers—and increases the number of words used in responding (Super, 1977). Schooled children have had more practice in figuring out what an adult is asking when the adult does not structure the problem or reveal what aspects of performance will be evaluated (Rogoff, Gauvain, & Ellis, 1984). Nonschooled children, having less experience with a testing situation, may be concerned with showing respectful behavior to the tester and trying to figure out the tester rather than to figure out the problem.

An example of how conventions for social interaction can influence memory performance is provided by a study on story recall by Rogoff and Waddell (unpublished ms). While story recall involves memory for material embedded in a meaningful context, and non-Western people have in some studies shown impressive prose recall (Cole & Scribner, 1977; Dube, 1977; Mandler, Scribner, Cole, & DeForest, 1980), in this study 9-year-old Guatemalan Mayan children remembered far less of the stories than did U.S. children. The Mayan children averaged 54.3 information units from the two stories, and the U.S. children recalled 79.0 information units. This was despite extensive efforts to make the task culturally appropriate for the Mayan children. The stories were adapted from the Mayan oral literture, told to the children by a familiar teenager speaking the local Mayan dialect, in a testing room in which they had become comfortable through prior play sessions, parties, and several tests which they had enjoyed. In the effort to make story recall more like telling the story rather than being tested by the same person who had just told it to them, the children told the stories to another local person (an older woman with whom they were familiar and comfortable) who had not been present when the teenager told them the story. With such efforts to make the task culturally appropriate to the Mayan children, why then was their performance so poor compared with Western children and non-Western groups whose performance on story recall is impressive?

While not obvious from the outset, there were important social features of the test situation that made the Mayan children very uncomfortable. It is culturally inappropriate for Mayan children to speak freely to an adult. When carrying messages to adults, they must politely add the word "cha" ("so I have been told") in order to avoid conveying a lack of respect by impertinently claiming greater knowledge than the adult. Though the Mayan children heard stories told by their elders, and talked freely among peers, it was a strange and uncomfortable experience for them to attempt to tell a story to an adult—no matter how comfortable they were with the content of the story, the testing situation, and the adult.

The Mayan children's recall performances were excessively bashful and contrasted with their eager performance on other tests. Some of them could barely be induced to speak at all; many spoke in whispers, fidgeting and looking at their knees; often their utterances were punctuated with the word "cha." They responded as if being grilled rather than narrating a story. Although the Mayan children usually mentioned a fact from each of the main episodes of the story, they did so in a disjointed fashion as if they were listing the answers to questions regarding the facts of the story. And the experimenter found it continually necessary to ask "What happened next?" This may relate to the closest experience of some of the Mayan children: being tested on Bible stories in church school. In contrast to the Mayan children's performance, the U.S. children's more fluent recalls were marked by much more narrative connection between pieces of information and less need for prompting questions. (About 75% of the Mayan children's recalls were rated as disjointed rather than cohesive, compared to 8% of the U.S. children's recalls. The listening adult averaged four "what else happened" questions and three prompting questions (e.g., "What did the judge say?") for the Mayan children, compared with an average of one "what else" and one prompting question for the U.S. children.)

The following examples are average recalls for U.S. and Mayan children on the first story, about a bad boy who lost his father's cattle. Remarks in parentheses indicate "what else" or prompting questions by the listening adult; these were standardized with criteria for when they could be used. An average performance by a U.S. child:

(Go ahead) . . .
There was once a boy named Michael and . . . and he . . . (what happened?) . . .
(What did they do in Tooele?) Um, they, um, he, he had bulls. He didn't tie them up too good, and the bulls got away and were eating some corn and so Michael goes

home and his dad got mad, and . . . they go to the judge . . . and, ah, and the judge said they had to pay $10 for each bull. And then the man said he, um, he would pay $10 for both bulls. And . . . he . . . and then the judge said that he would have to make up for the corn that the bulls ate. So he took the bulls home, and when they got home, Michael's dad spanked him real hard.

An average performance by a Mayan child:

(Go ahead) . . . (Say it) . . .
Manuel went to San Juan; he brought two bulls. He tied them up; he didn't tie them up well. Two bulls got away. The people from San Juan were very angry . . .
(What else did they do?) They went to San Juan . . . (What else?) . . .
(What did Manuel's father do?) He went to San Juan . . . They went . . . they went to the court in San Juan . . . (What else did they do?) . . .
(What else happened?) . . . . .
(What did the mayor say?) It's fine, said the mayor . . .
(What else did they do?) They returned, they went home . . .
(And then?) They brought the bulls.

The Mayan children included less information from the stories, but their recalls were also marked by hesitance, reciting of facts rather than narrating a story, and need for prompting by the adult listener, fitting with cultural restrictions on how children address adults. Whether Mayan children's story recall would appear more complete and fluent if they were recounting a story to a peer under comfortable circumstances is a matter of speculation. This research illustrates the inseparability of memory performances from the social circumstances of the performance as well as the cultural background molding the use of memory.

In line with this observation, McNamee suggests that "research on memory for connected text, especially with children, needs to incorporate data on the human environment where these processes develop and get used" (1981, pp. 6–7) because, for young children, story schemas develop between adults and children as they converse. It is one of the tasks of the early school years to teach children to produce school-style narratives during show-and-tell and class lessons (Cazden, 1979).

Far from school-style narrative being a natural mature form of discourse, it develops in the context of school and middle-class U.S. culture. For children from other cultural backgrounds attending school, it may be a challenge to adopt this form of recounting events. Research on story grammars documents that in different cultural groups, the format of stories varies (Matsuyama, 1983).

The organization of recall of stories or events is guided by the use of such activities in cultural practices. American and Greek students who were asked to recall a cinematically presented story differed in their approach to the task (Tannen, 1980): The American students treated it as a recall task, worrying about temporal sequence and inclusion of details, and reporting technical details pertaining to the cinematic presentation. The Greek students treated it as a story-telling task, interpreting events and actor's motives, frequently omitting details that did not contribute to the story theme, and focusing on the events depicted without commenting on the cinematic technique. Tannen provides evidence that these differences relate to cultural values: Published reviews by prominant American and Greek film critics reviewing the same films showed similar differences in approach, with the American critics focusing on the film director's technical accomplishments, while the Greek critics focused on the film's message and artistic vision rather than its technique. Nadel (1937) also found cultural differences in approaches to prose recall in terms of elaboration of the story's logical links versus emphasis on facts and description without an effort to preserve the cohesion of the story, which he related to broader cultural patterns.

Thus story recall is embedded in the immediate and the broader social context. The performance of a subject in an experiment cannot be considered a window on some pure aspect of memory functioning; it is inherently grounded in the social situation of the current performance and the situations in which the subject is used to remembering things.

Theoretical Perspectives on the Sociocultural Context of Remembering

The research we have reviewed in this chapter can be used to support theoretical perspectives which stress that remembering is integrally related to the social and cultural contexts in which it is practiced. To elaborate this point we rely especially on the writings of Bartlett, Vygotsky, and the Laboratory of Comparative Human Cognition.

Half a century ago, Bartlett (1932) argued that memory is a socially structured process. His work has been slow to gain influence, perhaps because the traditional definition of memory attempted to separate mental processes from the social substrate (e.g., using nonsense syllables). Bartlett argued that studying memory as a "pure" process, attempting to avoid the influence of previous knowledge and background experience, only complicates rather than simplifies matters, since memory is in its essence a social phenomenon. Bartlett's work has recently generated great interest in the reconstructive nature of recall and the influence of schemas on remembering. Thus researchers now acknowledge and study the influence of prior knowledge in reconstructing information, demonstrating that omissions and additions are often made in accord with inferences from prior knowledge (schemas). However, Bartlett emphasized not only the reconstructive nature of recall, but also stressed that "both the manner and the matter of recall are often predominantly determined by social influences" (p. 244).

Using examples of remembering by people of other cultures, Bartlett argued that remembering for non-Western as well as Western people is "a matter of social organization, with its accepted scales of value (p. 248)." He pointed to the role of preferred, persistent group tendencies in channeling memory, citing how a young Swazi boy was no better or worse than his Western counterpart in carrying a message of 25 words, but a Swazi herdsman's memory for cattle transactions made over the previous year was accurate in almost every detail. This was so, according to Bartlett, because of the tremendous social significance of herds in Swazi economic activity.

Within the traditional theory of memory which attempts to separate the mental process from the social, Bartlett's anecdotes may well be assimilated but dismissed as trivial or peripheral. That is, most people are probably willing to accept the idea that people remember better what is important to them, or what is well practiced. This may be regarded as a diversion from the mission of memory research if the role of experience or interest is viewed as simply an amplifier of a pure process of memory, which operates separately from experience and cultural patterns. But Bartlett's point (and the point we hoped to make through our review of research) is that the process of remembering is intimately tied up with what is being remembered, under what circumstances, and how that relates to the organized social and cultural background experience of the subject.

The Soviet view of the development of higher mental processes similarly stresses the social genesis and structuring of memory (Meacham, 1977; Vygotsky, 1962, 1978). Leont'ev stipulated that "the role of the social medium is not limited . . . simply to its emerging as a central factor of development; man's memory . . . remains associated with it in its very functioning (1981, p. 363)." In the Soviet approach, memory and other higher mental processes develop from experience in socially structured activity through the internalization of the processes and practices provided by society and its members. As discussed earlier, the social context influences the individual's patterns of behavior through cultural, institutional tools of action and thought such as arithmetic and writing systems, mnemonic strategies, and rules for the use of such tools. The cultural context is personified for the developing child in interactions with more experienced members of the society who transmit information and who structure practice with the skills and tools of society. In such social interaction, "culture and cognition create each other" (Cole, 1981). The Soviet perspective focuses on the social unit of activity and regards individual functioning as derived from that, rather than first explaining individual functioning and then adding sociocultural influences.

The notion that individual functioning is derived from social activity suggests that the particular culturally guided learning experiences of individuals are crucial for understanding memory development. While there is nothing surprising in the idea that people develop skills through practice, there are differences in how general the learning experiences and the resulting performances are expected to be, and hence in how cultural differences are explained.

The Laboratory of Comparative Human Cognition (1983) has distinguished a central-processor approach to learning from a distributed-processor approach. They characterize the central-processor approach as fitting the assumptions of existing developmental theory and research: The events which an individual experiences contribute to the strength or power of a central processor consisting of general skills. Subjects faced with particular tasks make use of their general skill contained in the central processor to perform the task, regardless of the nature of the task. The problem with the central-processing approach is that it assumes generality of processing, while numerous studies including many reviewed in this chapter find memory and other processes to be more context-specific (see also Rogoff, 1982; Rogoff, Gauvain, & Ellis, 1984). Such research suggests that memory does not involve context-free competences which may be applied indiscriminantly across widely diverse problem domains, but rather involves skills tied to somewhat specific activities in context. While researchers may refer to a variety of tasks under the label "memory tasks," this is a classification made by the researchers rather than an inherent definition of the activity for those carrying it out. As the Laboratory for Comparative Human Cognition puts it, "memory and reasoning are defined by the tasks we employ to specify them" (1979, p. 830).

The contrasting distributed-processing approach emphasizes that skills are closely tied to the context of practice, as the individual develops skills in particular tasks through experience in related activities. Skills are customized to the task, with experiences linked to task performance through discrete schemata. The problem with this approach is that it leaves unanswered the question of how people transfer knowledge and strategies from familiar contexts to new problems. To make use of their skills, people must be able to generalize them to new situations which differ in at least some details from the problems they have previously experienced. Thus, while performance is somewhat specific to the context of practice, the notion of strict specificity of skills will not account for the flexibility of application of skills in new situations. Transfer cannot be accounted for in mechanical terms, focusing on formal or physical similarities of the problems themselves without taking into account the systems nature of contexts—involving not only the form of the problem but also the purpose of solving it and the social context in which the activity is embedded.

From the perspective that memory develops in sociocultural context, the systems nature of memory activities assists in accounting for transfer from specific learning activities. People transform novel problems to resemble familiar ones by actively seeking analogies across problems. Thus the person's interpretation of the problem is important in applying skills already developed in another context. Bartlett asserted that generalization "is not in the least likely to occur . . . unless there is active exploration of the situation that offers it an opportunity" (1958, p. 95). Several studies have demonstrated that unless subjects are aware of underlying similiarities and the applicability of existing knowledge to new problems, they are unlikely to generalize (Duncker, 1945; Gick & Holyoak, 1980). Guiding the active role of the individual in bridging contexts are other people as well as cultural scripts for problem solution (Rogoff & Gardner, 1984).

A sociocultural approach to the development of memory skills examines memory performance using as the unit of analysis the whole activity, defined in terms of the meaning of the task and its materials to the subject group and its place in the social and cultural system. Memory processes are means by which people achieve practical results in specific culturally organized contexts.

Using *activity* as the unit of analysis contrasts with the independent-variable/dependent-variable approach which separates individual responses from environmental stimuli as the units of analysis. Precedents for using activity as the unit of analysis occur in theoretical work of Vygotsky (1978), Leont'ev (1981), Gibson (1979; see also Michaels & Carello, 1981) and the philosophical writings of Pepper (1942; see also Rogoff, 1982).

The cultural practice theory of the Laboratory of Comparative Human Cognition (1983) and Scribner and Cole (1981) focuses on activity by identifying "socially assembled situations" as the unit for analysis, rather than working from characteristics of individuals or of cultures. "Socially assembled situations" are cultural contexts for action and problem solving that are constructed by people in interaction with each other. Cultural practices employed in socially assembled situations are learned systems of activity in which knowledge consists of standing rules and technologies for thought and action appropriate to a particular situation, embodied in the interaction of individual members of a culture. The Laboratory of Comparative Human Cognition argues that descriptions of what people know how to do are distorted if they do not consider the social circumstances in which that knowledge is displayed and interpreted.

Summary

In order to understand the process of memory in cultural context we need to examine the practices of children and those around them in their usual activities. Memory skills develop for the purpose of solving practical problems which vary according to the specific situation and the cultural context. Memory skills develop as children adopt mnemonic tools and skills used in the cultural situations they experience, in collaboration with other people as they remember things in practical activities. Sociocultural experience and individual memory skills are fundamentally tied to each other. Thus memory performance must be examined in the context of the familiarity of the organization of the material to be remembered, the subjects' interpretation of the tasks to be accomplished, the relation of the task goals to culturally important activities, and the relation with the social interactional and the broader sociocultural contexts of peoples' practice in remembering.

Acknowledgments. We are grateful to Jamie Germond and Barbara Radziszewska for their comments on a previous draft of this chapter.

References

Bartlett, F. C. (1932). *Remembering*. Cambridge: Cambridge University Press.

Bartlett, F. C. (1958). *Thinking: An experimental and social study*. New York: Basic Books.

Blount, B. G. (1972). Parental speech and language acquisition: Some Luo and Samoan examples. *Anthropological Linguistics, 14*, 119–130.

Brown, A. L. (1975). The development of memory: Knowing, knowing about knowing and knowing how to know. In H. W. Reese (Ed.), *Advances in child development and behavior* (Vol. 10). New York: Academic Press.

Cazden, C. B. (1979). Peekaboo as an instructional model: Discourse development at home and at school. In *Papers and reports on child language development* (No. 17). Stanford University, Department of Linguistics.

Cazden, C. B., & John, V. P. (1971). Learning in American Indian children. In M. L. Wax, S. Diamond, & F. O. Gearing (Eds.), *Anthropological perspectives in education*. New York: Basic Books.

Ciborowski, T., & Choy, S. (1974). Nonstandard English and free recall. *Journal of Cross-Cultural Psychology, 5*, 271–281.

Cole, M. (1981, September). *The zone of proximal development: Where culture and cognition create each other* (Report 106). San Diego: University of California, Center for Human Information Processing.

Cole, M., Gay, J., Glick, J. A., & Sharp, D. W. (1971). *The cultural context of learning and thinking*. New York: Basic Books.

Cole, M., Hood, L., & McDermott, R. P. (1978). Concepts of ecological validity: Their differing implications for comparative cognitive research. *The Quarterly Newsletter of the Institute for Comparative Human Development, 2*, 34–37.

Cole, M., & Scribner, S. (1977). Cross-cultural studies of memory and cognition. In R. V. Kail, Jr., & J. W. Hagen (Eds.), *Perspectives on the development of memory and cognition* (pp. 239–271). Hillsdale, N.J.: Erlbaum.

Cole, M., Sharp, D. W., & Lave, C. (1976). The cognitive consequences of education: Some empirical evidence and theoretical misgivings. *Urban Review, 9*, 218–233.

Das, J. P., Manos, J., & Kanungo, R. N. (1975). Performance of Canadian native, black, and white children on some cognitive and personality tests. *Alberta Journal of Educational Research, 21*, 183–195.

D'Azevedo, W. A. (1982). In U. Neisser (Ed.), *Memory observed: Remembering in natural contexts* (pp. 258–268). San Francisco: W. H. Freeman.

Drinkwater, B. A. (1976). Visual memory skills of medium contact Aboriginal children. *Australian Journal of Psychology, 28*, 37–43.

Dube, E. F. (1982). Literacy, cultural familiarity, and "intelligence" as determinants of story recall. In U. Neisser (Ed.), *Memory observed: Remembering in natural contexts* (pp. 274–292). San Francisco: W. H. Freeman.

Duncker, K. (1945). On problem solving. *Psychological Monographs, 58*, 85–93.

Fahrmeier, E. D. (1975). The effect of school attendance on intellectual development in Northern Nigeria. *Child Development, 46*, 281–285.

Franklin, A. F. (1978). Sociolinguistic structure of word lists and ethnic group differences in categorized recall. *The Quarterly Newsletter of the Institute of Comparative Human Development, 2*, 30–34.

Gibson, J. J. (1979). *The ecological approach to visual perception*. Boston: Houghton Mifflin.

Gick, M. L., & Holyoak, K. J. (1980). Analogical problem solving. *Cognitive Psychology, 12*, 306–355.

Gladwin, T. (1970). *East is a big bird.* Cambridge, MA: Belknap Press.

Goodnow, J. J. (1976). The nature of intelligent behavior: Questions raised by cross-cultural studies. In L. B. Resnick (Ed.), *The nature of intelligence.* New York: Erlbaum.

Goody, J. (1977). *The domestication of the savage mind.* Cambridge: Cambridge University Press.

Hall, J. W. (1972). Verbal behavior as a function of amount of schooling. *American Journal of Psychology, 85*, 277–289.

Hall, W. S., Reder, S., & Cole, M. (1975). Story recall in young black and white children: Effects of racial group membership, race of experimenter, and dialect. *Developmental Psychology, 11*, 628–634.

Harkness, S., & Super, C. M. (1977). Why African children are so hard to test. In L. L. Adler (Ed.), *Issues in cross-cultural research. Annals of the New York Academy of Sciences, 285*, 326–331.

Hasher, L., & Zachs, R. T. (1979). Automatic and effortful processes in memory. *Journal of Experimental Psychology: General, 108*, 356–388.

Hatano, G. (1982). Cognitive consequences of practice in culture specific procedural skills. *The Quarterly Newsletter of the Laboratory of Comparative Human Cognition, 4*, 15–17.

Hunter, I. M. L. (1979). Memory in everyday life. In M. M. Gruneberg & P. E. Morris (Eds.), *Applied problems in memory.* N.Y.: Academic.

Irvine, J. T. (1978). Wolof "magical thinking": Culture and conservation revisited. *Journal of Cross-Cultural Psychology, 9*, 300–310.

Irwin, M. H., & McLaughlin, D. H. (1970). Ability and preference in category sorting by Mano school children and adults. *Journal of Social Psychology, 82*, 15–24.

Irwin, M. H., Schafer, G. N., & Feiden, C. P. (1974). Emic and unfamiliar category sorting of Mano farmers and U.S. undergraduates. *Journal of Cross-Cultural Psychology, 5*, 407–423.

Istomina, Z. M. (1977). The development of voluntary memory in preschool-age children. In M. Cole (Ed.), *Soviet developmental psychology.* White Plains, N.Y.: Sharpe.

Kagan, J., Klein, R. E., Finley, G. E., Rogoff, B., & Nolan, E. (1979). A cross-cultural study of cognitive development. *Monographs of the Society for Research in Child Development, 44* (5, Serial No. 180).

Kearins, J. M. (1981). Visual spatial memory in Australian aboriginal children of desert regions. *Cognitive Psychology, 13*, 434–460.

Kintsch, W., & Greene, E. (1978). The role of culture-specific schemata in the comprehension and recall of stories. *Discourse Processes, 1*, 1–13.

Kleinfeld, J. (1971). Visual memory in village Eskimo and urban Caucasian children. *Arctic, 24*, 132–137.

Laboratory of Comparative Human Cognition. (1979). Cross-cultural psychology's challenges to our ideas of children and development. *American Psychologist, 34*, 827–833.

Laboratory of Comparative Human Cognition. (1983). Culture and cognitive development. In J. H. Flavell & E. M. Markman (Eds.), *Handbook of child psychology: Vol. III. Cognitive develoment.* New York: Wiley.

Lancy, D. F., & Strathern, A. J. (1981). Making twos: Pairing as an alternative to the taxonomic mode of representation. *American Anthropologist, 83*, 773–795.

Leont'ev, A. N. (1981). The development of higher forms of memory. In A. N. Leont'ev (Ed.), *Problems of the development of the mind.* Moscow: Progress Publishers.

Lewis, D. (1976). Observations on route finding and spatial orientation among the Aboriginal peoples of the Western Desert region of Central Australia. *Oceania, 46,* 249–282.

Levy-Bruhl, L. (1926). *How natives think* (pp. 109–116). London: George Allen & Unwin.

Lord, A. B. (1965). *Singer of tales.* New York: Atheneum.

Mack, J. E. (1976). *A prince of our disorder: The life of T. E. Lawrence.* Boston: Little, Brown.

Mandler, J. M., Scribner, S., Cole, M., & DeForest, M. (1980). Cross-cultural invariance in story recall. *Child Development, 51,* 19–26.

Matsuyama, U. K. (1983). Can story grammar speak Japanese? *The Reading Teacher, 36,* 666–669.

McNamee, G. D. (1981, April). *Social origins of narrative skills.* Paper presented at the meetings of the Society for Research in Child Development, Boston.

Meacham, J. A. (1975). Patterns of memory abilities in two cultures. *Developmental Psychology, 11,* 50–53.

Meacham, J. A. (1977). Soviet investigations of memory development. In R. V. Kail, Jr. & J. W. Hagen (Eds.), *Perspectives on the development of memory and cognition* (pp. 273–295). Hillsdale, N.J.: Erlbaum.

Michaels, C. F., & Carello, C. (1981). *Direct perception.* Englewood Cliffs, N.J.: Prentice-Hall.

Nadel, S. F. (1937). Experiments on culture psychology. *Africa, 10,* 421–435.

Neisser, U. (Ed.). (1982). *Memory observed: Remembering in natural contexts.* San Francisco: W. H. Freeman.

Nerlove, S. B., & Snipper, A. S. (1981). Cognitive consequences of cultural opportunity. In R. L. Munroe, R. H. Munroe, & B. B. Whiting (Eds.), *Handbook of cross-cultural human development.* New York: Garland.

Newcombe, N., Rogoff, B., & Kagan, J. (1977). Developmental changes in recognition memory for pictures of objects and scenes. *Developmental Psychology, 13,* 337–341.

Pepper, S. C. (1942). *World hypotheses: A study in evidence.* Berkeley: University of California Press.

Price-Williams, D. R. (1962). Abstract and concrete modes of classification in a primitive society. *British Journal of Educational Psychology, 32,* 50–61.

Price-Williams, D. R. (1981, August). *Culture, intelligence and metacognition.* Presented at the meetings of the American Psychological Association, Los Angeles.

Rice, G. E. (1980). On cultural schemata. *American Ethnologist, 7,* 152–171.

Rogoff, B. (1981). Schooling and the development of cognitive skills. In H. C. Triandis & A. Heron (Eds.), *Handbook of cross-cultural psychology* (Vol. 4, pp. 233–294). Boston: Allyn & Bacon.

Rogoff, B. (1982). Integrating context and cognitive development. In M. E. Lamb & A. L. Brown (Eds.), *Advances in Developmental Psychology* (Vol. 2). Hillsdale, N.J.: Erlbaum.

Rogoff, B., & Gardner, W. (1984). Adult guidance of cognitive development. In B. Rogoff & J. Lave (Eds.), *Everyday cognition: Its development in social context.* Cambridge, MA: Harvard University Press.

Rogoff, B., Gauvain, M., & Ellis, S. (1984). Development viewed in its cultural context. In M. H. Bornstein & M. E. Lamb (Eds.), *Developmental Psychology.* Hillsdale, N.J.: Erlbaum.

Rogoff, B., & Waddell, K. J. (1982). Memory for information organized in a scene by children from two cultures. *Child Development, 53,* 1224–1228.

Rogoff, B., & Waddell, K. J. The social context of recalling stories: A cross-cultural study. Unpublished manuscript, University of Utah, Salt Lake City, Utah.

Ross, B. M., & Millsom, C. (1970). Repeated memory of oral prose in Ghana and New York. *International Journal of Psychology, 5,* 173–181.

Sanford, E. C. (1917, reprinted 1982). Professor Sanford's morning prayer. In U. Neisser (Ed.), *Memory observed: Remembering in natural contexts* (pp. 176–177). San Francisco: W. H. Freeman.

Scribner, S. (1974). Developmental aspects of categorized recall in a West African society. *Cognitive Psychology, 6,* 475–494.

Scribner, S., & Cole, M. (1981). *The psychology of literacy.* Cambridge, MA: Harvard University Press.

Sharp, D., Cole, M., & Lave, C. (1979). Education and cognitive development: The evidence from experimental research. *Monographs of the Society for Research in Child Development, 44* (1–2, Serial No. 178).

Smirnov, A. A., & Zinchenko, P. I. (1969). Problems in the psychology of memory. In M. Cole & I. Maltzman (Eds.), *A handbook of contemporary Soviet psychology.* New York: Basic Books.

Stevenson, H. W., Parker, T., Wilkinson, A., Bonnevaux, B., & Gonzalez, M. (1978). Schooling, environment, and cognitive development: A cross-cultural study. *Monographs of the Society for Research in Child Development, 43* (3, Serial No. 175).

Super, C. M. (1977). *Who goes to school and what do they learn?* Paper presented at the meeting of the Society for Research in Child Development, New Orleans.

Super, C. M., & Harkness, S. (in press). Looking across at growing up: The expressions of cognitive development in middle childhood. In E. S. Gollin (Ed.), *Developmental plasticity: Social context and human development.* New York: Academic Press.

Tannen, D. (1980). A comparative analysis of oral narrative strategies: Athenian Greek and American English. In W. L. Chafe (Ed.), *The pear stories: Cognitive, cultural and linguistic aspects of narrative production* (pp. 51–87). Norwood, N.J.: Ablex.

Vygotsky, L. S. (1962). *Thought and language.* Cambridge, MA: MIT Press.

Vygotsky, L. S. *Mind in society.* (1978). Cambridge, MA: Harvard University Press.

Waddell, K. J., & Rogoff, B. (1981). Effect of contextual organization on spatial memory of middle aged and older women. *Developmental Psychology, 17,* 878–885.

Wagner, D. A. (1974). The development of short-term and incidental memory: A cross-cultural study. *Child Development, 45,* 389–396.

Wagner, D. A. (1978). Memories of Morocco: The influence of age, schooling, and environment on memory. *Cognitive Psychology, 10,* 1–28.

Wagner, D. A. (1981). Culture and memory development. In H. C. Triandis & A. Heron (Eds.), *Handbook of cross-cultural psychology* (Vol. 4, pp. 187–232). Boston: Allyn & Bacon.

Weisner, T. S. (1976). Urban–rural differences in African children's performance on cognitive and memory tasks. *Ethos, 4,* 223–250.

Whiting, B. B. (1976). The problem of the packaged variable. In K. F. Riegel &
    J. A. Meacham (Eds.), *The developing individual in a changing world*. Chicago:
    Aldine.
Worden, P. E., & Sherman-Brown, S. (1983). A word-frequency cohort effect in young
    versus elderly adults' memory for words. *Developmental Psychology, 19*, 521–530.

5. Figure and Fantasy in Children's Language

Valerie F. Reyna

Introduction

Figurative Language: Memory and Understanding

This chapter concerns the development of two types of understanding: understanding of metaphors and understanding of fantasy-based language. Both metaphorical and fantasy-based language are figurative in the sense that they involve unconventional interpretations. In lieu of the more detailed definitions of memory and fantasy-based language given below, I offer some examples for the purpose of preliminary discussion. Speaking conventionally, we can call a tabby a "cat," but we speak figuratively if we refer to Maggie of *Cat on a Hot Tin Roof* as a "cat"; this use of "cat" to describe a woman is metaphorical. Similarly, referring to a collie as a "dog" is conventional usage, whereas referring to the cartoon character Huckleberry Hound as a "dog" is fantasy-based language.

The study of figurative language was traditionally undertaken primarily by philosophers and literary critics, often under the rubric of rhetoric where it had been placed by Aristotle. Until recently, linguists generally did not devote themselves to lengthy theorizing about figurative language. Psycholinguistics (the psychological study of language) tended to be swept along by the currents of linguistics, reflecting its origins as a reaction to revolutionary theoretical developments in linguistics. The linguist Noam Chomsky's views at at the time were representative. He emphasized conventional, rule-consistent meaning and assumed that figurative interpretation could be accounted for with only minor modification of theories designed for conventional meaning. In discussing such sentences as the now famous "Colorless green ideas sleep furiously," Chomsky (1965) allowed that "sentences that break . . . rules can often be interpreted metaphorically," but he maintained that these sentences are "interpreted by *direct* analogy to well-formed sentences" (italics added, p. 149).

Around the early 1970s, attention shifted in linguistics and psycholinguistics to "a concern with linguistic performance and pragmatics [the use and functions of language] in contrast to the emphasis on linguistic competence so characteristic of the Chomskyian revolution" (Ortony, 1979a, p. 4). With this shift came an increasing interest in figurative interpretation since such interpretation was taken to represent the operation of pragmatic rules as opposed to the syntactic and semantic rules that determined conventional interpretation. The assumption was that conventional interpretations could be rejected in favor of figurative ones depending on an utterance's context of use, and it was the use of utterances in context that began to intrigue many theorists in the 1970s.

Mathews' (1971) paper is an interesting transitional effort, incorporating aspects of both the pre- and the postshift periods. For example, although his was one of the earliest papers in modern linguistics devoted mainly to metaphor, he explains it by extending Chomsky's ideas about the selectional rules that govern conventional language. As papers on figurative language accumulated in the postshift period, figurative language was acknowledged to be ubiquitous in both ordinary and academic discourse and to be an important phenomenon to consider in theories of understanding.

Much of the work on metaphor in the postshift period, including that of psychologists, has been done using the methodologies of linguistics and philosophy. For example, Ortony (1979b) did not support his theory of "nonliteral similarity" with experimental data (although he was writing for a psychological journal), but relied instead on intuitions in the manner traditional in linguistics. Some of the current work on figurative language, however, is done using methods and approaches endemic to psychology, for example the information-processing approach of this chapter. Although methods originating outside of psychology may provide important insights about figurative language, an information-processing approach facilitates consideration of how phenomena observed under the heading of metaphor are related to such cognitive phenomena as memory.

Memory and understanding have long been associated theoretically (e.g., Bartlett, 1932). Most recent theories of memory emphasize encoding processes (e.g., Craik and Lockhart, 1972; Tulving and Thomson, 1973); as Bransford (1979) notes, "Questions about effective encoding processes lead us into an examination of processes of comprehension" (p. 86). One of the most successful instantiations of the idea that encoding affects memory is Tulving's encoding specificity hypothesis (e.g., Tulving, 1983). Especially significant here in connection with our discussion of figurative language is Tulving's observation that theorists have difficulty appreciating that "a highly familiar word could be seen from a particular viewpoint or perspective . . . or that its encoding could take the form of biasing some of its aspects" (p. 225). Recalling our examples, figurative language provides a dramatic illustration of Tulving's point. Words as familiar as "cat" and "dog" can have aspects of their meaning biased (indeed suppressed as when "cat" is applied to a woman) in order to derive figurative interpretations (e.g., Reyna, 1981).

The encoding specificity principle suggests that a theoretical account of how retrieval cues are effective is incomplete without some specification of encoding processes, and it is interpretative processs that affect how meaningful linguistic stimuli are encoded. If transfer-appropriate processing does indeed apply to many aspects of learning and memory as Bransford (1979) suggests, the specification of interpretative processes is even more broadly relevent than the encoding specificity principle allows.

An experiment by Stein (1977) illustrates the difficulty of accounting for memory performance in the absence of specific knowledge about interpretative processes. Stein presented subjects with statements such as "A pen is like a nail" and instructed one group to process them as similes and another group to rate the nouns according to their relative hardness or softness (e.g., "same"). In a cued-recall task, subjects who interpreted the statements as similes (a kind of figurative language according to some accounts) performed much better than those who rated hardness or softness. Both groups, however, were equally proficient at recognizing individual nouns that had appeared in the statements. Although Stein's results are intriguing, they leave open the question of which mental processes contributed to the superior memory performance of subjects encoding the statements as similes, and why an advantage was obtained for cued-recall but not individual-item recognition.

Studies other than Stein's and constructs other than encoding specificity could also be used to argue for more explicit theoretical treatments of those comprehension processes tapped in memory tasks and implicated in memory performance. Relating memory performance to figurative comprehension processes in particular may prove to be especially informative. Figurative, compared to conventional, language has been described as relatively more distinctive, more context-specific, more imagery evoking, more difficult to comprehend, and as requiring nonautomatic processing, requiring more active elaboration, evoking a greater multiplicity and complexity of associations, as well as other similarily controversial descriptions. Each of these characteristics has been linked to changes in memory performance.

Figure and Fantasy: Definitions and Relations

I plan to discuss the apprehension of both fantasy and figurative language in childhood; I discuss these phenomena together because I believe they are cognitively related. It is important to define these two phenomena, fantasy and figurative language, however, especially as their definitions have varied in the literature. Fantasy, for the purposes of this chapter, consists of imagining the impossible; it is the consideration of concepts that violate known constraints imposed by reality. Imagining a talking rabbit is an example of fantasy as such an entity has properties that are incompatible in reality.

Figurative language is a collection of phenomena all of which share the property of violating the conventional usage of language. For example, a metaphor such as "The volcano *burped*" violates selectional restrictions governing the proper combination of subjects and verbs: "Burped" conventionally requires an animate subject. Instances of figurative language sometimes undergo an historical process of becoming conventionalized; once-fresh metaphors (e.g., "leg of a table") can become part of the general lexicon, but their conventionalization makes them literal rather than figurative expressions.

Most developmental research on figurative language has been focused on metaphor. Figurative language includes a range of other phenomena, however, such as irony, hyperbole, indirect speech acts, and so on. One type of figurative language use hitherto unacknowledged in the literative occurs in works of fantasy. In a fairy tale or cartoon, for example, familiar words may take on unconventional interpretations, and their ordinary reference may be extended: Yogi Bear may be "smarter than the average bear," but he is not a bear at all in the usual sense of the term. When words are given fantasy-based interpretations that extend conventional meanings, I call this usage magical. My research to be reported here includes an investigation of children's magical interpretations for words.

Metaphor is a commonly used type of figurative language, and I will also focus on its development. A metaphor implicitly compares two concepts, and this comparison is couched in a statement that, if taken literally, is absurd, factually false, or contextually inappropriate. The metaphor "Juliet is the *sun*" is literally absurd on its surface, but the anomalous surface form leads an interpreter to search for reasons behind this statement of identity, that is, the ways in which Juliet could be *like* the sun (Miller, 1979). In fresh metaphors, interpretation includes, at least temporarily, modifying conventional meanings. In our examples, interpretation of "burped" and "sun" require modification of their conventional meanings in order to make sense of their application to such topics as "the volcano" and "Juliet," respectively.

With some specification of the phenomena to be examined, fantasy and metaphor, we can now turn to the reasons why they can be considered to be related. The ability to engage in fantasy and the appreciation of novel metaphor both require imagination, the mind's ability to rise above well-worn intellectual ruts: In fantasy, we eschew conventional concepts, those that adhere to reality's rules. In metaphor, we eschew conventional interpretations, those that adhere to linguistic rules (e.g., selectional restrictions).

Introspective evidence also associates fantasy with metaphor (Black, 1979; Miller, 1981; Reyna, in press; Verbrugge, 1979). Based on such introspective evidence, fantasy may be a preliminary or intermediate stage in metaphorical interpretation, a stage at which a metaphor is entertained as though it were true. Because the metaphor is literally false, anomalous or incongruent, it cannot be true in reality, but it can be imagined as true in fantasy. Considering a metaphor to be true produces a fantastic image, of a volcano actually burping, and so on. Through fantasy, an interpreter can accomplish some of the mental work involved in metaphorical interpretation, notably the breaking down of conventional category boundaries (Reyna, in press).

An association between fantasy and metaphor can also be demonstrated from analysis of extant fantastic creations. In other words, certain metaphors can be related not only to their corresponding literal concepts, but also to corresponding fantastic concepts (Reyna, in press). Consider the relations among the literal concept of a pig, the fantasy character Porky Pig, and a (once fresh) metaphorical interpretation for "pig," that is, a fat person. All three entities, a real pig, Porky Pig, and a fat person presumably share the property of plumpness. However, real pigs and Porky Pig share properties not applicable to people, pig-like or not, for example having a curly tail. Also, Porky Pig and pig-like people share properties not applicable to real pigs, for example being able to speak. In other words, Porky Pig is an amalgam of porcine and human properties and is thereby a conceptual compromise between the literal and metaphorical categories of "pig" (Figure 5-1).

Porky Pig is not, of course, the only possible conceptual compromise between these literal and metaphorical categories. The particular combination of porcine and human qualities embodied in Porky Pig is arbitrary; a pig–human fantastic creation could vary in the emphasis placed on one category of properties versus another. Also, not all combinations of properties from ordinarily exclusive categories are fantastic. Such a creation is fantastic to the extent that it includes properties that are conceived of as incompatible in reality (e.g., curly tails and speech).

Thus far, I have proposed that fantasy and metaphor can be related based on varying types of arguments: (a) that both are, by definition, exercises in creative

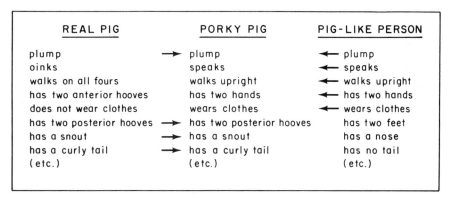

Figure 5-1. Relations among properties for three conceptions of a "pig," a literal interpretation (a real pig), a fantastic interpretation (Porky Pig), and a metaphorical interpretation (a pig-like person).

imagination, (b) introspective evidence that fantasy is a stage in metaphorical interpretation, and (c) an analysis of the intersecting properties of corresponding literal, fantastic, and metaphorical categories. Below, I present empirical evidence about the development of fantasy and metaphor, and about their possible relations.

Background

Evidence for Early Competence

The beginnings of fantasy and metaphor can be traced to early childhood. During the second year of life, children engage in enactive fantasy, symbolic play (e.g., Piaget, 1962). For example, a child will pretend to feed a doll despite awareness that in reality dolls do not eat. Shortly thereafter, at about 2 years of age, children have been observed to produce metaphors spontaneously, as in calling a piece of string "my tail" (e.g. Winner, McCarthy, and Gardner, 1980). As symbolic play presumes awareness of reality's constraints, so a designation of language use as metaphoric is based on evidence of the child's awareness of linguistic constraints, that is, that the child is aware that the metaphorically renamed object has an appropriate literal name. Most importantly, these early metaphors occur primarily in the context of fantasy (Gardner, Winner, Bechhofer, & Wolf, 1978; Winner, McCarthy, & Gardner, 1980). Although the development of metaphor as an outgrowth of symbolic play has been noted in the literature, this early association between metaphor and fantasy has not been explored in subsequent research.

Consistent with observations of early production of metaphors, preschoolers have been found to possess at least a rudimentary metaphorical competence, including the ability to demonstrate comprehension in experimental tasks (Billow, 1977; Gardner, Kircher, Winner, & Perkins, 1975; Gardner, Winner, Bechhofer, & Wolf, 1978; Pollio, Barlow, Fine, & Pollio, 1977; Winner, 1979; Winner, McCarthy, Kleinman, & Gardner, 1979). Preschoolers are particularly adept, exhibiting adult-like competence, when successful performance does not require verbal explanation of the metaphor (e.g., Gardner, 1974; Gentner, 1977; Milchman & Nelson, 1976).

The metaphorical competence attributed to preschoolers, however, is a limited competence. In Gardner's (1974) experiments, for example, a child was presented with pairs of opposite adjectives, such as "hard–soft" or "cold–warm," and was to match each member of a pair with a pair of visual stimuli, such as a picture of a smile and of a frown. Adult-like matching, matching "hard" to a frown and "soft" to a smile, however, does not indicate whether the child can appreciate anything other than the broad polarity connotations of the adjective. The interpretation of a corresponding metaphor such as "a hard frown" presumably requires derivation of additional, subtler aspects of meaning.

The metaphorical competence of the preschooler, and of the younger school-aged child, is also limited by the content of a metaphor. Children as young as 3 or 4 can appreciate a metaphor based on perceptual similarity, such as a description of snow as shaving cream (Winner, McCarthy, & Gardner, 1980; Winner, McCarthy, Kleinman, & Gardner, 1979). The ability to interpret metaphors based on a nonperceptual resemblance, such as a description of a psychological property, cruelty, in terms of a physical one, hardness, does not emerge until 9 or 10 years of age (Asch & Nerlove, 1960; Lesser & Drouin, 1975; Mendelsohn, Winner, & Gardner, 1980; Winner, Rosenstiel, & Gardner, 1976).

Little research has been done on the development of fantasy or on the magical interpretation of language. Fantasy play has been used as an experimental device, for example to investigate whether play training produces advances in the acquisition of Piagetian concepts (e.g., Brainerd, 1982.) These studies indirectly speak to the issue of the development of fantasy per se by consistently demonstrating that even very young preschoolers will engage in elaborate pretend activities organized around themes suggested by the experimenter. Young children's propensity for engaging in spontaneous fantasy play has also been noted in some clinical and observational studies which have been used to stress children's appreciation of fairy tales, and their playful exercise of, and fascination with, fantasy (Bettleheim, 1977; Chukovsky, 1968; Koch, 1970). Investigators using experimental techniques, however, have tended to question the preschool child's ability to appreciate the nature of the boundary between fantasy and reality, as did Piaget (1929). Scarlett and Wolf (1979), for example, examined children's enactment of fantasy stories using props, and found that children younger than 5 were unable to clearly separate the fictional world of a story from the everyday world of reality.

Slightly older children, 6 and 7 years old, tend to produce magical interpretations for sentences adults and older children treat as metaphors, for example interpreting "The prison guard had become a *hard rock*" as "A witch turned the guard into a rock" (Winner, Rosenstiel, & Gardner, 1976). Again, metaphor and fantasy are developmentally associated, but the nature of their association is unclear. The lack of clarity stems from experimental procedure: Winner et al. (1976), for example, did not instruct children that magical interpretations would be inappropriate. As Ortony, Reynolds, and Arter (1978) note, younger children may have offered magical interpretations because of "a response bias in favor of interpretations consistent with the kinds of stories children read—young children are frequently exposed to stories about magical worlds" (p. 928). Given an unspecified context for interpretations, fantasy or reality, younger children may have used fantasy as a default context. The fantasy-as-default-context hypothesis is highly plausible given the story-telling procedure used in the experiment and because younger children are more frequently exposed to fantasy stories as compared to older children.

During the early school years, children may also go through a period of animism "which consists in attributing to things characteristics similar to those which the mind attributes to itself such as consciousness, will, etc." (Piaget, 1929, p. 237). Thus, human properties are applied to inanimate objects so that the sun is said to "see" and tables "hurt" when they are broken. Although Piaget's observations have been challenged (Huang, 1943; Klineberg, 1957; Margand, 1977), most studies (using a variety of measures) have confirmed the finding of childhood animism (e.g., Laurendeau & Pinard, 1962). Carey (1978), for example, concludes that children as old as 6 or 7 will not only insist that objects such as the sun are alive, but also that these objects "eat" and "have bones." In fact, older subjects who should no longer exhibit animistic thinking often adamantly insist that certain inanimate objects are alive. The tendency to think animistically appears to prevail against many contradictory inputs, including courses in biology. In younger children this phenomenon may be an example of egocentrism, or an inability to distinguish fantasy from reality, or it may simply be due to a lack of knowledge about realistic properties of certain objects.

Later Performance: The Literal Stage of Middle Childhood and Beyond

The frequency of spontaneous metaphor declines in middle childhood, around 9 years of age (Billow, 1981; Marti,1979; Snyder, 1979). In both production and comprehension, children resist the use of figurative language, for example responding to "The prison guard had become a *hard rock*" with "I wouldn't say that because a person can't be a rock" (Gardner, Kircher, Winner, & Perkins, 1975; McCarthy, Winner, & Gardner, 1979; Pollio & Pollio, 1974; Rosenberg, 1977; Silverman, Winner, & Gardner, 1976; Winner, Rosenstiel, & Gardner, 1976). Gardner, Winner, Bechhofer, and Wolf (1978) refer to this period as a "literal stage—a time when children are consolidating the literal meanings of words and the community definitions of categories and are . . . reluctant to countenance any violations of these recent acquisitions" (p. 13). The apparent preference for literal language at this age is not uniformly obtained (Koch, 1970; Winner, McCarthy, & Gardner, 1980). Also, the literal stage is followed by significant improvements in metaphorical competence, including the ability to appreciate nonperceptual resemblances, as noted earlier. Given the lack of uniform results, and subsequent rapid improvement, the literal stage is typically attributed to the child's declining motivation to be unconventional (e.g., Winner, 1982). One reason for the declining motivation may be traditional schooling, with its emphasis on rules and correct responses (Rosenberg, 1977). Although not systematically investigated, fantasy might also be expected to decline during the literal stage, for similar motivational reasons, because it, too, involves unconventionality.

The final stage of development, full metaphorical competence, involves a complex set of skills, which can sometimes be acquired or implemented separately. These components of competence may include an ability to recognize metaphor (e.g., to discern literal anomaly), to appreciate disparate concepts as comparable, to modify interpretation of one lexical concept in terms of another, and finally to constrain interpretation based on the truth conditions that obtain (e.g., possible states of affairs in the real world).

Although research is lacking, we can speculate that magical interpretation may require a set of skills similar to those necessary for metaphorical interpretation. Magical interpretation may require an ability to recognize fantasy (e.g., "Once upon a time . . . "), to appreciate that disparate concepts can be combined in novel ways (e.g., pigs and people), to modify conventional concepts by fusion of ordinarily exclusive categories or by unconventional inclusion or exclusion of properties, and finally to recognize that interpretations must conform to the truth conditions that obtain (e.g., what is allowed in such specific genres as fairy tales as opposed to science fiction).

Measures and Materials

Assessing Interpretative Competence

Whether it is the distinction between "primitive" and "genuine" metaphor (Winner et al., 1976) or the designation of spontaneous speech as "misclassification" as opposed to "metaphor" (Winner, McCarthy, & Gardner, 1980), the classification of qualitative data leads to an unavoidable opacity. Systems for classifying qualitative data are not necessarily ill-defined or lack specificity, although they are especially susceptible to these problems; such systems may in fact achieve high interrater reliability. Nevertheless, it is sometimes difficult to reconstruct essential aspects of the eliciting stimuli and the subject's actual response from such interpretative categories as "metaphor." The problem of recapturing data from interpretative categories is more acute if controversy exists about the definition of a phenomenon, as is the case with metaphor. Qualitative data from researchers employing differing definitions often cannot be compared. In assessing a child's ability to interpret metaphor, then, the ideal measure would maximize transparency, that is, it would allow more complete reconstruction of data. Transparent measures would also enhance the historical durability of observations because data would be accessible for reinterpretation in the light of subsequent theoretical refinements.

An ideal measure of a child's ability to interpret metaphor would also minimize the contribution of extraneous performance factors. (In considering performance factors, it is necessary to point out that I have applied the measures and materials to be discussed to children at 6 and 9 years of age.) For example, an ideal measure should not be biased by a child's inability to articulate interpretations adequately. As noted earlier, requiring explanatory skill on the part of the child for successful performance has affected assessments of underlying metaphoric competence.

In studies of metaphoric competence, the most common forms of qualitative data consist of (a) observations of spontaneous productions and (b) responses to relatively open-ended questions about the meaning of verbal stimuli. In examining interpretative ability, the free or unconstrained response method can

be contrasted with the method of offering subjects a choice among interpretations. In the latter multiple-choice procedure, the experimenter controls
the range of possible responses. This method has the advantage of minimizing
the need for explanatory skill; it is also relatively transparent in that actual
responses, the limited set of subjects' choices, are easily obtained. The
alternatives, however, may be unrepresentative of the underlying population of
possible responses; the alternatives selected may only roughly approximate the
types of responses children would give in the absence of the experimenter's
suggestions. The multiple-choice method, then, can over- or underestimate
competence depending on the nature of choices offered.

In taking into account these considerations, I have designed a method for
assessing children's interpretative ability. In the first phase of the procedure, a
verbal stimulus is presented and the free-response method is used to obtain a
child's interpretation. Thus, the first phase produces qualitative data that are
uncontaminated by experimenters' suggestions. In the second phase, the child is
asked a series of yes–no questions about his interpretation of the verbal
stimulus. (Both the first and second phase of questioning are completed for a
given stimulus before proceeding to subsequent stimuli.) The constellation of
yes–no responses in the second phase, the response pattern, defines an
interpretative category. That is, the response pattern allows classification of
interpretations as metaphorical, literal, and so on. The use of response patterns
to assign interpretations to categories is only possible with specially constructed
verbal stimuli.

In these experiments, the verbal stimuli consist of sentences incorporating
semantic conflicts, as in "The volcano *burped*" example. Moreover, each
sentence incorporates a human-nonhuman semantic conflict, for example by
combining a nonhuman noun with a verb requiring a human noun. Consider a
child who is presented with a story about a father and a misbehaving son, with
the concluding, critical, sentence being "The *thunderstorm* spanked the boy."
Interpretation of "thunderstorm" depends on resolution of the conflict between
the nonhuman properties of "thunderstorm" and the human properties implied
by the verb "spanked." There are four logically possible outcomes to such a
conflict. First, human properties can be denied to "thunderstorm" and its
nonhuman properties affirmed. (I have classified such a response pattern as
literal because conventional meaning is preserved; further rationale for the
classification scheme will be discussed below.) For example, if asked "In the
story, is the thunderstorm a person?" the child's response is "no," and if asked
"In the story, is the thunderstorm something full of rain?" the child's response is
"yes." In a second pattern, human properties are attributed to "thunderstorm"
while nonhuman properties are denied. The remaining patterns include
affirming both human and nonhuman properties, and denying both human and
nonhuman properties. Thus, a pair of yes–no questons can be constructed for
each critical sentence that assess the child's resolution of the semantic conflict
(Table 5-1).

Table 5-1. Yes–No Questions

Noun Interpretation: "The *thunderstorm* spanked the boy"

Human?	*Nonhuman?*
In the story, is the thunderstorm a person?	In the story, is the thunderstorm something with rain?

Response Patterns

Human?	*Nonhuman?*	
1. no	yes	(Literal, "something full of rain")
2. yes	no	(Metaphorical, "the angry father")
3. yes	yes	(Magical, "a hand made of thunder clouds)
4. no	no	

As all critical sentences involve a human–nonhuman conflict, some yes–no questions could be standardized across sentences. For example, one yes–no question in each pair asks whether the to-be-interpreted term refers to a person (for nouns) or to what a person did (for verbs). The individual questions do not presuppose any particular definition of metaphor or any other interpretative categories. The combinations of responses to questions are assigned to interpretative categories, but the reader can examine the data at face value without accepting the classification scheme. Thus, given knowledge of the questions asked and the set of stimuli, data can be faithfully reconstructed, that is, the measure is transparent. In addition, the yes–no questions do not require explanatory skill, and results from these questions can be cross-validated with results from the free-response method.

Classifying Response Patterns

Consider again the example of interpreting "The *thunderstorm* spanked the boy" in the context of a story about a father and a misbehaving son. If a child says "yes," the thunderstorm is something with rain, and "no," it is not a person, as the verb "spanked" implies, the literal or conventional interpretation of "thunderstorm" is maintained. Note that this classification of an interpretation as literal is conservative: In order to classify a child's response pattern as literal, the child has to both deny a possible metaphorical interpretation and to assert that a literal interpretation is correct. Classifying this response pattern as literal is consonant with virtually all relevant theories. For example, Ricoeur (1978) states that given a sentence incorporating a "semantic impertinence," or semantic conflict, literal meaning is "the meaning which obtains if we rely only on the common or usual lexical values of our words" (p. 46).

If a child responds, on the other hand, that the thunderstorm is a person and is not something with rain, I classify this response pattern as metaphorical. Thus, in metaphorical interpretations of nouns, the child denies the category conventionally associated with the noun, and infers the opposing category required by the verb. Similarly, according to Ricoeur (1978), metaphorical interpretation involves "violation of the code of pertinence or relevance which rules the ascription of predicates in ordinary use. The metaphorical statement works as the reduction of the syntagmatic [categorical] deviance by the establishment of a new semantic pertinence" (p. 46). In interpreting "thunderstorm" as metaphorically referring to a person, then, properties pertinent to one category, thunderstorms, are taken to be appropriate to another category, humans.

Two response patterns remain to be identified with types of interpretations. A child might also respond affirmatively to both yes–no questions. Given the way critical sentences were constructed, the literal and implied categories (for example, thunderstorms and humans) are always mutually exclusive; there is no object that belongs to both categories simultaneously in the real world. When the child responds "yes" to both questions, then, he is asserting something not possible in the real world, for example, that something can be both a person and full of rain. These response patterns were classified as magical, as per the definition of magical interpretation proposed in the introduction. This classification was corroborated by children's interpretations in the first, free response, phase: A child offering an interpretation of the "thunderstorm" as "a hand made of clouds," for example, tended to subsequently respond "yes" to both questions. Fully 80% of such double-affirmative response patterns could be cross-validated in this way, with the remaining 20% randomly distributed among the remaining interpretative categories.

The last response pattern consists of "no" responses to both questions. This response pattern was extremely rare, around 1% of all responses, and cannot be assigned an interpretation type on theoretical grounds. Children who responded "no" to both questions typically offered a literal interpretation in the first phase, but disputed the literal characterization proposed in the second phase. On empirical grounds, therefore, this infrequent and mystifying response pattern was classified as literal.

Thus far, we have examined assignment of interpretation types to response patterns for nouns; similar considerations apply to classifying responses for verbs. Consider interpretation of "laughed" as in "The pig *laughed*" in the context of a story about a girl playing with animals on a farm (Table 5-2). Again, yes–no questions concern human and nonhuman properties, in the case of verbs querying whether the activity is a human one or a nonhuman one. Note that in Table 5-2 the pattern of yes and no answers for literal and metaphorical classifications is the reverse of the corresponding patterns for noun classifications. In other words, a literal interpretation of "laughed" requires affirming (rather than denying) that it is something people do while denying that it refers to a nonhuman activity in the story.

I should point out that the stimulus sentences I have discussed illustrate a

Table 5-2. Yes–No Questions

Verb Interpretation: "The pig *laughed*"

Human?	*Nonhuman?*
In the story, is the laughing something people do?	In the story, is the laughing something an animal does?

Response Patterns

Human?	*Nonhuman?*	
1. no	yes	(Metaphorical, "oinking")
2. yes	no	(Literal, "giggling")
3. yes	yes	(Magical, "what Porky Pig does")
4. no	no	

nonhuman noun as a subject combined with a human-requiring verb; other examples of this form are "The nightmare whispered" and "The mountain yelled." In addition to this form, in some studies I paired human nouns with verb phrases requiring nonhuman nouns, as in such combinations as "The fat lady oinked" and "The angry man struck the boy with lightning."

Interpretation: Many Competencies

A child presented with sentences of the forms noted above is faced with a problem-solving task, namely, to resolve the apparent semantic conflict. A literal interpretation, because it preserves that conflict, represents a failure to solve the problem. A metaphorical interpretation, on the other hand, resolves the conflict by modifying conventional meaning. A magical interpretation, because it too involves modifying conventional meaning, may also represent appropriate conflict resolution depending on the context in which a sentence occurs. (I will discuss contextual factors in greater detail below.) Appropriate conflict resolution, however, requires multiple skills, and can be influenced by various cognitive, linguistic, and pragmatic factors. Given the earlier discussion of measures and materials, we can now focus on factors that may influence children's performance with the specific stimuli and tasks I have employed.

Confronted with a sentence incorporating semantic conflict, a child must first recognize that there is a conflict among conventional meanings. In my research, pilot testing was used to ensure selection of terms with which children were familiar. Since children in the experiments proper were familiar with the conventional meaning of terms, a recognition of conflict can be assumed in most instances. Upon recognizing conflict, a child must then address that conflict. A child may be able to recognize conflict, but be unable to effect the reconstrual of literal meanings that the structure of the sentence implies. Such a child may produce a literal interpretation, but such an interpretation does not directly suggest a dissociation between ability to recognize conflict and ability to modify meaning. Evidence for this dissociation, however, can be gleaned by examining free responses: Some children offer what I call thematic interpretations; the child rearranges and sometimes adds to the words in an input sentence, using their conventional senses, into an internally coherent proposition. For example, given "The pig *laughed*," one 9-year-old said "Someone behind the pig was laughing." Thematic interpretations are a subtype of literal interpretations because all conventional meanings in the sentence are preserved. Also, children who offered a thematic interpretation in the first phase produced a literal response pattern to questions in the second phase. Thematic interpretations were rare, constituting 7.5% of all literal free responses in one study (10% for 6-year-olds and 5% for 9-year-olds). Thematic responses are, nevertheless, theoretically interesting because they represent an intermediate level of competence—resolution of semantic conflict, but failure to modify meaning in concert with the structure of the sentence.

There are several possible sources of difficulty for the child who recognizes the conflict, and the necessity to resolve it, but is unable to successfully modify meaning. Linguistic factors might include complexity of word meanings. For example, verb meanings may be, in general, more complex than noun meanings, and thus may be more difficult to modify. Prior to the present studies, there has been no systematic investigation of the relative difficulty of metaphorically modifying noun meanings (e.g., "thunderstorm") as opposed to verb meanings (e.g., "laughed"). As Verbrugge (1979) has noted, "Most of the metaphors used in developmental research are grounded on objects and their properties" (p. 81); that is, they involve noun interpretation. Verbrugge called for attention to verbs because such attention "will probably alter the pattern of stages proposed for metaphoric development" (p. 81). Although Verbrugge mentions that children are sensitive to "events" and "dynamic relations," he makes no specific predictions about how the picture of metaphorical competence in children will change if verb interpretation is assessed.

Indirect evidence on this point can be obtained from research concerning mastery of literal verb meaning. As E. Clark (1981) points out, "Children are much slower in mastering well-established verb meanings than they are in mastering noun meanings" (p. 304) (see also Gentner, 1978, 1981a, in press; and Huttenlocher, 1974.) The later acquisition of verbs has been observed across diverse languages (Gentner, in press). Gentner (1978, 1981a,b, in press) has explained such results by proposing that verbs are more semantically complex than nouns, that is, that verbs have more relational, complexly connected, semantic structures. Verbs are said to be relational because they act as a semantic frame that is used to assign such roles to nouns as agent, instrument, and recipient; these roles are (often hierarchically) related to express such concepts as causation, change of location, and change of possession. "Give," for example, implies roles for an agent, object, and recipient. The relation of possession, for example, applies between the agent and the object at some time t_0; the agent then does something to cause a change of possession so that the possession relation applies to the object and recipient at some later time t_1. This complexity of verbs produces a range of empirical effects: "Verbs are harder to remember, more broadly defined, more prone to alter meaning when conflict of meaning occurs, less stable in translation between languages, and slower to be acquired by children" (Gentner, 1981a, p. 161).

Additional evidence suggesting that verb interpretation may be more challenging than noun interpretation comes from a study with adults. I constructed 36 metaphors requiring noun interpretation and 36 requiring verb interpretation, sampling a broad range of semantic domains and word frequencies in each type. Adults were asked to rate the ease with which each metaphor could be interpreted. Verbs were consistently rated as more difficult to interpret compared to nouns (Reyna, 1981). Because the available evidence suggests that nouns and verbs may differ in terms of interpretive difficulty, I have included interpretation of both in my experiments.

Cognitive factors may also influence a child's ability to interpret semantically inconsistent sentences. Metaphors express an implicit comparison, for example between thunderstorms and angry fathers. In order for a child to modify the meaning of "thunderstorm" so that it can be interpreted to refer to an angry father, the child must appreciate the underlying similarity between these disparate objects. Although similarity judgment is "a basic psychological function" (Miller, 1979, p. 245), it can be made more or less difficult. According to Tourangeau and Sternberg (1981), for example, the comprehensibility of a metaphor for adults declines as the distance between the domains of compared objects increases. In other words, metaphorically comparing a person to an animal (e.g., a pig) should be less difficult than comparing a person to an event (e.g., a thunderstorm). I have obtained results with adults similar to those of Tourangeau and Sternberg; as distance between domains increased for objects metaphorically compared, reaction time to verify interpretations increased significantly (Reyna, 1981).

Previous developmental studies have demonstrated, as noted earlier, that children find metaphors expressing perceptual resemblances easier to interpret than those expressing nonperceptual resemblances (e.g., between physical and psychological properties). This finding has been explained in terms of the differing levels of abstractness in the two types of comparison. As domains become more disparate, however, their resemblances become more abstract. A ball and the sun are both concrete, inanimate objects and a child calling the sun a ball does so on the basis of shared concrete properties, for example shape (Gardner, Winner, Bechhofer, & Wolf, 1978). A person, Romeo's Juliet, and the sun are more disparate categories, however, and the resemblances noted between them tend to be more abstract. The claim, then, is that comparisons become more abstract as the distance between domains increases because increasing distance correlates with increasing dissimilarity of corresponding properties.

Ortony (1979b) makes a similar point in discussing metaphorical comparisons of objects from distant domains. Commenting on "Blood vessels are . . . aqueducts," Ortony questions whether the similarity between these objects has to do with whether they are "both channels through which liquids move" (p. 166). He goes on to say that "It is certainly the case that a blood vessel is a very different kind of channel from an aqueduct. But if this is so, on what basis can it be claimed that "being a channel" is the same attribute for both?" (p. 167). Ortony suggests that this "attribute inequality" problem between distant domains can be solved by appealing to "higher order matches" (p. 167), that is, more abstract similarities. (See also Black, 1962 and Tourangeau & Sternberg, 1981 for similar arguments.)

Thus, a child's difficulty with nonperceptual resemblances may indeed involve their abstractedness, but difficulty having to do with differences in abstractedness may be a by-product of difficulty in dealing with increasingly disparate categories. To address this hypothesis, I presented children with sentences in which the distance between domains of objects that could be metaphorically compared was systematically varied. For example, in sentences of the form "The *thunderstorm* spanked the boy," four categories of nonhuman nouns were assigned to human-requiring verbs: animals, inanimate objects, events, and abstractions. These domains are increasingly psychologically distant from the metaphorically implied domain of humans (Keil, 1979).

Pragmatic factors that may affect children's ability to interpret language figuratively include whether or not the child is able to recognize contextual cues. For example, we come to recognize such contextual cues as "Once upon a time . . . ," and mention of castles, knights, and damsels in distress in identifying a fairy tale. I include the ability to recognize such discourse contexts under pragmatic factors because it seems to be related to the child's increasing experience with different genres through the early school years, rather than with changes in fundamental cognitive competence (Winner, 1982).

Rather than test whether children can infer that a context signals reality or fantasy, I am more interested in whether children who are aware of the context can appropriately constrain their interpretations to what is possible in that context. Although Winner, Rosenstiel and Gardner (1976) observed magical interperations among 6- and 7-year-olds' responses, and counted these as incorrect, no research has addressed the child's competence if context is clearly signaled. Thus, in my experiments, children were explicitly told whether the stories they heard concerned something that happened in real life or something that happened in a fantasy context, specifically in a cartoon. Cartoons, rather than a literary genre, were selected as a fantasy context since they are highly familiar to children and because they vividly portray magical actions, as well as magical entities, supporting both verb and noun interpretations. Given this manipulation of context, reality or fantasy, we can determine if children are sensitive to the fact that interpretations must conform to a universe of possible states of affairs; figurative as well as literal interpretations are subject to such contextual constraints on truth conditions. For example, in my experiments, if a story is placed in a realistic context, its critical sentence can admit metaphorical, but not magical, interpretations. When the fantasy world of a cartoon is being referred to, however, a magical interpretation can be a contextually appropriate resolution of semantic conflict.

Method

Subjects

Thirty-two children, 16 6-year-olds (mean age, 6;5) and 16 9-year-olds (mean age, 9;7), participated in an experiment conducted in Princeton, New Jersey. These children were predominantly from families in which at least one parent was a professional, and many parents were affiliated with Princeton University. The second experiment was conducted in Kilgore, Texas. Sixty children participated in the Kilgore study, 30 6-year-olds (mean age, 6;8) and 30 9-year-olds (mean age, 9;5). Children were recruited through their public elementary school, and came primarily from middle-class backgrounds.

Materials

In the Princeton study, children received eight critical stimuli of the form "The *thunderstorm* spanked the boy," that is, stimuli combining nonhuman nouns with human-requiring verbs. Nonhuman nouns were selected from each of the categories of animals, inanimate objects, events, and abstractions. The following critical sentences exemplify the use of each category of nonhuman noun: "The pig laughed at the girl," "The mountain yelled at the man," "The thunderstorm spanked the boy," "The fun danced with the woman." Each critical sentence was preceded by several conventional sentences establishing a story line concluded by the critical sentence. For four critical sentences, the story directed children to interpret nouns; in the remaining four cases, children interpreted verbs.

In the Kilgore study, children received 16 critical stimuli. Eight stimuli were of the same form as used in the Princeton study: nonhuman nouns combined with human-requiring verbs. Nonhuman nouns were drawn from three categories: animals, inanimate objects, and events, that is, the category of abstractions was eliminated. Except for sentences with abstract nonhuman nouns, the Princeton stimuli were included as a subset of the Kilgore stimuli. Because 16 stimuli were presented in the Kilgore study, it was necessary to construct 10 new critical sentences to supplement the subset of stimuli from the Princeton study.

As mentioned above, in the Kilgore study, eight stimuli combined nonhuman nouns with human-requiring verbs. The remaining eight stimuli combined human nouns with nonhuman-requiring verbs, for example "The fat lady oinked at the man," and "The angry man struck the boy with lightning." Note that the latter set of sentences preserve the human–nonhuman conflict found in the former set but the sources of conflict are reversed across parts of speech. The latter set of stimuli was also yoked to the former set in terms of content. For example, consider noun interpretation for "The *thunderstorm* spanked the boy" and "The *angry man* struck the boy with lightning," which are yoked sentences. Based on free responses in the Princeton study, the most likely metaphorical interpretation for "thunderstorm" is "angry father." Based on pilot data, the most likely metaphorical interpretation for "angry man" in "The *angry man* struck the boy with the lightning" is "storm." Thus, it is possible to compare the relative difficulty of, for example, interpreting "thunderstorm" as an angry father and interpreting "angry man" as a storm. By yoking the content of the two sets of sentences, it is possible to separately evaluate effects of content, the nature of objects compared, from the direction of the comparison. In other words, because the objects implicitly compared in yoked sentences are equivalent in most cases, but the direction of comparison is the opposite, the effect of direction of comparison can be examined separately.

As in the Princeton study, for half the stimuli, stories directed children to interpet nouns and, for the other half, to interpret verbs. If a child experienced any difficulty focusing on the correct word, the experimenter repeatedly reminded the child of the story. For example, given "The *thunderstorm* spanked the boy," and directed to interpret the noun, the experimenter would remind the child that the story indicated that the boy was spanked: "The story says that the boy was spanked. What could the thunderstorm be that spanked the boy? In the story, what could the thunderstorm be?," and so on. Also, critical sentences requiring noun interpretation and those requiring verb interpretation in the Kilgore study were both yoked. In other words, the factors of word interpreted (noun or verb) and direction of comparison (human to nonhuman or nonhuman to human) were crossed with one another.

Procedure

In both the Princeton and Kilgore studies, all 6-year-olds were tested orally and individually. In the Princeton study, 9-year-olds were also tested orally and individually, but in the Kilgore study 9-year-olds responded to a written questionnaire. At the outset, each child was reminded that a word can mean "a whole lot of different things."

In both studies, children participated in two sessions separated by a rest period. The stimuli in a session were presented to each child in a different random order. In the Kilgore study, a constraint was imposed on randomization: The nonhuman noun–human verb and the human noun–nonhuman verb critical sentences were presented in separate blocks, with presentation order counterbalanced across subjects. (No effect of order of presentation was observed, so results were collapsed across the two orders.) Children interpreted nouns and verbs in separate sessions. The order of interpretation, nouns first or verbs first, was counterbalanced across subjects and within age groups.

As discussed earlier, two classes of questions were asked for each stimulus: a free response question and specific yes–no questions (Tables 5-1 and 5-2). If children offered literal responses or seemed unsure of their responses, they were reminded of the story, the experimenter repeated questions, and the child was probed with such open-ended questions as "Why do you think that?"

In the course of a story, and again with each question, children were informed of the context for interpretation. The child was told either that the story was about something that happened in real life or about something that happened in a cartoon. Each interpretation was made with respect to both contexts, with the reality context always preceding the fantasy context. Thus, a child would complete the first phase, free response, and the second phase, yes–no questions, with the context described as real life. Then, the same story was re-presented as referring to a cartoon, and the child again offered a free response and answered yes–no questions.

Results and Discussion

Overview of Figurative Competence

In order to minimize redundancy, I will present the Princeton study's results in detail, introducing the Kilgore study when results conflict or require clarification. Thus, the reader can assume replication of results across the two studies, unless otherwise noted. The data to be focused on are response patterns to the yes–no questions.

To examine overall performance with sentences incorporating semantic conflict, consider literal response patterns for the 6- and 9-year-olds in the Princeton study. Random responding by children would distribute responses evenly across the four possible response patterns (Tables 5-1 and 5-2). Thus, chance level performance for literal response patterns is 50% (patterns 1 and 4 in Tables 5-1 and 5-2) and is 25% each for metaphorical and magical response patterns. Children's performance exceeded these chance levels. Literal response patterns accounted for only 25% of all responses; of this 25%, 2% were accompanied by thematic interpretations in the first phase of questioning. Therefore, 23% of all responses represent a wholesale failure to resolve semantic conflict, and an additional 2% represent a resolution of conflict without modification of meaning.

Regarding the competence of school-aged children, it is important to note that the overwhelming majority of responses, 75%, did involve modification of meaning, that is, most responses consisted of figurative interpretations. However, the level of competence demonstrated here is certainly affected by the stimuli presented. In particular, because performance was assessed with respect to verbs and abstract nouns, as well as with concrete nouns, overall percentages are not directly comparable to other studies in which only concrete nouns were employed. In addition, no attempt was made to sample verbal materials according to their representation in everyday discourse; thus, overall percentages in my studies do not necessarily predict the extent of successful performance in everyday life. Instead, the aim is to assess the degree to which interpretative ability approaches ideal competence, ideal competence being defined as the ability to interpret a full range of stimulus types in a full range of contexts.

By focusing on ideal competence, we need not abandon concerns about what constitutes realistically realizable levels of performance. For example, we can compare performance levels in children to adult levels, that is, the degree to which adults achieve ideal competence. Given analogous materials incorporating the same proportions of noun and verb interpretations and a similar sampling of noun categories, including abstract nouns, the percentage of literal responses for adults is around 11% (Reyna, 1981), clearly superior to the 25% level for children.

Turning to a more fine-grained analysis, the overall performance of the school-aged children can be assessed with respect to four levels of competence. We have already discussed the percentage of responses at the two lowest levels of competence, wholesale failure to resolve conflict (23%) and conflict resolution without meaning modification (2%), the latter most likely representing a transitional phase in interpretative competence. More advanced competence is demonstrated by reponses that modify meaning, that involve figurative interpretation, but fall short of ideal competence because contextual constraints are not respected. (For example, a child offering a magical interpretation in a realistic context has failed to constrain interpretation to what is possible in the given context.) Twenty-eight percent of response patterns fell into this class. The largest percentage of response patterns, however, involved contextually sensitive figurative interpretation, 47%. About the same overall percentage of contextually correct metaphorical responses and magical responses were given, 46% and 48%, respectively.

Although most studies have suggested that metaphorical competence undergoes significant development in the early school years (e.g., Winner et al., 1976) some studies have attributed adult-like competence to children at this age (e.g., Gentner, 1977). My results, that correct metaphorical responses occur with a frequency of 46%, are consistent with those studies that characterize the competence of younger school-aged children as much better than chance but far from mature.

Age Differences

Table 5-3 shows the percentage of response patterns at each level of competence separately for 6- and 9-year-olds. An analysis of variance conducted on frequencies of literal response patterns indicated that there is a significant main effect of age. Six-year-olds produced more literal responses than 9-year-olds ($F(1, 28) = 7.51, p < .05$, Figure 5-2). A separate analysis of variance conducted on frequencies of magical, as opposed to metaphoric, responses indicated an interaction of age with context. In other words, 9-year-

Table 5-3. Percentages of Response Patterns at Different Competence Levels According to Age: Princeton Study

Age	Competence Levels		
	Literal (incorrect)	Figurative (incorrect)	Figurative (correct)
6	32	30	38
9	19	26	55

olds produced more contextually appropriate figurative responses than 6-year-olds ($F(1, 28) = 4.72, p < .05$). The age difference and ordering of percentages within age groups in Table 5-3 for literal, incorrect figurative, and correct figurative responses are consistent with a theoretical characterization of these categories as representing increasing levels of competence.

In order to examine developmental differences in greater detail, I will use frequencies of literal responses as an index of interpretative difficulty. As discussed above, the Princeton study indicated that 9-year-olds produced fewer literal responses than 6-year-olds, 18% versus 32%. In the Kilgore study, however, the age pattern reversed. Thirty-six percent of 9-year-olds' responses were literal compared to 16% for 6-year-olds ($F(1, 56) = 7.40, p < .01$). The superior performance of 6-year-olds in the Kilgore study compared to the Princeton study is easily accounted for by a change in verbal stimuli. Abstract

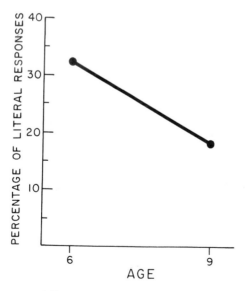

Figure 5-2. Percentage of literal response patterns for 6- and 9-year-olds in the Princeton study.

nouns were eliminated from the Kilgore stimuli. As I will discuss in detail below, sentences with abstract nouns proved more difficult to interpret than other sentences.

The inferior performance of 9-year-olds in the Kilgore study vis-à-vis the Princeton study is more problematic. These conflicting results can be accounted for in at least three ways. First, 9-year-olds in the Kilgore study may have been in the midst of the "literal stage" of middle childhood, which the Princetonians were not subject to. This hypothesis is more plausible if we can assume, for example, that schooling is more traditional in Kilgore, Texas compared to Princeton, New Jersey (Rosenberg, 1977). Evidence for such a difference in traditionalism is, however, anecdotal at best. Another explanation involves differences in populations; children in the Princeton study had more highly educated parents compared to the Kilgore children. If we assume, again speculatively, that more highly educated parents are more accepting of figurative language, perhaps their children can avoid a literal stage. (I should point out that a broadly facilitative effect on figurative language due to parents' educational levels cannot be easily supported given the magnitude of the superior performance by 6-year-olds in Kilgore.) Finally, performance by 9-year-olds in Kilgore could have been influenced by presentation medium—responding to written questions may have been more challenging than responding to the same questions orally, the latter procedure having been used with 9-year-olds in Princeton. In order to evaluate this hypothesis, an additional group of 18 9-year-olds in Kilgore, from the same school, were tested orally using the same materials employed in the written questionnaire. In other words, the procedure for the Oral Group of 9-year-olds was the same as that for the 9-year-olds in Princeton and for the 6-year-olds previously tested in Kilgore. The percentage of literal responses for the 9-year-olds tested orally was 33%, almost the same level of performance as 9-year-olds given a written questionnaire, 36%.

Because the differences between 9-year-olds in Kilgore and in Princeton cannot be attributed to differing presentation media, we are left with two possible, though speculative, explanations. Both explanations posit a literal stage, attributable to extrinsic motivational factors precisely because performance declines for one population, whose younger members are more advanced, but improves for another population. Whether these extrinsic motivational factors consist of differences in parental attitudes, styles of schooling, or other motivational factors is indeterminate. Thus, these contradictory results for 9-year-olds in Kilgore and Princeton are reminiscent of the extant literature on the elusive literal stage of middle childhood.

Linguistic and Cognitive Factors

Returning to the Princeton study and the analysis of literal responses, age was found to interact with an apparently linguistic factor, the word interpreted, noun or verb ($F(1, 28) = 8.73, p < .01$, Figure 5-3). The overall difference in literal

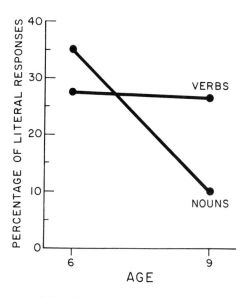

Figure 5-3. Percentage of literal response patterns for 6- and 9-year-olds in the Princeton study according to the word interpreted, noun or verb.

responses for 6- and 9-year-olds, then, derives from differences with nouns rather verbs. Six- and 9-year-olds do not differ in their percentage of literal responses to verbs, about 27% for both ages; however, 6-year-olds give far more literal responses to nouns than 9-year-olds do, 35% versus 11%. (Nouns and verbs do not differ significantly for 6-year-olds, $t(15) = 1.46, p > .05$.)

Figure 5-4 shows percentages of literal responses given to semantically inconsistent sentences across a wider age range. The data for 6- and 9-year-olds are presented again in Figure 5-4, along with data from the analogus experiment with adults mentioned earlier (Reyna, 1981). It should be noted that adults were not given explicit instructions about the context for their interpretations, reality or fantasy, whereas responses for the children are collapsed across context. This difference in procedure between children and adults, however, does not affect our comparison of literal responses across ages. For children, the percentage of literal responses in the two contexts is identical, 25%; moreover, literal responses for nouns and for verbs each differ by only 1% across the contexts.

Figure 5-4 illustrates the position of the 9-year-olds, poised between the competence of 6-year-olds and adults. For nouns, 9-year-olds given exactly the same percentage of literal responses as adults do, 11%. For verbs, on the other hand, 9-year-olds give about the same percentage of literal responses as 6-year-olds do, 27%. Thus, 9-year-olds evince a sort of décalage with respect to figurative competence, resembling adults with nouns, but resembling 6-year-olds with verbs.

The Princeton results indicate that interpretation of nouns is easier than that

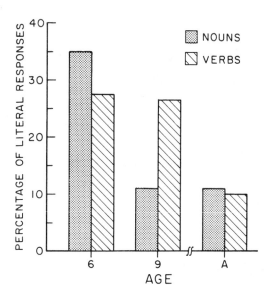

Figure 5-4. Percentage of literal response patterns for 6- and 9-year-olds in the Princeton study and for adults in a comparable study according to the word interpreted, noun or verb.

of verbs since children improve in their ability to interpret nouns before they improve in their ability to interpret verbs. The Kilgore study also supports the conclusion that nouns and verbs differ in interpretative difficulty: Nineteen percent of responses to nouns were literal compared to 33% for verbs ($F(1, 54) = 7.23, p < .01$). This difference between nouns and verbs obtained for 6-year-olds as well as 9-year-olds.

This better performance with nouns than with verbs in the Princeton study can be accounted for by two kinds of explanations, emphasizing either that noun interpretation is easier due to cognitive factors or verb interpretation is harder due to linguistic factors. An explanation emphasizing the difficulty of verbs could point to their greater semantic complexity which apparently contributes to their being acquired later by children than nouns are. In this view, verbs would be interpreted literally more often than nouns because children have greater difficulty manipulating the complexly related elements of meanings that make up verbs; because figurative modification of meaning requires manipulating these meaning elements, verbs would prove a greater challenge than nouns.

On the other hand, noun interpretation in the Princeton study could have been favored because of the form of the critical sentences. All critical sentences consisted of a nonhuman noun paired with a human-requiring verb; figurative interpretation of such nonhuman nouns always involved some degree of personification. A magical or metaphorical response pattern, in contrast to the literal patterns, included a yes response to the question about whether the noun referred to a person. In both types of figurative interpretation of nouns, then, the nonhuman is viewed in terms of the human. In interpreting the verbs figuratively, however, an opposite process is required. The verb, ordinarily applying to humans, must be construed as applying, to some degree, to nonhumans. In other words, the human must be viewed in terms of the nonhuman, a process I will call depersonification. If personification were an easier cognitive process than depersonification, figurative interpretation of nouns in the Princeton study would be favored compared to verbs. The question, then, as stated by Verbrugge (1979), is "whether children are equally adept at, or prone to, using metaphors in either direction—viewing people in terms of inanimate objects and viewing objects as human" (p. 82).

As noted in the introduction, younger school-aged children often exhibit animistic thinking, investing nonhuman objects with human properties. If animism characterizes children's thinking at this age, then noun interpretation in the Princeton study should be facilitated because it can rely on the child's natural tendency to personify, to see the nonhuman in terms of the human. Interpretation that requires an opposing process, suppressing human properties in order to see the human in terms of the nonhuman (as in verb interpretation), would not enjoy this advantage. Indeed, adult metaphor seems to exhibit the same sort of bias that Piaget attributed to children's thinking. In an extensive survey of literary metaphor, Brook-Rose (1958) found that viewing the nonhuman as human, personification, was far more common than comparison in the opposite direction. Animistic thinking is egocentric in the sense that objects in the world are perceived as like oneself. Children have been characterized as egocentric in a variety of ways, including being unable to understand that there are physical, conceptual, or social persepectives other than their own. The more general claim that children are egocentric, as opposed to the more specific claim about childhood animism, would be sufficient to suggest an advantage for personification.

In order to separate contributions of the linguistic factor, semantic complexity of verbs versus nouns, and the cognitive factor, personification versus depersonification, we can examine responses to the yoked materials in the Kilgore study. Recall that in the yoked materials part of speech was crossed with direction of comparison, with content of comparisons held relatively constant. If personification enjoys a cognitive advantage, and this advantage accounts for superior performance with nouns in the Princeton study, fewer literal responses in the Kilgore study should be elicited from materials that can be figuratively interpreted through personification. In the Kilgore study, however, slightly *more* literal responses were given to the personification materials than to the depersonification materials, 28% to 24%.

Perhaps the advantage for personification, however, only obtains for 6-year-olds, who could be expected to be more susceptible to animistic thinking, as opposed to 9-year-olds. Again, results are counter to the personification hypothesis. For 6-year-olds, 18% of responses to personification materials are literal, compared to 14% for depersonification materials (Table 5-4). Retreating from a strong personification hypothesis, one might argue that the effect of personification is potentiated by investing it in a noun as opposed to a verb. In other words, the Princeton results might be due to an interaction between personification and part of speech. As Table 5-4 shows, however, once again there is no evidence in the Kilgore study for any contribution of personification, alone or in combination, to ease of interpretation. (Similarly poor support has been obtained for other claims that could be based on egocentrism; Brainerd, 1982.)

Thus, results from the Princeton and Kilgore studies implicate a linguistic factor, relative semantic complexity of nouns and verbs, in the interpretative difficulty of semantically inconsistent sentences. The contribution of a cognitive factor, the direction of an implicit comparison in these sentences, was discounted.

Although the direction of comparison may not contribute to the difficulty of figurative interpretation, other cognitive factors may do so. I have mentioned that the content of implicit comparisons seems to affect ease of interpretation and age of acquisition of particular types of metaphor. Metaphors comparing objects whose resemblance is nonperceptual are more difficult and are correctly interpreted later than metaphors comparing objects whose resemblance is perceptual. The disadvantage for nonperceptual resemblances has been explained in terms of their abstractness. Research with adults, on the other hand, has demonstrated the increasing difficulty of metaphorically comparing objects from more disparate domains. According to theories concerned with this finding, increasing abstractness of resemblances inheres in increasing distance between domains; as domains become more disparate, resemblances between objects in those domains become more abstract. Thus, explanations for findings with children stress abstractness as a basis for difficulty, whereas theories for findings with adults stress distance between domains as a basis for difficulty. In the latter theories, abstractness is one by-product of greater domain distance.

Table 5-4. Percentage of Literal Response Patterns to Stimuli Allowing Either a Personification or Depersonification Figurative Intepretation by Age and Part of Speech

	Stimuli	
Age	Personification	Depersonification
6	18	14
9	37	35
Part of Speech		
noun	21	17
verb	34	32

I believe that there are several considerations that favor extending the theory for adults to findings with children. First, it is more parsimonious to employ one theory rather than two, especially when the one subsumes the other. Second, it is important to bring ideas about adult competence to bear on the child literature. This has benefits in terms of increasing opportunities to allow data to refine theories, and empirical research with children can be more profitably guided by a greater investment in theory. Third, domain distance seems to be less difficult to define then abstractness of resemblances. Domain distance is a variable that can be independently assessed before applying it to a particular metaphor. Admittedly, the domain of an object can shift from context to context. For example, a piano can be treated as belonging to the domain of musical instruments for some purposes and treated as a piece of furniture for other purposes. Nevertheless, the set of possible domains for an object are, for the most part, predictable and consensual within speech communities. Abstractness, on the other hand, seems to have a post hoc quality. Once we know how a metaphor is interpreted, we can describe the basis for that interpretation in terms of abstract or nonabstract resemblances. Also, abstractness as a variable tends to be applied in a dichotomous fashion. Resemblances are characterized as either abstract (nonperceptual) or concrete (perceptual). Domain distance, in contrast, because it is a continuum, allows predictions for intermediate cases.

My proposal to account for findings with children, currently explained in terms of abstractness, using theories of domain distance requires two kinds of empirical justification. It is necessary to demonstrate that abstractness and domain distance consistently covary, that increasing domain distance inevitably leads to greater abstractness of resemblances, and vice versa. If this were not the case, both theories would be necessary or it would be necessary to supplement one theory so that it accounted for both variables. If abstractness and domain distance are inherently related, however, it would be impossible in principle to unconfound their contributions to interpretative difficulty; conclusions about the relation between these variables could only be reached inductively. Also, to apply theories of domain distance to children, we need some evidence that varying domain distance affects interpretative difficulty for children in the same manner that nonperceptual resemblance does.

Domain distance was systematically varied in the Princeton and Kilgore studies. The domains of nonhuman nouns, in sentences combining nonhuman nouns with human-requiring verbs, varied in their distance from the metaphorically implied domain of humans. Animals, inanimate objects, events, and abstractions are increasingly distant from the category of humans (Keil, 1979). Regarding the claim that domain distance and abstractness of resemblance should covary, we can examine the bases for children's metaphorical interpretations offered in the free-response phase of questioning. As domain distance increased, children offered fewer metaphorical interpretations mentioning physical characteristics, and citation of emotional and other abstract properties increased. For example, metaphorical interpretations for "pig" in "The *pig* laughed at the girl" almost exclusively mentioned physical characteristics (e.g., fatness). In interpreting "thunderstorm," an event, in "The *thunderstorm* spanked the boy," emotional properties were by far the most common properties cited (e.g., anger). As children were not explicitly questioned about the bases for their interpretations, this type of evidence for covariance is merely suggestive.

The remaining evidence bears on the question of whether domain distance affects interpretative difficulty in children in a manner similar to the effects of abstractness. If results here conform to the pattern hitherto observed for perceptual versus nonperceptual resemblances, we should observe that (a) increasing domain distance leads to greater interpretative difficulty, and (b) greater domain distances should create more difficulty for younger children compared to older children (unless the older children are in a literal stage). Table 5-5 shows the percentages of literal responses, again used as an index of interpretative difficulty, for nonhuman nouns varying in distance from the domain of humans. For 6-year-olds and 9-year-olds in the Princeton study, and for 6-year-olds in the Kilgore study, the first prediction is confirmed. Increasing domain distance is associated with greater interpretative difficulty. For 9-year-olds in the Kilgore study, domain distance clearly has no effect, which is again consistent with the hypothesis that these children's inferior performance is caused by motivational rather than substantive factors. (Motivational factors usually act as multipliers on response strength; the motivational problem suggested in this case, however, seems to produce an unwillingness to even attempt a figurative response in the first place.) Regarding the second prediction, younger children in the Princeton study had greater difficulty than the older children at every level of domain distance. Also, the younger children in the Kilgore study generally performed at a lower level at each domain distance compared to older children in the Princeton study. As with the first prediction, the performance of the older Kilgore subjects does not fit the general pattern observed for the older children. The inferior performance for 9-year-olds in the Kilgore study, especially at the smallest domain distance, is again consistent with findings in the literature for children in a literal phase for

Table 5-5. Interpretative Difficulty According to Age and Domain Distance: Percentages of Literal Responses for Nonhuman Nouns

Age	Increasing Domain Distance			
	Animal	Inanimate Object	Event	Abstraction
	Princeton Study			
6	4	7	8	16
9	1	2	2	6
	Kilgore Study			
6	2	6	7	—
9	9	9	10	—

whom previous gains with metaphors expressing perceptual resemblances appear to be temporarily lost.

The data discussed above support applying theories of domain distance to findings with children; domain distance produces effects analogous to effects of abstractness, and there is some suggestion that increasing domain distance is associated with greater abstractness of resemblances. These conclusions, however, must be qualified. The number of stimuli on which the children's data is based is quite small; more members from each domain must be sampled in order to confidently generalize to entire domains.

Pragmatic Factors

I have discussed linguistic and cognitive factors that mediate a child's ability to figuratively modify meaning. If a child is capable of modifying meaning despite variations in linguistic and cognitive factors, that child may nevertheless fail to assign figurative interpretations to appropriate contexts. Thus, the data I will consider in this section are those response patterns that demonstrate figurative competence and the distribution of these response patterns according to context. For purposes of analysis, the number of magical response patterns for each child was divided by the total number of figurative response patterns (Figure 5-5). Therefore, if children randomly assigned magical and metaphorical responses to the two contexts, reality and fantasy, the percentage score in each context would be 50% (the chance level of responding is 50%). If children offered more magical responses than metaphorical, the score would exceed 50%; if more metaphorical than magical responses occurred, the score would be less than 50%.

I should point out that this analysis does not bear on the question of whether children can distinguish reality from fantasy. The nature of symbolic play in toddlers indicates that young children appreciate that there is a distinction

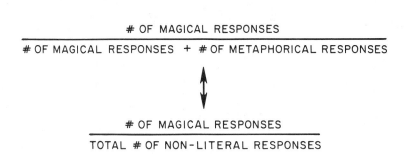

Figure 5-5. The derivation of scores used in analyses of variance of figurative response patterns and used in subsequent figures reporting percentages of magical response patterns.

between reality and fantasy. The observations regarding symbolic play, however, do not demonstrate that children fully appreciate the differing constraints that apply in realistic and fantastic contexts. As an analogy, a child may be able to distinguish a game of checkers from a game of chess, but that does not imply that the child is aware of the rules for each game.

Although children in the Princeton study produced the same percentage of literal responses overall, 25%, in both the fantasy and reality contexts, figurative responses differed in the two contexts: Children produced more magical responses in the fantasy context, 63%, and more metaphorical responses in the reality context, 60% (i.e., a score of 40% in the reality context), $F(1, 28) = 17.83, p < .01$ (Figure 5-6). Moreover, this differentiation between contexts increases with age, $F(1, 28) = 4.72, p < .05$. As Figure 5-7 shows, for 6-year-olds, 57% of figurative responses in the fantasy context are magical, slightly greater than the chance level of 50%, and 46% of responses in the reality context are magical, slightly less than chance. For 9-year-olds, in contrast, magical responses are far more frequent figurative responses in the fantasy context than in the reality context, 69% versus 34%.

These results indicate that the ability to assign figurative interpretations to appropriate contexts develops dramatically in the early school years. At 6 years of age, children appear to have a fragile appreciation of the differing constraints in realistic and fantastic contexts. This result is consistent with Scarlett and Wolf's (1979) finding that 5-year-old children often require concrete props in order to respect the boundary between a fantasy story they are enacting and the world of reality. In addition, my results clarify Winner,

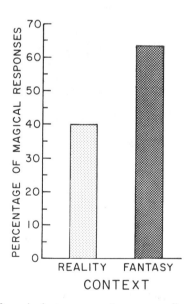

Figure 5-6. Percentage of magical response patterns according to context, reality or fantasy (cartoons), in the Princeton study.

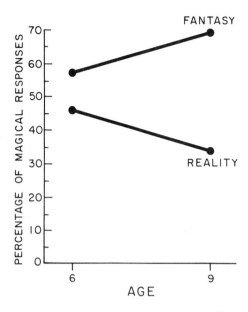

Figure 5-7. Percentage of magical response patterns according to context, reality or fantasy, and age, 6- or 9-year-olds, in the Princeton study.

Rosenstiel, and Gardner's (1976) finding that younger children, around 6 years old, offered more magical interpretations than older children to sentences considered by the experimenters to be metaphors. As you may recall, interpretation of Winner et al.'s results was problematical because they did not explicitly signal the context for interpretation. This procedure left open the possibility that younger subjects, failing to discern subtle cues about context, offered magical interpretations by default. Because children in my studies were informed of the context for their interpretations, and pilot testing showed that 6-year-olds clearly appreciate what was meant by real life and cartoons, we are in a position to conclude that younger children offer magical interpretations not simply because they fail to recognize contextual cues, but because they lack the ability to use contextual cues in deriving figurative interpretations. In contrast, by 9 years of age, children appear to appreciate that context constrains the nature of what is possible, and offer figurative interpretations that conform with constraints on possibility. It is reasonable that appreciation of contextual constraints on interpretation should develop significantly in the early school years. Schooling exposes children to a wider variety of genres, and extensive experience with objects and events is necessary in order to discover the limits of their possibilities.

Relations Between Metaphor and Fantasy

Born in the context of symbolic play, earliest metaphor is linked with fantasy. During the preschool years, children become able to produce and comprehend metaphors in contexts other than symbolic play. Researchers have not investigated, however, whether metaphorical competence is correlated with competent exercise of fantasy-based thought during the preschool period. The Princeton and Kilgore studies allow consideration of whether subsequent development of metaphor and fantasy, in the early school years, is correlated. Using comparable measures, derivation of appropriate linguistic interpretations, we can ask whether metaphor and fantasy exhibit a similar developmental trajectory. As Table 5-6 shows, the percentage correct for metaphorical and fantasy-based (magical) interpretations is virtually identical at age 6, and again at age 9; this correlation between the two types of interpretations obtains despite the dramatic change in percentage correct between the two ages. These data suggest that competence for metaphorical and magical interpretation develop together, that is, they increase at the same rate, during the early school years.

This association between metaphorical and fantasy-based interpretation is consistent with the hypothesis that they share certain underlying psychological similarities. These similarities may include that both require an imaginative leap, a rejecting of conventional categories, either conceptual or linguistic. In both cases, conventional categories are broken down by suppressing conventional features and replacing these with ordinarily inapplicable features (Reyna, 1981). Thus, both metaphorical and magical interpretations relate ordinarily disparate categories, a conventional category, and an imaginatively constructed category.

These broad similarities between metaphorical and magical interpretation do not imply that both involve exactly the same mental processes. Indeed, as I indicated in the introduction, there is some evidence, albeit introspective, that fantasy-based interpretation may be a preliminary stage in metaphorical interpretation. If fantasy-based interpretation is a preliminary stage, then if a person experiences difficulty completing a metaphorical interpretation, he or she may report the product of an intermediate stage, a magical interpretation. In this view, the incidence of magical interpretations would be systematically related to the difficulty of metaphorical interpretation.

In both the Princeton and Kilgore studies, children experienced greater difficulty metaphorically interpreting verbs as opposed to nouns. They also offered significantly more magical interpretations for verbs than for nouns. In the Princeton study, for example, 57% of figurative interpretations for verbs are magical compared to 46% for nouns ($F(1, 28) = 6.20$, $p < .05$, Figure 5-8).

Table 5-6. Percentage Correct of Contextually Sensitive Figurative Interpretations by Age: Princeton Study

Age	Metaphorical Interpretations	Magical Interpretations
6	37	39
9	54	56

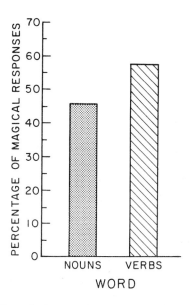

Figure 5-8. Percentage of magical response patterns to nouns versus verbs in the Princeton study.

More specifically, we can examine the incidence of magical responses when metaphoric interpretation failed, that is, when children offered other than metaphorical interpretations for sentences in the realistic context. The overall pattern of magical responses to verbs is reflected in the pattern for incorrect responses: Forty-five percent of figurative interpretations for verbs were magical, in the realistic context, as opposed to 34% for nouns. Similarly, in the comparable experiment with adults, metaphorically interpreting verbs was rated as significantly more difficult than interpreting nouns and, once again, significantly more magical interpretations were given for verbs than for nouns (Reyna, 1981).

Age itself can be considered a variable that contributes to the difficulty of interpreting metaphors. The percentage of contextually appropriate metaphorical interpretations rises from 37% at age 6 to 54% at age 9 (Table 5-6), reaching about 84% for adults (Pollio & Burns, 1977; Reyna, 1981). For adults, I count the 5% of magical interpretations offered overall in Reyna (1981) as contextually inappropriate because reality may be considered a default context for adults in the absence of specific instructions to the contrary. (If I were instead to allow magical interpretations as appropriate for adults in the absence of specific instructions, the trend would hold nevertheless.) Recall that the hypothesis we are considering predicts that incorrect magical interpretations will be offered in lieu of correct metaphorical interpretations as the latter's interpretative difficulty increases. Thus, given a trend of increasingly correct metaphorical interpretation with age, we should observe precisely the opposite pattern across age for percentages of incorrect magical interpretation. That is, magical interpretations offered for stimuli that should correctly receive metaphorical interpretations (because of sentential and contextual constraints) should decrease as age increases.

The percentage of incorrect magical interpretations does decrease from 46% of figurative interpretations at age 6 to 34% at age 9 (Princeton study), and finally to 6% of figurative interpretations for adults (Reyna, 1981). This difference between 6- and 9-year-olds was statistically evaluated and found significant ($F(1, 28) = 4.72, p < .05$); the reliability of the difference between 9-year-olds and adults is obvious by inspection. I should point out that this finding, that younger school-aged children offer more magical interpretations for stimuli that should be interpreted metaphorically, corroborates the results of Winner et al. (1976). The explanation proposed here for this finding, however, differs from other accounts. According to the hypothesis we have entertained, younger children offer more incorrect magical interpretations than adults do not so much because of a response bias as Ortony et al. (1978) speculated, but because children have greater difficulty interpreting metaphors compared to adults.

Summing up the results as they bear on the hypothesis we have considered, younger children who experience greater difficulty interpreting metaphors also tend to produce more magical interpretations for stimuli that should be treated as metaphors. In addition, for all age groups, conditions that increase the difficulty of interpreting metaphors also consistently increase the incidence of magical interpretations. These results are consistent with a hypothesis that magical interpretation is a preliminary stage in metaphorical interpretation, and therefore inappropriate magical interpretations are produced when interpretative difficulty prevents the completion of metaphorical processing. In order to support such a hypothesis, however, more direct evidence of underlying interpretative processes is required.

The development of metaphorical competence has hitherto received some research attention, whereas development of fantasy, especially after the preschool years, has received scant attention. I believe that metaphor and fantasy merit closer scrutiny from psychologists because they involve fundamental psychological processes such as those implicated in the apprehension of analogies, including the ability to relate apparently disparate elements, and because they represent exercises of imagination. Imaginative thinking, in turn, is the basis of such important human activities as problem solving. The role of imagination is particularly critical in the resolution of difficult and profound human problems. As Bertrand Russell said, "Imagination, not slavery to fact, is the source of whatever is good in human life."

Acknowledgments. I gratefully acknowledge the assistance of Jackie Loewy and Joy Woodruff in the data collection and of Jim Bartlett, Chuck Brainerd,

Jay Dowling, and Mike Pressley for comments on a draft of this chapter. I also thank the faculty and students of Stanford University's Psychology Department for their comments on my presentation of this material to them, and George A. Miller for his continued support and assistance.

Requests for reprints should be sent to Valerie F. Reyna, University of Texas at Dallas, P.O. Box 688, Psychology Department, GR 4.1, Richardson, TX, 75080.

References

Asch, S., & Nerlove, H. (1960). The development of double function terms in children. In B. Kaplan & S. Wapner (Eds.), *Perspectives in psychological theory*. New York: International Universities Press.

Bartlett, F. (1932). *Remembering: A study in experimental and social psychology*. London: Cambridge University Press.

Billow, R. (1975). A cognitive developmental study of metaphor comprehension. *Developmental Psychology, 11*, 415–423.

Billow, R. (1981). Observing spontaneous metaphor in children. *Journal of Experimental Child Psychology, 31*(3), 430–445.

Black, M. (1962). *Models and metaphors: Studies in language and philosophy*. Ithaca: Cornell University Press.

Black, M. (1979). More about metaphor. In A. Ortony (Ed.), *Metaphor and thought*. New York: Cambridge University Press.

Brainerd, C. (1982). Effects of group and individualized dramatic play training on cognitive development. In D. Pepler & K. Rubin (Eds.), *The play of children: Current theory and research*. Basel, Switzerland: Karger.

Bransford, J. (1979). *Human Cognition: Learning, Understanding and Remembering*. Belmont, CA: Wadsworth Publishing Company.

Brooke-Rose, C. (1958). *A grammar of metaphor*. London: Seeker and Warburg.

Carey, S. (1979). The child's concepts of animals and living things. In F. C. Keil, *Semantic and conceptual development*. Cambridge, MA: Harvard University Press.

Chukovsky, K. (1968). *From two to five*. Berkeley: University of California Press.

Chomsky, N. (1965). *Aspects of the theory of syntax*. Cambridge, MA: M.I.T. Press.

Clark, E. (1981). Lexical innovations: How children learn to create new words. In W. Deutsch (Ed.), *The child's construction of language*. London: Academic Press.

Craik, F., & Lockhart, R. (1972). Levels of processing: A framework for memory research. *Journal of Verbal Learning and Verbal Behavior, 11*, 671–684.

Gardner, H. (1974). Metaphors and modalities: How children project polar adjectives onto diverse domains. *Child Development, 45*, 84–91.

Gardner, H., Kircher, M., Winner, E., & Perkins, D. (1975). Children's metaphoric productions and preferences. *Journal of Child Language, 2*, 125–141.

Gardner, H., & Winner, E. (1978). The development of metaphoric competence. *Critical inquiry, 5*, 123–141.

Gardner, H., Winner, E., Bechhofer, R., & Wolf, D. (1978). The development of figurative language. In K. Nelson (Ed.), *Children's Language*. New York: Gardner Press.

Gentner, D. (1977). Children's performances on a spatial analogies task. *Child Development, 48*, 1034–1039.

Gentner, D. (1978). On relational meaning: The acquisition of verb meaning. *Child Development, 49*(4), 989–998.

Gentner, D. (1981a). Some interesting differences between verbs and nouns. *Cognition and Brain Theory, 4*(2), 161–178.

Gentner, D. (1981b). Verb semantic structures in memory for sentences: Evidence for componential representation. *Cognitive Psychology, 13*(1), 56–83.

Gentner, D. (in press). Why nouns are learned before verbs: Linguistic relativity versus natural partitioning. In S. Kuczay (Ed.), *Language development: Language, cognition, and culture*. Hillsdale, NJ: Lawrence Erlbaum Associates.

Huang, I. (1943). Children's conception of physical causality: A critical summary. *Journal of Genetic Psychology, 63*, 71–121.

Huttenlocher, J. (1974). The origins of language comprehension. In R. L. Solso (Ed.), *Theories in cognitive psychology: The Loyola symposium*. Hillsdale, NJ: Lawrence Erlbaum Associates.

Keil, F. C. (1979). *Semantic and conceptual development*. Cambridge, MA: Harvard University Press.

Klineberg, G. (1957). The distinction between living and non-living among 7–10 year old children, with some remarks concerning the animism controversy. *Journal of Genetic Psychology, 90*, 227–238.

Koch, K. (1970). *Wishes, lies, and dreams*. New York: Chelsea House.

Laurendeau, M., & Pinard, A. (1962). *Causal thinking in the child: A genetic and experimental approach*. New York: International Universities Press.

Lesser, H. & Drouin, C. (1975). Training in the use of double-function terms. *Journal of Psycholinguistic Research, 4*, 285–302.

Margand, N. A. (1977). Perceptual and semantic features in children's use of the animate concept. *Developmental Psychology, 13*, 572–576.

Mathews, R. (1971). Concerning a "linguistic" theory of metaphor. *Foundations of Language, 7*, 412–425.

Marti, E. (1979). *La pensèe analogique chez l'enfant de 2 à 7 ans*. Unpublished doctoral dissertation, University of Geneva.

McCarthy, M., Winner, E., & Gardner, H. (1979). *Early metaphors: An experimental investigation*. Unpublished manuscript, Harvard University, Cambridge, MA.

Mendelsohn, E., Winner, E., & Gardner, H. (1981). *Sorting out similarity*. Unpublished manuscript, Project Zero, Harvard Graduate School of Education, Cambridge, MA.

Milchman, M. & Nelson, K. E. (1976). *The development of pantomime comprehension and comprehension of verbal simile and metaphor*. Unpublished manuscript, New School for Social Research. New York, NY.

Miller, G. A. (1979). Images and models, similes and metaphors. In A. Ortony (Ed.), *Metaphor and thought*. Cambridge: Cambridge University Press.

Miller, G. A. (1980). *Language and speech*. San Francisco: W. H. Freeman.

Ortony, A. (Ed.). (1979a). *Methaphor and thought*. London: Cambridge University Press.

Ortony, A. (1979b). Beyond literal similarity. *Psychological Review, 86*, 161–180.

Ortony, A., Reynolds, R. E., & Arter, J. A. (1978). Metaphor: Theoretical and empirical research. *Psychological Bulletin, 85*, 919–943.

Piaget, J. (1929). *The child's conception of the world*. New York: Harcourt, Brace.

Piaget, J. (1962). *Play, dreams, and imitation in childhood*. New York: Norton.

Pollio, H., Barlow, J., Fine, H., & Pollio, M. (1977). *Psychology and the poetics of growth: Figurative language in psychology, psychotherapy, and education*. Hillsdale, NJ: Lawrence Erlbaum Associates.

Pollio, H. & Burns, B. (1977). The anomaly of anomaly. *Journal of Psycholinguistic Research, 6,* 247–260.

Pollio, M. & Pollio, H. (1974). The development of figurative language in school children. *Journal of Psycholinguistic Research, 3,* 138–143.

Reyna, V. F. (1981). *The animated word: Modification of meaning by context* (Doctoral Dissertation), Ann Arbor, MI: University Microfilms International, reference number 82-03153.

Reyna, V. (in press). Metaphor and associated phenomena: Specifying the boundaries of psychological inquiry. *Metaphor.*

Ricoeur, P. (1978). The metaphorical process as cognition, imagination, and feeling. *Critical Inquiry, 5*(1), 143–159.

Rosenberg, L. (1977). A study of figurative language production in traditional and open classrooms. Unpublished honors thesis, Harvard University.

Scarlett, W. G., & Wolf, D. When it's only make-believe: The construction of a boundary between fantasy and reality in storytelling. In E. Winner and H. Gardner (Eds.), *Fact, fiction, and fantasy in childhood: New directions for child development* (No. 6). Washington: Jossey-Bass.

Schaffer, L. F. (1930). Children's interpretations of cartoons. In *Contributions to education*. New York: Teachers College, Columbia University.

Silverman, J., Winner, E., & Gardner, H. (1976). On going beyond the literal: The development of sensitivity to artistic symbols. *Semiotica,* 291–312.

Snyder, J. (1979). The spontaneous production of figurative language and word play in the grade school years, Unpublished doctoral dissertation, Boston University.

Stein, B. (1977). The effects of cue-target uniqueness on cued recall performance. *Memory and Cognition, 5,* 319–322.

Tourangeau, R., & Sternberg, R. J. (1981). Aptness in metaphor. *Cognitive Psychology, 13*(1), 27–55.

Tulving, E. (1983). *Elements of episodic memory*. New York: Oxford University Press.

Tulving, E., & Thompson, D. (1973). Encoding specificity and retrieval processes in episodic memory. *Psychological Review, 80,* 352–373.

Winner, E. (1979). New names for old things. *Journal of Child Language, 6,* 469–491.

Winner, E. (1982). Invented worlds: *The psychology of the arts*. Cambridge, MA: Harvard University Press.

Winner, E., & Gardner, H. (1979). *Fact, fiction, and fantasy in childhood: New directions in child development* (No. 6). Washington: Jossey-Bass.

Winner, E., McCarthy, M., & Gardner, H. (1980). The ontogenesis of metaphor. In R. Honeck & R. Hoffman (Eds.), *Cognition and figurative language*. Hillsdale, NJ: Erlbaum.

Winner, E., McCarthy, M., Kleinman, S., & Gardner, H. (1979). First metaphors. In *New Directions for Child Development, 3,* 29–41.

Winner, E., Rosenstiel, A. K., & Gardner, H. (1976). The development of metaphoric understanding. *Developmental Psychology, 12,* 289–297.

Verbrugge, R. (1979). The primacy of metaphor in development. In E. Winner & H. Gardner (Eds.), *Fact, fiction, and fantasy in childhood: New directions in child development* (No. 6). Washington: Jossey-Bass.

6. Studying Student Cognition During Classroom Learning

Ronald W. Marx, Philip H. Winne, and John Walsh

Instructional psychology has been a field of study at least since William James (1907) based his *Talks to Teachers on Psychology* on the current theories of his time. Carried forward by researchers such as Cattell, Hall, Thorndike, Skinner, Gagne, and others, the field has blossomed in the last two decades. In concert with the cognitive revolution currently underway in the general field of psychology, instructional psychology has relied increasingly on a cognitive paradigm to interpret and explain instructional phenomena (see Calfee, 1981; Winne, in press a,b).

This chapter describes briefly the current state of cognitively oriented instructional psychology with particular emphasis on studies of cognition in classroom settings. To set the stage for such discussion, we begin by describing context variables which make studying students' cognitions during classroom instruction a unique enterprise. More precisely, the first section of the chapter makes explicit several assumptions about learners which are common to investigations of cognition in classrooms. Then, we characterize classroom tasks to illustrate some important differences between these tasks and those commonly found in nonclassroom studies of cognition. With this backdrop in place, we turn to an analysis of methods employed to study students' cognition. We hope this account will alert researchers to variables which influence the quality of the data obtained about learners' cognitions. The chapter closes with a brief review of current findings in this area and posits an agenda for future investigations.

Preparation of this chapter was supported in part by a fellowship to John Walsh from the Social Sciences and Humanities Research Council of Canada.

Classroom Settings

Over the course of public schooling, an average child spends approximately 12,000 hours in classrooms. This makes the classroom the most ubiquitous setting in which formal instruction takes place. Despite the opportunities classroom instruction presents as an occasion for studying learning and cognition, an exceptionally small amount of research on students' cognitive activity has been done in such settings. Indeed, most cognitively based instructional theory has been derived from nonclassroom investigations of cognition. This lacuna invites educators to criticize cognitively based theories of instruction on the grounds that they suffer from low ecological validity. The validity of these criticisms rests upon the extent to which classrooms are unique places. Although we cannot illustrate fully the distinct nature of classroom settings (e.g., see Hamilton, 1983; Mehan, 1979), this section highlights some significant differences which bear on the issue of ecological validity and on our later discussion of methods that researchers use to access students' cognitions in classrooms.

Assumptions About Students

Our description of classrooms necessitates some remarks about the nature of students. Along with others, we make four assumptions about the cognitive activities in which students engage while learning from instruction.

Reciprocity. Instruction and students' learning from instruction are complex and causally reciprocal phenomena. The intentions and behavior of teachers, coupled with instructional material, interact with the cognitive processes and behavior of students (Winne & Marx, 1977). In this view, students' cognitive activities are not simply responses to environmental events, nor are they sole determinants of students' behaviors. They are both effects produced by students' perceptions of events and causes or preconditions leading yet to other events in the classroom. This notion of reciprocity demarcates our perspective from others (e.g., see Rosenshine, 1983) who view classroom instruction as a unidimensional causal process. Unlike such perspectives, which have traditionally framed research questions in terms of the effect of specific teacher behaviors on students (Dunkin & Biddle, 1974), we assume that students affect instruction as much as instruction affects students.

Correspondence. Cognitive processes and states are given empirical meaning by operational definitions. The assumption of correspondence maintains that, other things being equal (*ceteris paribus*), an operational definition is uniquely and reliably associated with a given theoretical construct. For example, when a student fails to retrieve a proposition which was recalled on a previously administered test, the assumption of correspondence and the condition of *ceteris paribus* limits explanation to one theoretical reason. Whether a researcher's reason is proactive interference, insufficient depth of search, or low motivation will depend on the theory selected. Irrespective of which theory is selected, the assumption of correspondence holds that there is only one reason available within a given theory that accounts for the observed phenomeon.

Divisibility of the environment. Any characterization of the environment surrounding a specific phenomenon under study necessarily omits some variables from investigation. For instance, a study of reading comprehension is unlikely to include a description of the lunch students ate before participating in the study. In sharp contrast, most studies would report the number of words in the passages read by students. To exercise this selectivity, it is necessary to assume that there are aspects of the environment which can be set apart from other aspects. A theory is then called upon to select important variables from all those that could be observed. This assumption is exercised not only when naming theoretically unimportant variables, but also whenever researchers attempt to partition the effects of environmental variables under experimental investigation.

Divisibility of cognition. Corresponding to the previous assumption of divisibility of the environment are assumptions about the divisibility of cognition. For example, many theories describe memory as composed of several major operational units: buffers for sensory input and motoric output, short-term memory for information transformation, and long-term memory for permanent information storage. Implicit in such characterizations is the assumption that cognitive components can be separated. Furthermore, the assumption of divisibility of cognition engenders distinctions between types of knowledge, such as propositional and procedural (e.g., Anderson, 1980; Broudy, 1977; Ebel, 1982), and types of processes like metacognitive monitoring and attending (e.g., Brown, 1978).

Implications. These four assumptions have important ramifications for viewing students' cognitions in classrooms. One implication is that students determine not only teacher behaviors, but also their own cognition. In other words, students mediate between instructional cues and achievement by applying particular cognitive operations. Therefore, the cognitive activities that teachers intend students to use may or may not be those that students employ. Only under certain conditions, to be described shortly, will the correspondence between an instructional cue and students' actual cognitive processes match the intentions of teachers or researchers.

A second implication emerging from these assumptions is that models of students' cognitions in classrooms are arbitrary in a number of respects. First, the assumption of reciprocity makes it difficult to define units of observation for cognitive and environmental variables. This is because students' cognitions and instructional events are interdependent. Second, since students mediate instructional cues and cognitive activities, they may modify their cognitive procedures during studies which attempt to map such activities. Distinguishing between adaptive changes in students' cognitive activities and noise in data may be arbitrary. Third, variables that comprise the *ceteris paribus* features of a study based on one theory may be arbitrary or irrelevant when judged by another theory. One illustration of this issue is Clark's (1973) argument about the fallacy of treating samples of language as a fixed effect in research on acquisition and comprehension.

Classroom Tasks

Recent work by classroom researchers characterizes the classroom as a system of task environments (see Newell & Simon, 1972) or task structures. According to Berliner (1983, p. 2), task structures in classrooms "have *functions*—real or imagined—and *operations*—rules and norms—associated with them." Berliner's conception of task structures focuses on the social nature of classrooms, although there is also a clear implication for cognitive functions. Doyle (1983; see also Doyle, Sanford, Clements, French, & Emmer, 1983) has elaborated the cognitive nature of the classroom task environment in his characterization of academic tasks. According to Doyle (1983) academic tasks have three major features. First, they are established in instructional settings under a set of *conditions*. These can be characterized as parameters within which tasks are accomplished. Second, tasks require a set of coordinated cognitive *operations*, that is, a plan for their completion. Occasionally these plans are known by the teacher or student before the activity begins; more frequently, they evolve as part of instruction. Third, tasks require that a *product* be created. These products consist of more than mere answers to items on achievement tests, as we will discuss later. In addition, there is considerable variability from student to student and from time to time in the criteria teachers and students use to judge the quality of these products. The following sections discuss briefly the nature of the conditions, operations, and products of classroom tasks. A more complete description can be found in Marx (1984) and Winne (in press b).

Conditions. There are three major categories of variables which describe the conditions of tasks in classrooms. The first is content, the information in the curriculum delivered to students by instruction. The content of school curricula can be characterized in many different ways (Reigeluth & Stein, 1983). Recent characterizations have described both the amount of information and its structure (e.g., Meyer & Freedle, 1984). For example, Winne and Marx (1983) quantified the content students were taught by counting the number of concepts and their attributes in each lesson. Other methods include Kintsch's (1979) measures of propositions and Mayer's (1981) counts of idea units.

The second category of variables affecting classroom task conditions is setting. This category reflects one of the most salient differences between classroom research and nonclassroom studies of instruction. For example, settings for nonclassroom tasks almost universally have fixed time constraints and rarely consume more than an hour or two. On the other hand, classroom tasks typically extend over long periods of time. A science unit may last for 2 or 3 weeks, and the oral reading group as a task structure may extend over several years. Also, laboratory tasks are often designed to be novel. This allows researchers to gather data about basic processes that are uncluttered by participants' previous exposure to the task or its structure. In contrast, classroom task structures are usually very familiar to students. Indeed, it is rare to find a child who, after Grade 1, does not have a well developed script for task structures like oral reading, seatwork, group work, and a host of other academic and social routines.

Setting factors not only influence the duration and familiarity of classroom tasks, but may modify in different ways for different learners. It is not uncommon, for example, for students to negotiate some tasks with teachers (e.g., the content of a group project) or alternatively, for teachers to modify tasks for some learners (e.g., remedial tasks). Modifications to classroom tasks may also occur in more subtle ways. Some students may seek clarification of task demands from their fellow students, often with unpredictable results; others may rely on more institutionally legitimate sources of task demands, such as the teacher or notes on the blackboard. The important point is that setting factors may modify classroom tasks differentially and are often uncontrolled factors in classroom research. By sharp contrast, the tasks used in laboratory studies of cognition are not susceptible to such modifications.

The last category of variables which influences task conditions is the manner in which instruction is delivered to the learner. Although classroom instruction is delivered most frequently by teachers, a wide variety of media are also common (e.g., printed sheets, audio tapes, video recordings, and increasingly, microcomputers). There are three aspects of instructional delivery that warrant particular mention. The first concerns the medium of instruction. A large corpus of research exists in this area, particularly in regard to the cognitive operations students use as they learn from various media (Rigney, 1978; Winn, 1982). Second, the delivery of instructional tasks is governed by goals which are established early in a sequence of instruction. Goals which are not clear to students result in unfocused activities and promote variability in the cognitive operations used across individuals in a group of learners. Obviously, teachers should understand the goals which they are working toward if they expect students to achieve common products. There is evidence, however, that this understanding is not always present (Winne & Marx, 1982). Third, instructional cues delivered along with lesson content serve to constrain the cognitive plans students use to accomplish tasks. These cues are functional only to the extent to which they correspond to students' prior knowledge regarding classroom instruction in general and the content of the particular lesson (Winne, 1982, in press b).

Operations. The second aspect of classroom tasks discussed by Doyle (1983) concerns the cognitive operations which students apply to classroom demands.

We will not reiterate the basic research that forms the bulk of cognitive psychology. Rather, we will show once again that by their very nature, classroom settings influence the manner in which cognitive operations are conceptualized.

Most research in cognitive psychology explores the nature of cognitive operations, especially the basic processes that form building blocks in human cognition. The methodologies developed by experimental cognitive psychologists are predicated on exercising very strong control over the conditions participants experience. Classrooms, on the other hand, are not environments in which control can be exerted to the same extent. Hence, research on cognition in classrooms is not likely to achieve the same level of precision as laboratory research on cognition.

This lack of precision might seriously weaken research about students' cognitions were it not for the fact that questions asked by classroom researchers differ from those asked by experimental psychologists. The ultimate aims for research addressing the instructional psychology of classrooms embrace both the explanation and the improvement of the process of schooling. Because classroom research must eventually be prescriptive (Bruner, 1966), the theoretical constructs and data reflecting these constructs must be comprehensible and manipulable not only by researchers, but also by teachers. Thus, any discussion of cognitive operations which is pertinent to classrooms must occur at a level of aggregation that is somewhat above that which is typical of cognitive psychology.

To illustrate the level of aggregation we judge appropriate for analyses of cognition in classrooms, we once again refer to Doyle's (1983) review. He posits four general types of cognitive plans which guide students' operations in accomplishing various classroom tasks. The first class of cognitive operations is the memory plan. This is used when learners are required to recognize or reproduct information. The second type of plan Doyle describes is labelled procedural, which is used when tasks require students to apply predictable formulae or algorithms to perform classroom tasks. When learners apply previously learned procedures to new situations, select appropriate procedures for new problems or transform information, they are engaging in the third type of plan, called comprehension or understanding. This type of plan closely resembles what educators typically call higher-order cognitive activities (Winne, 1979). The fourth category of plan includes those cognitive operations students apply when they are required to state opinions.

Products. To complete the characterization of classroom tasks, we describe briefly the products toward which students' cognitive plans are directed. These products vary along two dimensions. The first dimension pertains to the nature of the criteria used to evaluate products. Such criteria may be few in number or many, and specific or vague. Irrespective of their precise nature, it is clear that this feature interacts with the cognitive plans that students employ (Calfee, 1981; Corno & Mandinach, 1983). The second dimension of the products of classroom tasks pertains to the quality of feedback delivered upon the completion of classroom products. The frequency, locus of feedback (student or teacher), timing (immediate or delayed), informativeness, and valence (negative, neutral, or positive) all serve to shape the cognitive plans of students.

This completes our description of the major classes of variables which influence students' completion of tasks in classroom settings. Although much more could be said about classrooms as venues for cognitive research, the preceding shows that investigations of students' cognitions in classrooms differ in several respects from analogous investigations in laboratories. Stark differences are apparent in the level of aggregation of students' cognitive activities, and in the nature of classroom tasks. We now turn to a discussion of the methods employed by reseachers to access cognition in classrooms.

Method and Methodology

In this section, we examine methods and methodologies used to study students' cognitive activities in classrooms. In particular, we review four basic methods used in representative research. We then propose variables that can be used to frame hypotheses about the validity of methods for studying cognition in classrooms.

Previously Used Methods

Most research to date has been conducted in classroom analogs. These settings permit one or more "nearly definitional" variables of typical classroom tasks to be held constant, sometimes at zero (i.e., some feature of classroom tasks is missing). An example is the absence of a student's opportunity to interact with the teacher when the lesson is presented on videotape. Four criteria were used to decide how analogous to real classroom settings a study has to be in order to be included here. First, the instructional treatment had to be delivered, at least in part, by a human, either live or on videotape. Second, students had to know before instruction that tests measuring their achievement would be administered. Third, and much less precise, the instruction had to be reasonably "classroom-like." By this we mean that characteristics of lessons could not be widely outside the bounds of normal classroom practice. For instance, if the study was about concept learning, the concepts had to be ones likely to appear in curricula appropriate for the age level of the students. Finally, the research had to include data in addition to measures of students' achievement of the objectives of instruction. Inferences about students' cognitions during instruction derived from achievement tests only are often overly speculative (e.g., see Winne, 1982). Collecting data about students' cognitive activities in addition to that provided by tests is a defining feature of studies reviewed here. The application of these four criteria to distinguish studies of students' cognitions in classrooms produces four families of methods in prior research.

Questionnaires. Several researchers have administered paper-and-pencil questionnaires to students after their participation in lessons. Weinstein and her colleagues (Weinstein & Middlestadt, 1979; Weinstein, Marshall, Brattesani, & Middlestadt, 1982) developed the Teacher Treatment Inventory to gauge upper-elementary-grade students' attention to, and perceptions about, their teacher's behavior toward other students. The questionnaire was administered to students about 6 or 7 months into the school year. On the questionnaire, students read one of four brief descriptions about a hypothetical student. The descriptions factorially vary the hypothetical student's sex and two levels of achievement (highest or lowest in the class). Using a 4-point scale (always, often, sometimes, never), the children then predicted how frequently their teacher would act in a specific manner toward each hypothetical student. Examples of teacher behavior from each of four subscales defined by factor analysis include "asks John easy questions" (supportive help); "scolds Anne for not listening" (negative feedback and teacher direction); "expects John to stick with his class work" (work and rule orientation); and "calls on Anne to explain things to the class" (high expectations, opportunity, and choice).

Another questionnaire has been developed by Peterson and her colleagues (Peterson, Swing, Braverman, & Buss, 1982; Peterson, Swing, Stark, & Waas, 1983). Their Cognitive Processes Questionnaire was used in two studies. In the 1982 study, it was administered to Grade 5 students following two lessons on probability. Sixth-grade students responded to the questionnaire after nine lessons about measurement in the 1983 study. Following the last lesson, students rated on a 5-point scale (usually, often, sometimes, never, don't know) the extent to which they typically engaged in cognitive activities such as "Do you listen closely to what the teacher says during the math lesson?" (attending subscale); "As you finish working a problem, do you think about all the things you should have done and then check to make sure you did them?" (specific cognitive strategies subscale).

Weinstein and her colleagues derived their items from the literature of research on teaching. Peterson and her colleagues also used this literature along with instructional psychological research based on settings which were not analogous to classrooms. Both teams' questionnaires were sufficiently general for use with different teachers and lessons. Except for a few items which refer specifically to mathematics in Peterson et al.'s work, these questionnaires also generalize across subject areas.

Winne and Marx (1983, Study 4) used a different approach to develop a questionnaire to tap students' cognitive activities. They videotaped each of three teachers delivering three lessons about human hearing. Following each lesson, the teachers were shown the videotape and asked to identify short segments during which time they cued students to engage in particular cognitive activities. The researchers then listed pairs of instructional cues and intended cognitive responses that were generated by each teacher. A fourth lesson was videotaped and short segments were labeled by the reseachers in these terms. Then the researchers' analysis was validated by showing each teacher his or her videotape and asking each of them to confirm the cue–response pairs located at points in the videotape.

This procedure yielded very high agreement (90% or better) between the teachers' and the researchers' analyses. Based on earlier work (Winne & Marx, 1982) to be discussed in the section on interviews, eight categories of students' cognitive activities were included in a 20-item questionnaire. Each item on the questionnaire consisted of a short segment of the videotape of the fourth lesson on hearing, an item stem-printed on the test paper ("How did Mrs. Christy want you to think now?"), and four alternatives; For example, "Check to see if you understand" (monitor comprehension); "Think what is the same about a term and a diagram" (compare codes); "Say this idea once or twice in your mind" (rehearse). Students viewed the videotape and responded to these multiple-choice items when the researcher stopped the playback.

Interviews. Many researchers have used interviews to gather data about students' cognitive activities in classrooms. Compared to questionnaires, there has been a greater variation in the way this method has been used.

At the most unstructured and inclusive level, and most removed from our focus, stand general interviews about students' reactions to learning. One example of this approach is Baird and White's (1982) investigation of three university students' approaches to learning genetics. Over 6 weeks, students judged the usefulness and difficulty of lectures, and recalled descriptions they had provided a week earlier about methods they had used to learn. Based on these and other data (e.g., preparing "maps" of content, attempts at solving problems) seven learning tendencies were induced. For example, the tendency labeled impulsive attention consisted of directing attention to incidental material and basing further cognitive processing on this information to the exclusion of more relevant content.

Winne and Marx (1982; Marx, Winne, & Howard, 1982) and Peterson et al. (1982, 1983) used structured interviews to stimulate students' recall of their cognitive activities. Figure 6-1 shows Winne and Marx's (1982) schedule. Upper elementary students were shown a videotape of a lesson in which they had just participated to stimulate their recollection of events that had occurred during instruction. A student was interviewed at preselected points in the playback, that is, where the teacher indicated that she had cued students to engage in a particular cognitive activity when she had viewed the videotape. Audiotape recordings of the students' responses to the interview were transcribed and analyzed to generate categories of students' cognitions. Peterson et al. followed a similar procedure except that they tabulated the frequency with which students' interview responses fell into categories the researchers had defined a priori.

Variations of this method have been used by Leinhardt (1983) and by Marx, Winne, and Howard (1982). Leinhardt used less-structured forms of interview in stimulated-recall situations. Also, she interviewed students during actual lessons by interrupting a student to probe aspects of thought. Marx et al.

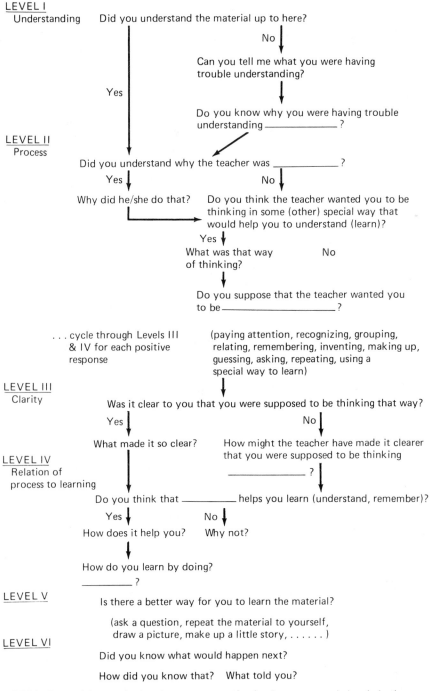

LEVEL I
Understanding   Did you understand the material up to here?

No ↓

Can you tell me what you were having
trouble understanding?

Yes

Do you know why you were having trouble
understanding _____ ?

LEVEL II
Process   Did you understand why the teacher was _____ ?

Yes ↓   No ↓

Why did he/she do that?   Do you think the teacher wanted you to be
                           thinking in some (other) special way that
                           would help you to understand (learn)?

                           Yes ↓   No

                           What was that way
                           of thinking?

                           ↓

                           Do you suppose that the teacher wanted you
                           to be _____ ?

. . . cycle through Levels III   (paying attention, recognizing, grouping,
& IV for each positive   relating, remembering, inventing, making up,
response   guessing, asking, repeating, using a
                                  special way to learn)

                                  ↓

LEVEL III
Clarity   Was it clear to you that you were supposed to be thinking that way?

                 Yes ↓   No ↓

                 What made it so clear?   How might the teacher have made it clearer
LEVEL IV   that you were supposed to be thinking
Relation of
process to learning   _____ ? ↓

                 ↓

                 Do you think that _____ helps you learn (understand, remember)?

                 Yes ↓   No ↓

                 How does it help you?   Why not?

                 ↓

                 How do you learn by doing?
                 _____ ?

LEVEL V   Is there a better way for you to learn the material?

                 (ask a question, repeat the material to yourself,
                 draw a picture, make up a little story, ...)
LEVEL VI
                 Did you know what would happen next?

                 How did you know that?   What told you?

NOTES: Be sensitive to whether the current question has been answered already in the
       student's answers to previous questions. If so, skip the question.

Figure 6-1. Student interview schedule. (From Winne and Marx, 1982, p. 499.
Reprinted with permission from *Elementary School Journal*, 82(5), 493–518. © The
University of Chicago Press.)

interviewed students in a stimulated-recall setting using a variation of the schedule shown in Figure 6-1. However, in their study, students had not actually participated in the lessons. They had watched a videotape of other students and a teacher participating in a lesson scripted to manipulate certain instructional variables.

Traces. Winne and Marx (1983) developed a method to operationalize students' cognitive responses to teachers' instructional cues. Their method consisted of two parts. In the first part, students were taught to produce physical traces of cognitive activities cued by the teacher. For instance, students might be trained to write in a notebook those words which they think might be the answers to subsequent test items. The second part of the method was to instruct the students and to measure traces they produced during the lesson. For example, a diagram might be scored for the extent to which it represents the use of a memory plan.

In a videotape analog study of classroom teaching (Winne & Marx, 1983), an instructional cue was defined a priori as a teacher's statement having either the form, "Make sure you understand concept *X*"; or, "Is concept *X* really clear now?" First, students were trained to identify these instructional cues when they were presented in the first set of videotaped recitation lessons. During training, and subsequently in a test phase of the experiment, students referred to worksheets while the videotape was being shown. In the next part of training, students were taught two cognitive operations that the teacher intended to be used upon delivery of a cue, and were instructed to mark the worksheet in ways that left traces of these cognitive activities.

Figure 6-2 displays a correctly marked worksheet. One cognitive plan that students were trained to perform (a comprehension plan) was to identify in an example instances of a concept's defining attributes. The trace for this cognition

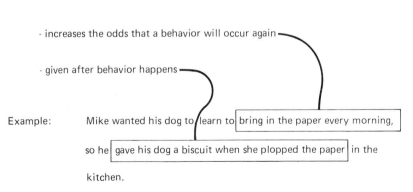

Figure 6-2. An example of a trace (From Winne, 1984, p. 89. Reprinted with permission from *Research on Teaching in Canada*, L. McLean, R. Crocker, and P. Winne (Eds.) Toronto: The Ontario Institute for Studies in Education (OISE) Press).

was a circle drawn around words in the example that represented the defining attribute. The other cognitive plan in which students were trained was a memory plan that required rehearsing the concept's defining attributes. The trace for rehearsing was drawing a line to connect the statement of a defining attribute to its instance in the example. We reasoned that the attribute had to be read silently and comprehended, that is, meaningfully rehearsed, in order for it to be connected to the correct circle in the example. (Admittedly, once one attribute had been rehearsed and the trace placed on the worksheet, an "efficient" student might draw the second trace for rehearsing by elimination rather than by rehearsing it.) The trace cannot be performed correctly (i.e., proper words circled and correctly connected to attributes) without at least comprehending and beginning to memorize propositions about the concept.

Unitizations of continuous events. The last technique to be discussed was used by Koopman and Newston (1981) in a study addressing students' perceptions of "units" of instruction. These researchers provided undergraduates with a button that operated a continuous event recorder. While watching a videotape of an instructor teaching a small group of undergraduates, the students were instructed to press the button whenever they thought that the teacher completed a "step" in the lesson that added to their understanding of the content. By coordinating these temporal divisions with the videotape, the students' conceptions of naturally perceived "whole" events could be investigated. Also, by instructing students beforehand to look for steps of a particular size, such as the smallest meaningful step, students' capacity to adapt their perceptions of units of instruction could be studied.

Methods in General

In research on students' cognitions while learning from classroom teaching, students perform two tasks: An instructional task that requires cognition and a researcher's task that investigates that cognition. In the course of performing the researcher's task, students generate data about the cognitive operations and plans they applied to perform instructional tasks. Students also had to apply cognitive operations to perform the researcher's task. Hence, the researcher's task must be justified methodologically in two ways: first, it should validly reveal features of the cognitive activities students used to accomplish the instructional task like those described in the prior section; second, the cognitions students used to perform the researcher's task should not distort their reports of the cognitions involved in performing the instructional task.

According to the general model of tasks described earlier, a researcher's task consists partially of conditions and a product. These set boundaries on the task introduced to a student. The researcher's plan also calls for students to use cognitive operations and plans. Thus, different methods researchers use to study students' cognitive performances relating to instructional tasks can be distinguished by values of variables that characterize these three parts of a researcher's task. In this section we describe these variables. In addition, speculations and, where possible, data are presented about issues pertinent to different methods. For ease of reference, we abbreviate instructional task at I-task and the researcher's task as D-task (data producing task).

For verbal methods, like interviews and questionnaires, Ericsson and Simon (1980) and Herrmann (1982) have already identified many variables which influence D-tasks. We will not repeat much of their findings here. However, a few alterations in conceptualization and several additional issues pertaining especially to the use of trace methods in classrooms are repeated or elaborated.

Conditions of D-tasks. Perhaps the most obvious variable characterizing the conditions of a D-task is the I-task students pursue. Only a few major variables need to be added to those previously described regarding I-tasks. One variable is the *timing* of the D-task relative to the I-task. The D-task can be administered prior to the I-task, during execution of the I-task, or following the student's completion of the I-task. A second variable characterizing an I-task that also frames part of the conditions of a D-task is the student's *familiarity* with the I-task. Familiarity is a joint function of prior exposure to the conditions of the I-task, the automaticity of operations for executing the I-task, and recognition of the products of the I-task. The final variable of an I-task bearing on the conditions of a D-task is the *size* of the I-task, which includes (1) the duration of the I-task, (2) the number of cognitive tactics or components of productions (Anderson, 1980) the I-task elicits, and (3) the number and organization of bits of declarative knowledge or steps of procedural knowledge constituting output from the I-task.

Timing, familiarity, and size can influence the relative allocation of cognitive resources to an I-task and a D-task (see Ericsson & Simon, 1980). When the D-task is nearly simultaneous with the I-task, students have to allocate cognitive resources between the two tasks, potentially distorting the execution of both. To our knowledge, neither the extent or type of distortion, nor how a student successively switches between tasks, is known.

The timing variable has received much attention recently, especially when the D-task calls for introspection and data are retrospective verbal reports (Ericsson & Simon, 1980; Nisbett & Wilson, 1977). Only two studies (Peterson, Swing, Braverman, & Buss, 1982; Peterson, Swing, Stark, & Waas, 1983) of students' classroom cognitions tested the consistency of retrospective verbal reports by comparing data obtained by this method with data obtained by another method, namely, questionnaire. These researchers studied fifth-grade and sixth-grade students participating in lessons on specially prepared mathematics unit. Following each lesson, students were interviewed about their cognitive activities using a structured interview schedule similar to that shown in Figure 6-1. Prior to the interview, students viewed a videotape of the entire lesson that served as a stimulus for them to reconstitute cognitive events which had taken place earlier during the actual teaching. At the end of the entire unit, students answered questionnaire items which asked them to rate the extent to which they typically engaged in certain cognitive practices during teaching.

Examples of these items are "During the math lesson, do you spend a lot of time thinking about things besides what the teacher is saying?" "As you finish working a problem, do you think of all the things you should have done and then check to make sure you did them?"

Peterson and her colleagues coded students' interview protocols with high reliability into five a priori categories: attending, understanding, reasons for not understanding, cognitive strategies, and description of teacher behaviors. The latter two categories were also divided into several more categories. Correlations between scores on three subscales of the questionnaire (attending, monitoring understanding, and the use of specific cognitive strategies) and scores derived from the stimulated recall interview ranged from $-.27$ to $.34$ (Md $= .13$) in one study (Peterson et al., 1982) and from $-.04$ to $.34$ (Md $= .12$) in the second study (Peterson et al., 1983). Although 11 correlations of 39 computed in the 1982 study and 4 of 12 in the 1983 study were reliably different from zero ($p < .05$), these validity coefficients are nonetheless weak. Therefore, in these two investigations, the timing of the D-task appeared to affect the data significantly.

This interpretation is weakened, however, by considering the familiarity and size of the I-tasks. In both studies, the teacher used a new teaching format that was required for the research. Systematic observations of the teacher revealed that major features of the teaching strategy were present in both studies. But these observations do not reflect the full range of variables that can influence I-tasks. No data were collected to described the students' familiarity with the kind of teaching they experienced in the study. If familiarity was low, students' cognitive operations applied to I-tasks could have varied considerably as they adapted to these relatively novel tasks.

The size of the I-tasks upon which the interview and questionnaire D-tasks were based is inconsistent across the questionnaire and interview data. In responding to the questionnaire, students performed an D-task referring to a modal version of all the I-tasks in all the lessons. The interviews tapped cognitive activities about segments of lessons (review, development of new content, controlled practice, and seatwork) and were gathered lesson by lesson. This method retains the variance in sizes of I-tasks tapped by the D-tasks. Thus, both within and across the two D-tasks the sizes of I-tasks were different.

One other explanation can account for these low-validity coefficients. Both D-tasks were not associated precisely with particular I-tasks. If a segment of a lesson, say development, contained several I-tasks (e.g., see Koopman & Newston, 1981), both the D-tasks which Peterson et al. used force students to pool responses across potentially unequivalent I-tasks to create scores. This feature of their methods may have added further noise regarding students' cognitive operations for accomplishing a given I-task.

Peterson and her colleagues merit praise for attempting to cross-validate their methods. Theirs is the only research in this field with this added quality. The low-validity coefficients they obtained now appear explainable partly in terms of variations in the timing, familiarity, and size variables discussed here. In addition, by pooling data obtained by one type of D-task across potentially heterogeneous I-tasks, variance is introduced to the data that can lower correlations. Because of the problems which result from the data-pooling procedure, we add *identification* of the I-task itself to our list of conditions of a D-task. Overall, four variables are needed to describe the I-task as part of the conditions of any D-task: identification of the particular I-task referred to by the D-task, the timing of the D-task relative to the I-task, the student's familiarity with the I-task, and the size of the I-task.

There are other features of D-task conditions which warrant attention. One of these is the student's familiarity with the D-task. To distinguish this from the students' familiarity with the I-task, we label this variable describing conditions of the D-task *prior experience*. Students' prior experience with most D-tasks is low. Although teachers ask questions like, "How did you get that?," these questions refer more to relations among categories of content rather than to cognitive operations per se (see Winne & Marx, 1982). In general, nonclassroom research suggests that students, particularly younger students, are not likely to be aware of their cognition (Flavell, 1981) nor to be articulate when introspecting about their cognitive operations (Winne & Marx, 1982). It is likely that low prior experience can contribute to unreliability in content analyses of students' verbal protocols.

Some of the problems associated with introspection can be solved by obtaining traces of students' cognitions. First, students must be trained to leave traces of cognition. When training is successful, the researcher knows that students are competent at the D-task. Winne and Marx (1983, studies 2 and 3) have shown that it is not difficult to train students to leave traces like that shown in Figure 6-2. In study 2, when this trace was scored for correct completion on a posttraining test, students achieved an average 87% level of performance. On another trace that required students to monitor worksheets for similarities and differences in the attributes of two related concepts (e.g., reinforcer and punisher), students' average trace scores were 100%. In study 3, students' average posttraining scores on these same traces were 74% and 90% respectively.

A second advantage of traces is that they do not require students to translate their cognitions into words. Instead, traces involve students in performances that reflect components of cognition. Therefore, the problem of reliably coding naive students' vague verbal descriptions is reduced. On the other side of the balance is the question of the construct validity of traces. If a trace can be produced by alternative cognitions, the extent to which this method accurately reflects a particular cognition is questionable. This problem plagued the interpretations relating to rehearsal of a concept's attributes in traces of the sort depicted in Figure 6-2, as discussed earlier.

Another variable describing the conditions of a D-task is the discrepancy between the information initially provided in the D-task and the information sought by the researcher. This variable is called *incompleteness*. Incompleteness might be assessed by counting the number of propositions or gauging the size of productions that must be added to the D-task to complete it. For instance, a forced-choice question about whether the student was engaging in one of four alternative cognitive operations requires recognizing only one proposition to satisfy the D-task. The trace pictured in Figure 6-2 calls for four productions (two analyses, two rehearsals).

Operations in D-tasks. D-tasks require that students execute cognitive operations to create a product. For the four methods used in the research discussed here, these products constitute descriptions of the cognitive operations used to accomplish I-tasks. The cognitive operations students use in D-tasks are the same processes they would use to accomplish I-tasks. There is only one "cognitive machine." What distinguishes D-tasks from I-tasks are the conditions (content, setting, and delivery) under which D-tasks are used and the products of these tasks.

In general, the content used to carry out D-tasks are units of academic content and cognitive operations applied to that content. A primary cognitive operation in most D-tasks is recognizing a chunk of academic conent and the operations applied to it. Hence, variables that affect the recognition of events in general also will likely influence operations carried out to complete D-tasks. When the D-task follows the I-task, recall can be added to recognition as a necessary cognitive operation. Variables that influence recall operations, especially features of the conditions of D-tasks, probably will also affect operations in delayed D-tasks.

One variable impinging on operations in D-tasks is the *accessibility* of cognitions used to perform I-tasks. Accessibility refers to the extent to which a student focuses conscious attention on the cognitive processing used to carry out an I-task while executing that I-task. When I-tasks are executed routinely, the production system is automatic and unitized (Anderson, 1980). This lowers accessibility to components of the production system because the entire system functions as one unit (Ericsson & Simon, 1980). Hence, to access the inner workings of routine I-task operations, steps must be taken to enhance students' opportunities to recognize or recall components of the chunks.

Traces are one method for gaining such access since each component of even an automatic and unitized trace is an operational definition for a component cognitive operation in the I-task. In this case, each D-task operation reflects an I-task operation. Verbal reporting methods, like interviews and questionnaires, take another approach to the problem of accessibility. In these methods, once students recognize a chunk of cognitive activity, they are asked force-choice questions in which component cognitive operations are named (e.g., see Level II in Figure 6-1). Because possible components are identified for them, students need only judge the similarity between the choice offered and the operations they applied to the I-task. This reduces the recognition task to only one operation, similarity judgment, instead of requiring students to identify components of cognition that are normally inaccessible and then judging the similarity between the researcher's probe and the cognitive operation (e.g., see Glass, Holyoak, & Santa, 1979, Chap. 2).

Simplifying the recognition features of a D-task risks several methodological problems (see Ericsson & Simon, 1980). One that has occurred in classroom studies is that students may acquiesce to the choices provided by the researcher if the operation is plausible to them. Marx, Winne, and Howard (1982) encountered this problem in stimulated-recall interviews. When students were asked to agree or disagree with each of four to six proposed, but quite varied cognitive operations, the proportion of agreements ranged from 70 to 98% in 47 of 50 cases (Md = 89%). Only three items showed low levels of agreement (20–25%).

The *set* adopted by a student will likely influence cognitive operations in D-task. Sets or "preemptive schemata" guide top-down processing. Operations for executing seemingly parallel D-tasks may vary both within and across students as a function of the set created either by the I-task or the D-task. For example, in the study by Winne and Marx (1982), students were interviewed after viewing one small segment of a videotaped lesson in which they had just participated. In their first trial with the D-task, students may have noted that they were asked to explain how a cognitive operation they had applied in an I-task "helped you learn" (see Level IV in Figure 6-1). This question may have established a set governing their search for operations to be identified for Level II in subsequent interview trials. The latitude intended by the open-ended probe in Level IV may have been restricted by exposure to other questions in the interview.

When a D-task is presented concurrently with an I-task, the *relative primacy* of the two tasks can affect cognitive operations applied to either or both tasks (Ericsson & Simon, 1980). Cognitive resources needed for complying with a D-task may not be available if a student's efforts are focused on an I-task. Leinhardt (1983) reported that probes delivered during class were perceived by "good" students to be intrusions. Winne and Marx (1983, study 4) found that teachers, half of whose students had been trained to leave traces of I-task cognitions, noticeably slowed the pace of lessons after delivering an instructional cue for an I-task. These teachers clearly were modifying the lesson to accomodate the demands of the D-task. Since the students in classrooms receive marks for executing I-tasks, and only thanks from the researchers for carrying out D-tasks, it is reasonable that they might neglect D-task operations which intrude on I-tasks. This is apparently what happened in a study by Winne and Marx (1980) with university students. It may also account for findings in studies 2 and 3 reported in Winne and Marx (1983). In these studies, students were trained to record traces to high levels of performance, as reported previously. However, students did not sustain these high levels of performance in lessons delivered after training. Trace scores declined from 87% to 71% and from 74% to 57% for the trace displayed in Figure 6-2. For the second trace involving monitoring similarities and differences across two concepts' attributes, a decline from 100% to 95% was observed in study 2, while an increase from 90% to 96% appeared in study 3. A logical response to this difficulty is to mark students' traces, too, but to our knowledge this has not been done.

A final variable that may affect cognitive operations in D-tasks is a student's *opportunity to revise* the D-task by practicing it. Winne and Marx (1983, study 4) trained students to a high level of competence to provide traces during regular classroom lessons. In a subsequent phase of the study, students' use of these cognitive operations to complete I-tasks was tested. In particular, students participated in several science lessons. At points selected by the teacher, students were cued to select and apply particular cognitive operations to accomplish an I-task. Over the course of the lessons, students' traces changed form and became less frequent. One interpretation of these observations is that students changed how they executed I-tasks, thereby making the D-task that was trained previously less appropriate. An equally plausible speculation is that students changed the D-task, adapting their traces to changing operations they applied in I-tasks. If this was the case, the traces were ambiguous since students rather than the researchers mapped the correspondences between the I- and D-tasks.

In summary, D-tasks call for students to recognize or recall features of cognition and then describe these features. Variables which influence recognition and recall operations in general have a potential to influence students' operations in the performance of D-tasks. Many of these variables were described by Ericsson and Simon (1980) and Herrmann (1982) in their reviews. Four such variables are particularly relevant to D-Tasks used so far in the studies of students' cognitions in classrooms: accessibility to the I-task, set for performing the D-task, the relative primacy of the I- and D-tasks, and opportunities to revise the I- and D-tasks.

Products of D-tasks. For the researcher, the product of a D-task is clear. For the student performing a D-task, however, the product of a D-task is likely to be quite unfamiliar. The general model of tasks presented earlier specifies that the *clarity of the product* is important in carrying out a task because it is a benchmark with which to judge progress during execution. Errors or distortions in completing the task may arise if a student does not know what the product of the D-task is.

The latitude of response format can determine the clarity of the product in a D-task. When students are freer to determine the content and the form of products for D-tasks, the heterogeneity of data is likely to increase. Consider the structured interview schedule in Figure 6-1. The first question at Level II allows extreme latitude in the product that results from carrying out the D-task. It was extremely difficult to generate reliable and valid rules for scoring the products students produced for this D-task. In addition, feedback to the student from the interview process is likely to modify the D-task idiosyncratically. In sharp contrast, questionnaire items like those Peterson et al. (1982, 1983) used resulted in more equivalent products. Other things being equal (i.e., variables defining the conditions and operations of D-tasks) the forced-choice questionnaire's restricted latitude in the product is preferable. Not only is the product of the D-task clearer to students, but the researchers' operational definition of the product of the D-task is more precise. The latter gain, however, can be offset if such restrictions of latitude in the product of a D-task also lessen its construct validity.

Summary. Like any task, D-tasks can be described in terms of conditions, operations, and products. Each of these categories contains variables which influence the quality of methods for obtaining data about how students execute cognitive work in classrooms. Variables associated with the conditions of D-tasks fall into two groups: those pertaining to the I-task, and those describing the D-task. In the former, the timing, familiarity, size, and identifiability of the I-task can influence students' approaches to D-tasks. In the latter students' prior experience with the D-task and the incompleteness of a D-task can affect data. Operations students use to perform D-tasks are also affected by several variables. We identified four variables which warrant attention in this respect: accessibility of cognitive operations applied in I-tasks, set for performing the D-task, the relative primacy of the I-task relative to the D-task, and students' opportunities to revise the D-task. Finally, a single variable relating to the product of D-tasks was hypothesized to affect data about students' cognitions, namely, clarity of the product.

Conclusion

We have written about two major topics. First, we discussed classrooms as settings for cognitive research. In this context, four assumptions were made explicit. These assumptions about reciprocity, correspondence, divisibility of the environment, and divisibility of cognition undergird current views of how students learn in classrooms. Should any one of these assumptions be untenable, common notions about how cognition relates to learning would be jeopardized.

These assumptions provided a background for analyzing classroom tasks. In the section on classroom tasks, we proposed a system of variables for characterizing the classroom task environment within which students think. Many of these variables are held constant in instructional research carried out in controlled contexts, and some variables describe features of classrooms that have not been represented in nonclassroom research. These facts highlight the need to corroborate the model of cognition developed from nonclassroom research in classroom settings. If cognition is partly a function of the task to which it is applied, as many cognitive scientists (e.g., Brown, Campione, & Day, 1981; Jenkins, 1979) point out, then empirical demonstrations of the model's generalizability are clearly warranted. The variables describing classroom tasks provide a map of this relatively uncharted territory that can guide early attempts at such corroboration. Refining this map is a major order of business for future research.

The second major topic we addressed was the juxtaposition of methods for studying students' cognitive activities in classroom task environments with concerns about the logic of such methods. Following the lead of Ericsson and Simon (1981), we analyzed methods as a second set of tasks which students perform for researchers. These tasks are used to investigate cognitive activities that students apply to accomplish classroom tasks. In this light, a system of variables was proposed to describe properties of methods. This system was used to discuss results researchers have obtained when using these methods to study students' cognitions in classrooms. Some success in understanding these findings was gained by using this system. What remains is a need for systematic investigations which refine and validate the methodological properties we proposed. Only when techniques for representing students' cognitions in classrooms are understood in terms of their relative strengths and weaknesses will it be reasonable to place faith in the research that uses these procedures.

In closing, we take up a point of social concern introduced earlier. Classroom instruction is a widespread enterprise in which society invests vast resources. To the extent that students must engage in cognition to profit from instruction and achieve the goals society sets for education, it behooves us at least to understand the cognitive dynamics of instructional phenomena. If students merely needed to be told what to learn, to be exposed to the content of education, instruction would be logically unnecessary. But there is little doubt that students need guidance from instruction to achieve the goals of education. Therefore, if cognition underlies learning and if students' unguided cognitive processing of content is not sufficient to promote learning, instruction therefore must aim to shape students' cognitive operations on content. In brief, successful instruction must influence the cognitive activities students apply to classroom tasks. Thus, not only is the study of students' cognitions in classrooms a scientific challenge, it is also fundamental to bettering education.

References

Anderson, J. R. (1980). *Cognitive psychology and its implications*. San Francisco: W. H. Freeman.

Baird, J. R., & White, R. T. (1982). Promoting self-control of learning. *Instructional Science, 11*, 227–247.

Berliner, D. C. (1983). Developing conceptions of classroom environments: Some light on the T in classroom studies of ATI. *Educational Psychologist, 18*, 1–13.

Broudy, H. S. (1977). Types of knowledge and purposes of education. In R. C. Anderson, R. J. Spiro, and W. E. Montague (Eds.), *Schooling and the acquisition of knowledge*. Hillsdale, N.J.: Erlbaum.

Brown, A. L. (1978). Knowing when, where, and how to remember: A problem of metacognition. In R. Glaser (Ed.), *Advances in instructional psychology* (Vol. 1). Hillsdale, N.J.: Lawrence Erlbaum Associates.

Brown, A. L., Campione, J. C., & Day, J. D. (1981). Learning to learn: On training students to learn from texts. *Educational Researcher, 10*(2), 14–21.

Bruner, J. S. (1966). *Toward a theory of instruction.* Cambridge, MA: Harvard University Press.

Calfee, R. (1981). Cognitive psychology and educational practice. In D. C. Berliner (Ed.), *Review of research in education* (Vol. 9). Washington, D.C.: American Educational Research Association.

Clark, H. H. (1973). The language-as-fixed-effects fallacy: A critique of language statistics in psychological research. *Journal of Verbal Learning and Verbal Behavior, 12,* 335–359.

Corno, L., & Mandinach, E. B. (1983). The role of cognitive engagement in classroom learning and motivation. *Educational Psychologist, 18,* 88–108.

Doyle, W. (1983). Academic work. *Review of Educational Research, 53,* 159–199.

Doyle, W., Sanford, J. P., Clements, B. S., French, B. A. S., & Emmer, E. T. (1983). *Managing academic tasks: An interim report of the junior high school study* (R & D Report 6186). University of Texas, Research and Development Center for Teacher Education.

Dunkin, M. J., & Biddle, B. J. (1974). *The study of teaching.* New York: Holt, Rinehart, and Winston.

Ebel, R. L. (1982). Proposed solutions to two problems of test construction. *Journal of Educational Measurement, 19,* 267–278.

Ericsson, K. A., & Simon, H. A. (1980). Verbal reports as data. *Psychological Review, 87,* 215–251.

Flavell, J. H. (1981). Cognitive monitoring. In W. P. Dickson (Ed.), *Children's oral communication skills.* New York: Academic Press.

Glass, A. R., Holyoak, K. J., & Santa, J. L. (1979). *Cognition.* Reading, Mass.: Addison-Wesley.

Hamilton, S. F. (1983). The social side of schooling: Ecological studies of classrooms and schools. *Elementary School Journal, 83,* 313–334.

Herrmann, D. J. (1982). Know thy memory: The use of questionnaires to assess and study memory. *Psychological Bulletin, 92,* 434–452.

James, W. (1907). *Talks to teachers on psychology.* New York: Holt.

Jenkins, J. J. (1979). Four points to remember: A tetrahedral model of memory experiments. In L. S. Cermak and F. I. M. Craik (Eds.), *Levels of processing in human memory.* Hillsdale, N.J.: Lawrence Erlbaum.

Koopman, C., & Newston, D. (1981). Level of analysis in the perception of ongoing instruction. *Journal of Educational Psychology, 73,* 212–223.

Kintsch, W. (1979). On modeling comprehension. *Educational Psychologist, 14,* 3–14.

Leinhardt, G. (1983, April). *Student cognitions during instruction.* Paper presented at the annual meeting of the American Educational Research Association, Montreal.

Marx, R. W. (1984, April). *Self-regulation of cognitive strategies during classroom learning.* Paper presented at the meeting of the American Educational Research Association, New Orleans, LA.

Marx, R. W., Winne, P. H., and Howard, D. C. (1982). *Influence of cognitive style on students' perception of instruction* (Final Report, SSHRC Grant 410-80-0605;

Research Report No. 82-05). Burnaby, B.C.: Instructional Psychology Research Group, Simon Fraser University.

Mayer, R. E. (1981). *Structural analysis of science prose: Can we increase problem solving performance?* (Report No. 81-3). Santa Barbara, CA: Department of Psychology, University of California.

Mehan, H. (1979). *Learning lessons.* Cambridge, Mass.: Harvard University Press.

Meyer, B. J. F., & Freedle, R. O. (1984). Effects of discourse type on recall. *American Educational Research Journal, 21,* 121–144.

Newell, A., & Simon, H. A. (1972). *Human problem solving.* Englewood Cliffs, N.J.: Prentice-Hall.

Nisbett, R. E., & Wilson, T. D. (1977). Telling more than we can know: Verbal reports on mental processes. *Psychological Review, 84,* 231–259.

Peterson, P. L., Swing, S. R., Stark, K. D., & Waas, G. A. (1983, April). *Students' reports of their cognitive processes and affective thoughts during classroom instruction.* Paper presented at the annual meeting of the American Educational Research Association, Montreal.

Peterson, P. L., Swing, S. R., Braverman, M. T., & Buss, R. (1982). Students' aptitudes and their reports of cognitive processing during instruction. Journal of Educational Psychology, 74, 535–547.

Reigeluth, C. M., & Stein, F. S. (1983). The elaboration theory of instruction. In C. M. Reigeluth (Ed.), *Instructional-design theories and models.* Hillsdale, N.J.: Lawrence Erlbaum.

Rigney, J. W. (1978). Learning strategies: A theoretical perspective. In H. F. O'Neil, Jr. (Ed.), *Learning strategies.* New York: Academic Press.

Rosenshine, B. (1983). Teaching functions and instructional programs. *Elementary School Journal, 83,* 335–352.

Weinstein, R. S., Marshall, H. H., Brattesani, K. A., & Middlestadt, S. E. (1982). Student perceptions of differential teacher treatment in open and traditional classrooms. *Journal of Educational Psychology, 74,* 678–692.

Weinstein, R. S., & Middlestadt, S. E. (1979). Student perceptions of teacher interactions with male high and low achievers. *Journal of Educational Psychology, 71,* 421–431.

Winn, W. (1982). Visualization in learning and instruction: A cognitive approach. *Educational Communication and Technology, 30,* 3–25.

Winne, P. H. (in press a). Cognitive processing in the classroom. In T. Husen and T. N. Postlethwaite (Eds.), *International encyclopedia of education.* Oxford: Pergamon Press.

Winne, P. H. (in press b). Steps toward promoting cognitive achievements. *Elementary School Journal.*

Winne, P. H. (1984). Motivation, macrotreatments and methodology. In L. D. McLean, R. K. Crocker, & P. H. Winne (Eds.), *Research on teaching in Canada* (pp. 81–93). Toronto: OISE Press.

Winne, P. H. (1982). Minimizing the black box problem to enhance the validity of theories about instructional effects. *Instructional Science, 11,* 13–28.

Winne, P. H. (1979). Experiments relating teachers' use of higher cognitive questions to student achievement. *Review of Educational Research, 49,* 13–49.

Winne, P. H., & Marx, R. W. (1983). *Students' cognitive processes while learning from teaching* (NIE Final Report, NIE-G-79-0098). Burnaby, B.C.: Instructional Psychology Research Group, Simon Fraser University.

Winne, P. H., & Marx, R. W. (1982). Students' and teachers' views of thinking processes for classroom learning. *Elementary School Journal, 82*, 493–518.

Winne, P. H., & Marx, R. W. (1980). Matching students' cognitive responses to teaching skills. *Journal of Educational Psychology, 72*, 257–264.

Winne, P. H., & Marx, R. W. (1977). Reconceptualizing research on teaching. *Journal of Educational Psychology, 69*, 668–678.

7. Some Methodological and Statistical "Bugs" in Research on Children's Learning

Joel R. Levin

This chapter provides me with the opportunity to discuss a number of methodological and statistical "bugs" that I have detected creeping into psychological research in general, and into research on children's learning in particular. Naturally, one cannot hope to exterminate all such bugs with but a single essay. Rather, it is hoped that this chapter will leave a trail of pellets that is sufficiently odorific to get to the source of these potentially destructive little creatures. It also goes without saying that different people in this trade have different entomological lists that they would like to see presented. Although all cannot be presented here, I intend to introduce you to nearly 20 of my own personal favorites. At the same time, it must be stated at the outset that present space limitations do not permit a complete specification and resolution of the problems that these omnipresent bugs can create for cognitive-developmental researchers. Consequently, in most cases I will only allude to a problem and its potential remedies, placing the motivation for additional inquiry squarely in the lap of the curious reader.

A couple other prefatory remarks are in order. First, most of the bugs considered here are "old friends,' or at least they should be. The issues they encompass have been discussed time and again in widely cited treatments of psychological research methodology and data analysis (e.g., Campbell & Stanley, 1966; Cook & Campbell, 1976; Kirk, 1982; Winer, 1971). Based on a perusal of our journals and other scholarly research reports, however, it is clear to this writer that such issues bear reiteration—even at the risk of offending the competent veteran reseacher. Second, it should be mentioned that many of the present methodological and statistical concerns are shared by Salthouse and

Kausler (1985) in the companion volume to this one. Consequently, I give this single hearty recommendation of their chapter to the reader seeking additional related information (see also the recent chapter by Appelbaum & McCall, 1983).

The chapter comes at an extremely opportune time. First of all, the bugs have surfaced in a wide variety of substantive research contexts, and so I have seized the moment to round them all up for public inspection in one place. Secondly, the confines of a chapter provide an especially apropos vehicle both for synthesizing the already assembled bug traps and for hinting in the direction of building additional and bigger traps in the future. Finally, with this piece my 6-year term as Associate Editor of the *Journal of Educational Psychology* comes to a close. With it, I have some particularly recent and salient memories of submitted manuscripts that were infested with one or more species of these nasty little bugs. And so with a nod of priority to John Seeley Brown (e.g., Brown & Burton, 1978), let us begin our "buggy" adventure.

Bugs Associated with Developmental Comparisons

The first genus of methodological and statistical bug to be considered is that associated with developmental comparisons (typically, age or grade-level differences) with respect to memory performance. In studies of this kind, subjects at different developmental levels may be presented with a common word list, picture list, or text, which they study and are subsequently asked to recall. Developmental differences in recall levels and patterns, as well as their interaction with experimental manipulations, are typically of interest to the researcher. The bug here stems from the extremely likely possibility that a single set of materials does not lend itself to the kind of logical and statistical analyses that the researcher wishes to conduct.

Consider, for example, the means and standard deviations associated with the hypothetical study presented in Table 7-1. (The means are also plotted in Figure 7-1). In that study, subjects at four developmental levels were randomly assigned to two different conditions in order to study and recall a 10-item list.[1] In the control condition subjects were left to their own devices while studying the list, whereas in the experimental condition subjects were first instructed in the use of a thought-to-be-effective cognitive strategy. Suppose that one question of interest focuses on developmental increases in recall per se, and a second question focuses on the interaction of conditions and developmental level (i.e., whether the effect of cognitive-strategy instruction on recall is more pronounced at certain developmental levels than at others).

---

[1] Of course it must be realized that simple cross-sectional comparisons of this kind create a host of additional interpretive bugs for developmental researchers (see, for example, Baltes, Reese, & Nesselroade, 1977).

Table 7-1. Means and Standard Deviations, by Developmental Level and Experimental Condition

		Developmental Level			
		1	2	3	4
Control	*M*	1.00	4.00	6.00	7.00
	SD	.50	2.00	2.00	2.00
Experimental	*M*	1.00	6.00	8.00	9.00
	SD	0.50	2.00	1.00	0.50

Several aspects of these hypothetical data should be highlighted with reference to the present discussion. First, from Figure 7-1 it appears that in both conditions there is a curvilinear (viz., linear plus quadratic) relationship between developmental level and performance. In particular, recall increases most between the first two developmental levels, with lesser recall increments at each successive level. Second, it appears that there is indeed an interaction between conditions and developmental level, such that a difference between the two condition means is apparent at Levels, 2, 3, and 4, where none is at Level 1. Third, no such interaction appears between Levels 2 and 4, where the 2-point mean recall advantage in favor of the experimental group remains constant. It will now be argued that *even if statistically significant*, each of these conclusions is unwarranted given the nature of the present data.

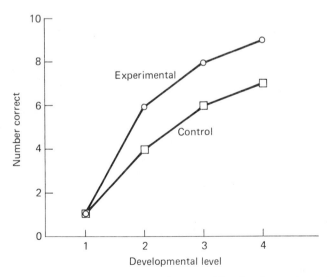

Figure 7-1. Mean number correct, by developmental level and experimental condition.

Methodological Bugs

The use of a common stimulus list at all developmental levels often produces attenuated performance at one or both extremes of the levels included in the study. In the present study, a 10-item stimulus list was administered to all subjects, and it certainly appears that attenuated performance resulted at both developmental extremes. In this case, the problem is exacerbated by the inclusion of two experimental conditions that differ in their effectiveness.

1. The "floor" bug. Note that in both the experimental and control conditions, subjects at Level 1 correctly recalled an average of only one item. Such a low performance suggests that a "floor effect" was present, namely that the task was simply too difficult for these youngest subjects. Floor effects mask between-subject differences that might have emerged if a less difficult task—here, a shorter list—had been administered. In particular, floor effects reduce the range (and variance) of obtainable scores, and are usually accompanied by a change in the shape of the distribution (such as from normal or symmetrical to positively skewed)—see Campbell and Boruch (1975) for an enlightening discussion of the potentially devastating effects of this methodological bug. Assume that in the present context, a task of appropriate difficulty produces a standard deviation of about 2 items. This is the value that in fact appears in four of the of the eight cells (see Table 7-1). In contrast, in the two Level 1 cells, the standard deviation is only .5, or a value 4 times lower than "normal." (This corresponds to a *variance* that is *16* times lower than "normal.")

The suspected floor effect has especially important implications for the interpretation of what looks like a noneffect of conditions at Level 1. Overlooking the floor effect, one would certainly conclude that the cognitive strategy was not effective for Level 1 subjects. But is such a conclusion justified? Is it not possible that the difficulty of the stimulus list per se (i.e., the number of items included, the items' complexity, or the amount of study time allotted) mitigated whatever strategy effects would have occurred with a less difficult list? Perhaps yes, perhaps no; the important point is that the present data do not permit one to distinguish between a real strategy noneffect and an artifactual one. That is, unintended list characteristics *may be* obliterating the potential benefits of the strategy among Level 1 subjects and, as such, the findings at that level are ambiguous.

That same little floor bug also affects our interpretation of what looks like an interaction between conditions and levels. Given the arguments in the preceding paragraph, let us assume for the moment that with a less difficult list subjects at Level 1 would have benefitted from the cognitive strategy. Further assume that they would have benefitted to *exactly the same extent* as would have Level 2 subjects who were given a list that was matched in difficulty to their levels.[2] In

---

[2]"Matched lists" can be operationally defined as yielding equivalent performance distributions (in terms of, say, percentage correct) in control conditions at different developmental levels. One such recommended strategy is to create longer lists by adding parallel "filler" items to the shorter

particular, assume that with two lists of "equal difficulty" at the two age levels, the same strategy advantage of two points—which is currently present among Level 2 subjects but masked among Level 1 subjects—would have materialized. Were that the case, what looks like an interaction in the company of floor effects no longer is when the floor is swept clean. The converse argument can turn apparent noninteractions into interactions, as will now be seen in the context of the floor bug's close kin, the "ceiling" bug.

2. The "ceiling" bug. If floor effects result from too difficult a task, "ceiling effects" result from too easy a task. Ceiling effects are suspected from very high means, negative skewness, and reduced variability. Refer again to the summary data in Table 7-1, where the maximum possible on this list is 10 items correct and the expected standard deviation is 2 points. Note in the experimental condition that perhaps by Level 3 and certainly at Level 4, high means and low variability are evident. (At Level 4 the experimental group's standard deviation is once again 4 times less than "normal.") The effect of this ceiling bug is that it prevents one from determining precisely how high the strategy would have carried these subjects had, say, a longer list of items been presented. Suppose in this case that with such a list, Level 4 experimental subjects would have exhibited more than the present 2-item advantage over control subjects. If that were the case, then a potential interaction is being suppressed by the administration of a "too-easy" list. Thus, still another set of ambiguous findings is associated with the present hypothetical study, which this time can be traced to the possibly artifactual *non*interaction observed between conditions and Levels 2–4.

Statistical Bugs

Over the years I have encountered a number of author conclusions that follow from either dubious or blatantly incorrect applications of statistical techniques. Discussion of such statistical misapplications will constitute a substantial part of the remainder of this chapter. In this section, I will mention what I view as unwarranted conclusions regarding (either the presence or absence of) developmental differences in the performance of some task.

3. The "heterogeneous" bug. As is pointed out even in an initial inferential statistics course, the valid application of the parametric independent-sample t-test of means—as well as its analysis-of-variance (ANOVA) F extension to K

---

list. If only the items "common" to each developmental level are included in the data analysis, there is no confounding of developmental level and tested-for list content. Using different lists at each developmental level naturally invalidates the search for developmental differences per se (i.e., developmental main effects), but such differences are clearly not of concern in the present example. If developmental main effects were of primary concern (as they are in the following section), then one would need to administer the same list at each developmental level.

samples—depends on a number of assumptions being met. In addition to the assumption that the dependent measure is normally distributed within each experimental condition or population, an integral statistical assumption is that the dependent measure's variability is the same in each population. This is the "homogeneity-of-variance" assumption of both the t- and the F-test. One also learns early on that Monte Carlo investigations of the behavior of the t- and F-test have documented that violations of this latter assumption are not particularly consequential when equal (or near-equal) numbers of subjects are included in each of the experimental conditions [e.g., Glass, Peckham, & Sanders (1972)—but see Tomarken & Serlin (in press) for some recent contradictory evidence.] In other words, in the equal-N situation parametric tests of mean differences are "robust" in the presence of variance heterogeneity. Thus, given equal sample sizes (as can often be arranged), it would seem that the existence of different degrees of variability at different developmental levels should be of little concern to the parametric hypothesis tester.

I have a couple of concerns over this lack of concern, however. In the first place, if variance heterogeneity *artificially* results from a full performance range in one condition and a restricted range (due to ceiling or floor effects) in the other, then we are back to our previous discussion of methodological bugs, which no statistical justification in the world can alleviate. That is, the just-mentioned robustness studies are based on comparisons of distributions with *genuine* variance differences, and their findings certainly cannot be applied to situations where variance differences may be traced to methodological inadequacies.

My second concern is more subtle, and can best be illustrated with reference to the control group's data in Table 7-1. Suppose that a common 10-item list was administered to the four groups of control subjects represented by the four developmental levels. Recall that the variability of Level 1 subjects ($SD = 0.50$) was considerably lower than that of Level 2 through Level 4 subjects ($SD = 2.00$). Ignoring for the moment that the reduced Level 1 variability is a byproduct of floor effects, let us construct the typical statistical analysis procedure followed by a researcher. An omnibus F-test is performed, and suppose it proved to be statistically significant. What happens next? Usually "post hoc comparisons" are conducted to determine which developmental levels differ significantly from one another. It is clear from the data presented in Table 7-1 that when comparing Levels 2, 3, and 4 the appropriate error to be used is that based on the common variance (squared standard deviation) of 4.00. Yet, when such groups are in fact compared according to standard multiple-comparison procedures, that error will be pooled with the much lower Level 1 variance of 0.25. Assuming equal sample sizes in this example, the appropriate mean square error for comparing Levels 2–4 is clearly 4.00, but when the Level 1 data are incorporated this becomes 3.06 (about a 25% reduction). The consequences of this deflated error term are to produce an invalid t- or F-ratio, which will lead to the declaration of differences being "significant" that might not have been had the more face-valid error term been applied.

Exactly the same problem arises when not all the means being compared come from normal distributions with genuine (i.e., nonartificial) variance differences. In such multiple-comparison situations, it has been shown empirically that one's nominal and actual Type I error probabilities do not correspond (as they do when the homogeneity-of-variance assumption is met). Researchers can avoid reaching unjustified conclusions, however, by employing multiple-comparison procedures that either incorporate separate (rather than pooled) variance estimators (see Kirk, 1982) or are based on nonparametric analogs (see Marascuilo & McSweeney, 1977).

4. The "Type IV" bug. Also known as the "inference-leaping" bug, this persistent pest belongs to the general family of *Type IV errors* (Marascuilo & Levin, 1970). In common parlance, a Type IV error is a mismatch between what one is *entitled* to conclude on the basis of a performed statistical test and what one *actually* concludes on the basis of that test. In this manifestation—and again with reference to the control group's data in Figure 7-1—the main effect of developmental level is assessed via a proper statistical test, and suppose it proves to be significant. Based on such a test, a researcher would be entitled to conclude that not all means associated with the different developmental levels are equal to one another or, equivalently, that there exist developmental differences somewhere in the data. Yet, the verbal interpretation that often follows from such a test is that "there is a significant increase in performance with increases in developmental level," or that "there is an increase from one developmental level to the next," or some such claim of specific developmental differences. For the present example it is likely that a significant main effect would also be associated with a significant linear trend. However, one can conceive of—and I have in fact seen—developmental data sets with statistically reliable mean differences that do not include statistically reliable linear increases or decreases in performance (see Figure 7-2 for a hypothetical example). Similarly, in the present data set perhaps all pairs of adjacent mean differences would be statistically significant, but perhaps only some of them would be; and it is even possible that none of them would be! The point is that conclusions about specific trend components or levels differences follow from statistical tests of specific contrasts, and not from omnibus statistical tests of main effects.

Other species of the inference-leaping bug will also be briefly mentioned here. One of these is following up a significant omnibus F-test with multiple-comparison procedures that are not consistent or "coherent" (Gabriel, 1969) with the initial difference-screening test. In the one-way ANOVA model, for example, it is easily demonstrated that the Scheffé multiple-comparison procedure is logically tied to the omnibus F-test, whereas all others are not. In particular, a nonsignificant F-ratio *guarantees* that no significant Scheffé

J. R. Levin

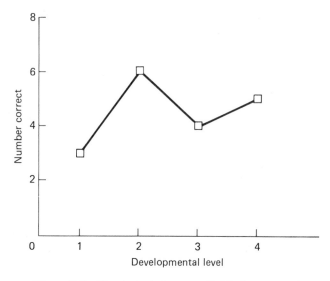

Figure 7-2. Graph depicting a negligible linear trend.

contrast exists in the data, whereas a significant F-ratio *guarantees* that at least one significant Scheffé contrast exists. Although one may hesitate to adopt the Scheffé procedure because of its typically lower statistical power in comparison to other procedures, it is nonetheless the only procedure that is coherent with the omnibus F-test. Exactly the same kind of coherence relationship holds between the lesser-known studentized range test and the Tukey method of multiple comparisons (Kirk, 1982), as well as between the MANOVA application of Roy's criterion and the Roy–Bose multiple-comparison procedure (Marascuilo & Levin, 1983). As will be pointed out later in this section and in others (see Bugs 15 and 16), an especially problematic situation arises when hypothesis-testing incoherence inflates the Type I error probability, as happens when omnibus statistical tests are followed by uncontrolled comparisons of means.

A final inference-leaping bug of note infests factorial analysis-of-variance designs, where a lack of coherence between "interaction" and "simple-effect" conclusions runs rampant (see Marascuilo & Levin, 1970, and Betz & Levin, 1982). To illustrate this type of Type IV bug, let us consider the means associated with the 2×2 design in Table 7-2. Note that a classic "disordinal" interaction is apparent (Lubin, 1961), where the difference between means within one column (or row) is reversed in sign and of the same absolute magnitude as the difference between means in the other column (or row). Such a pattern is always characterized by its zero sum of squares (and F-ratio) for both main effects. For this example, suppose that eight subjects were tested in each of the four cells, and that the mean square error associated with the data was equal to 4.00. With these stipulations, it is found that a significant interaction (a "difference in differences" or "differential effect") is present here,

Table 7-2. Hypothetical Disordinal Interaction

	Condition	
	A1	A2
B1	6.5	5.0
B2	5.0	6.5

Note: Cell $Ns = 8$; $MSE = 4$.

$F(1,28) = 4.50, p < .05$. So far, so good. But enter the type IV bug when a researcher concludes on the basis of this interaction that at Level B1 performance in Condition A1 is superior to that in Condition A2, whereas at Level B2 performance in Condition A2 is superior to that in Condition A1. Note that these two statements refer to the significance of each difference *separately*, rather than to the significance of the difference in differences produced by the four means *collectively*. Thus, these simple-effect conclusions are not coherent with the statistical interaction just detected and—even worse—for the present data set neither of the simple effects alluded to in the researcher's statement is statistically significant, $F(1,28) = 2.25$, $p > .10$, in each case. Case closed for now, although it should be noted that the converse situation is also possible; that is, nonsignificant interactions can be associated with statistically reliable simple effects (see Marascuilo & Levin, 1970, for an actual research example).[3]

Although such bugs (i.e., Type IV errors) are viewed by some as being inconsequential in contrast to Type I and Type II errors (e.g., Games, 1978), the present author has demonstrated that in many applications Type IV errors in fact *are* Type I and Type II errors (Levin, 1977). That is, errors stemming from inconsistent applications of statistical procedures (Type IV errors) can be identified precisely as incorrect null hypothesis rejections (Type I errors) and nonrejections (Type II errors). Thus, to the extent that controlling Type I and Type II errors is a valued standard in psychological research, so too should be controlling—or even better, eliminating—inference-leaping bugs, alias Type IV errors.

5. The "trendy" bug. Another not-so-obvious problem occurs when developmental researchers attempt to apply statistical "trend analysis" to a set of data whose independent variable is quantitatively defined (such as in the present example, where Levels 1–4 represent increasing amounts of some cognitive-developmental variable). Trend analysis proceeds on the basis of applying

[3]Note that throughout this section I have avoided the issue of whether interaction effects should be conceptualized in the traditional "absolute" sense or rather in a "relative" sense (e.g., Bogartz, 1976). That is, does a two-item difference on a short List A (or at a particular level of performance on List A) mean the same thing as a two-item difference on a longer List B (or at a different level of performance on List A)? Traditional analysis-of-variance models assume that it does (see Loftus, 1977, for additional discussion).

standard "orthogonal polynomial coefficients" to investigate linear, quadratic, and higher-order trend components in the data (see, for example, Kirk, 1982, p. 830). There are several assumptions underlying the valid application of standard orthogonal polynomial coefficients, however, and aye, there's the bug!

In the first place, the independent variable must constitute at least an interval scale (where distances between scale values are known), in contrast to simply an ordinal scale (where scale-value distances are not known).[4] In the present example, if all that can be assumed is that the four developmental levels are monotonically increasing (i.e., that Level 4 represents "more" cognitive development than Level 3, which represents "more" than Level 2, which represents "more" than Level 1), then the developmental-level factor is ordinal. If, on the other hand, the numbers 1–4 represent subjects' ages or grade levels, then the developmental factor is at least interval (actually ratio). Standard trend analysis and resulting interpretations would be appropriate in the latter case, though not in the former.

Given an interval scale for the independent variable, a second issue that must be considered is the distance between each scale value represented in the study. Standard tables of orthogonal polynomial coefficients assume that all scale values are equally spaced. Thus, the inclusion of first, third, fifth, and seventh graders in a study (Example A) would satisfy the "equally spaced" criterion, whereas the inclusion of first, fourth, fifth, and sixth graders (Example B) would not. Over the years, I have encountered several studies where the latter situation obtained, and yet standard tables of trend coefficients were applied. It is easily shown that applying standard trend coefficients in the presence of unequally spaced intervals leads to a misspecification of the actual trend that is present, through either an augmentation or a diminishment of it.

This point can be illustrated graphically via Figure 7-3. In the upper portion of that figure, the four levels of Example B are plotted incorrectly as equally spaced intervals, and it appears that the associated means trace out a perfect positive linear trend. In the lower portion of that figure, where the same four means are associated with the correctly spaced levels of Example B, the "perfect" linear tend is not so perfect.

The preceding statements should not be interpreted as implying that trend analysis must be avoided in cases where scale values are not equally spaced. In such cases, it is possible to derive appropriate coefficients to test for the various trend components. For instance, in the just-mentioned Example A the correct linear trend coefficients are the standard tabled values of -3, -1, $+1$, and $+3$; in contrast, for Example B the corresponding coefficients are -3, 0, $+1$, and $+2$.

A final concern in this domain is whether the sample sizes at each developmental level are equal. If they are, and if more than one trend

---

[4] Although trend analysis can be applied to factors with ordinal scales, the resulting trends cannot be termed "linear," "quadratic," "cubic," etc. (see Levin, Marascuilo, & Hubert, 1978).

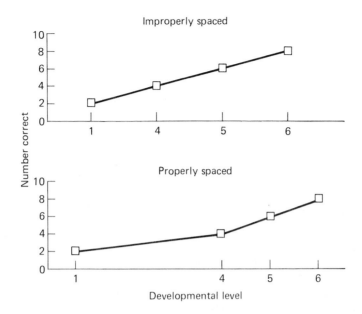

Figure 7-3. Examples of improperly (top) and properly (bottom) scaled independent variables.

component is investigated in the same study (e.g., if both linear and quadratic trends are assessed), then the application of standard trend coefficients will yield trend components that are mutually orthogonal (uncorrelated). In contrast, if sample sizes at the different developmental levels are not all equal, then orthogonality among trend components will not be present. If orthogonality is desired—as is usually the case—then, as in the previous example, alternative sets of trend coefficients need to be derived. A general procedure for handling both the unequally spaced interval situation and the unequal sample size situation was proposed by Gaito (1965)—see also Kirk (1982, pp. 773–777).

6. The "unthinking" bug. Let me conclude this section by briefly describing a few bugs associated with hypothesis testing in general. One such bug occurs whenever a researcher has a very precise hypothesis in mind, and yet assesses the validity of that hypothesis in a very imprecise fashion. Imprecise hypothesis testing usually stems from a researcher's routinely applying a textbook statistical test (or having a computer do it) without first considering the optimality of that test for his or her particular research question. One such unthinking bug is conducting a multiple-degree-of-freedom F-test when a t- or F-test of a specific contrast would be much more appropriate. Recall the previously mentioned Type IV bug, where a researcher unjustifiably concluded that there was a significant linear trend following the obtainment of a significant main effect. Given that the linear component of the developmental main effect was of primary interest to the researcher—as is often the case with a developmental factor—then why wasn't the omnibus test of the developmental main effect bypassed in favor of a one-degree-of-freedom test of the linear trend contrast? With the latter strategy, one could efficiently assess the linear developmental effect via a single contrast, accompanied by an assessment of all "residual effects" (departures from linearity) via a test incorporating the remaining degrees of freedom.

Shifting from an omnibus test of the main effect to a localized test of the linear trend contrast (or some other contrast dictated by the researcher's major hypothesis) invariably adds statistical power to a study (see Cohen, 1977, and Levin, 1975). In an attempt to eradicate the unthinking bug, even more statistical power can be added when contrasts are evaluated directionally (i.e., as one-tailed tests). Contrary to what many researchers seem to think, when formulated appropriately (i.e., prior to data collection), directional tests are not "more liberal" than nondirectional tests; they are *equally* liberal if based on the same Type I error probability. What they are is "more powerful," resulting from the assignment of all the Type I error probability to one distributional tail on the basis of prior knowledge, careful planning, and just plain *thinking* about one's research hypothesis. I have yet to read the study in which cognitive-developmental differences were being assessed and the researcher could not specify whether *higher* or *lower* levels of performance would be expected with increases in development. With such positive or negative linear trends (or any other contrasts) firmly in mind, to conduct two-tailed tests of them is to throw away statistical power; yet, in the cognitive-developmental literature, this certainly appears to be the rule rather than the exception.

7. The "null" bug. A second hypothesis-testing bug to be inspected in this section is one arising from a researcher's desire to "prove" the null hypothesis, that is, to permit the conclusion that there are no mean performance differences between two (or among more than two) developmental levels. In the first place, the business of proving the null hypothesis is not a straightforward task, from either a philosophical or a statistical standpoint (see, for example, Cohen, 1977; Morrison & Henkel, 1970; Serlin & Lapsley, 1983; and Walster & Cleary, 1970). In this context, however, what often occurs is that a "no difference" conclusion follows from a comparison of two means based on small sample sizes (and hence, the "proof" is associated with low statistical power).

Alternatively, consider a situation where two treatments are being compared at two different developmental levels. Further suppose that for unstated or unknown reasons, more subjects were tested at one developmental level than at the other. Statistical tests reveal that there is a significant treatment effect at one developmental level (the one with the larger sample sizes) but not at the other. Based on such evidence, would you "buy" the researcher's conclusion that there are different treatment effects (nonnull and null, respectively) associated with the two developmental levels? Many developmental researchers have attempted to convince us of this in the past.

To this list may be added the problem of "proving" that the respective ANOVA or analysis of covariance (ANCOVA) assumptions of homogeneity of variance or homogeneity of regression have been met when tests of these assumptions were based on inadequate sample sizes. It is well known that such tests are not likely to detect even moderate differences unless sample sizes are quite large. A similar argument may be applied to situations in which a researcher claims support for a theoretical position on the basis of not rejecting a statistical test designed to assess departures from the theory ("residual effects"). Obviously, those who are aware of the role that sample size plays in statistical hypothesis testing also realize that conclusions based on insufficient Ns are suspect.

As a footnote to this section, it goes without saying that the "flip-side" of the just-discussed hypothesis-testing problem must be considered as well. That is, *any* difference—however trivial—may be shown to be real (i.e., nonzero) if sample sizes are large enough. Despite having received a good deal of publicity in recent years (e.g., Cohen, 1977; Glass, 1977), concern for "practical" as opposed to "statistical" significance and the magnitude of one's "effect sizes" needs to be more seriously heeded by cognitive-developmental researchers. Only unless decisions about *optimal* sample sizes are taken into account during the design of a study (e.g., Serlin & Lapsley, 1984; Walster & Cleary, 1970) will subsequent hypothesis-testing conclusions be credible. In this context, "optimal" sample sizes refer to those that will provide a researcher with sufficient statistical power to detect practically important effects, but not so much power that trivial effects will be detected.

8. The "interactive" bug. In the just-mentioned example of comparing a treatment effect at two developmental levels, an additional potential problem should be identified. This is the problem of inferring that an interaction exists on the basis of two tests that were separately conducted. This particular bug stems from many researchers' lack of awareness of the distinction between interactions and simple effects in factorial ANOVA designs (see, for example, Marascuilo & Levin, 1976). With reference again to the Type IV bug (Bug 4), a simple effect involves comparing two or more levels with respect to their mean performance, whereas an interaction (or differential effect) involves comparing those levels with respect to mean performance *differences*.

For the present two-level, two-treatment example, it was stated that the researcher conducted two separate treatment comparisons, one at each developmental level: these are two simple-effects tests (of the treatment effect within each developmental level). Given optimal sample sizes (see above), such tests would allow a researcher to conclude whether or not there exists a reliable treatment effect at Level 1 and whether or not there exists a reliable treatment effect at Level 2. Suppose that at Level 1 the treatment effect is found to be statistically reliable, whereas at Level 2 it is not. Does this entitle the researcher to conclude that the treatment exerts a different effect at the two levels? Indirectly, from a logical perspective, perhaps "yes"; but directly, from a statistical perspective, definitely "no." The "differential-effect" conclusion requires that one conduct a direct statistical comparison of the treatment effect at the two different developmental levels. That is, an interaction between treatments and developmental levels must be assessed via a statistical test that compares the difference between experimental and control subjects at Level 1 with the same difference at Level 2. Should such an interaction contrast prove statistically significant, then a "differential-effect" conclusion is justified. This conclusion would allow one to claim that there was a *larger* treatment effect at one developmental level than at the other.

Note, at the same time, that the interaction conclusion does not enable one to claim that the treatment effect was statistically *real* at one developmental level but not at the other (refer back to Bug 4 and the data in Table 7-2). Putting on the other hat, a researcher who wished to make such a claim would need to perform more than one simple-effects test rather than a single test of the interaction. As should be apparent from this discussion, the moral is simply that the kind of conclusions that a researcher wishes to make should dictate (and be compatible with) the particular statistical model adopted, which in the present case is either the interaction or the simple-effects model. Humphreys (1980) provides a similar discussion of the direct versus indirect statistical-inference problem.

Other Bugs in Research on Children's Learning

I will now discuss a variety of other methodological and statistical bugs that have surfaced in the children's learning literature over the years. Classifying these bugs as either "methodological" or "statistical" is done more out of concern for providing some superordinate structure to this section, rather than because the two classifications are conceptually distinct. For instance, and as will become apparent in the discussion that follows, there are many cases in which a methodological bug has direct implications for the subsequent statistical analysis and interpretations.

Methodological Bugs

9. The "control" bug. Imagine once again a study in which subjects who are taught a presumably effective learning strategy (experimental group) are compared with subjects who are not taught the strategy (control group). Given random assignment of subjects to the two conditions, conclusions stemming from such an "internally valid" (Campbell & Stanley, 1966) study would seem to be straightforward enough. But are they really? The credibility of any resulting strategy effects depends critically on the manner in which the control group has been operationalized. And I have seen control-group operationalizations that have run the gamut, in terms of their representing either extremely trivial or extremely challenging tests of the treatment manipulation. On the extremely trivial side, for example, I have encountered studies in which the learning of experimental subjects who have applied a cognitive strategy to an instructional unit is compared with that of "control" subjects *who were never even exposed to the to-be-learned material*. Although such studies may be useful in indicating whether or not some *relevant instruction* and/or *exposure to the instructional unit* is better than none, they do not permit a disentanglement of these two plausible sources of the resulting treatment effect. Neither are they helpful in permitting an evaluation of the potency of the particular strategy investigated relative to a situation in which subjects are allowed to apply *whatever strategies they normally use* to study the material. If provided with an equivalent amount of exposure time to the instructional unit, this latter control condition can be thought of as representing an ecologically valid, "natural" comparison for the experimental strategy under consideration.

The bottom line of this discussion is simply that for any particular experimental treatment, virtually an infinite variety of control treatments can be devised (e.g., some controlling for practice, some controlling for time, some controlling for novelty, etc.). In children's-learning research, it is even common practice to include "negative" control groups, where subjects are in fact prevented from employing any potentially useful strategy that is part of their normal repertoire (see, for example, Levin & Pressley, 1983, and Rohwer, 1973). As long as researchers in this field show an awareness for such variations in control-group quality and rigor—and temper their enthusiasm for treatment effects accordingly—then this bug will cease being a bug of concern.

10. The "spurious" bug. The label for this bug was born out of the common description for empirically demonstrated relationships that are not what they might appear to be. That is, what looks like an interesting relationship between two variables may sometimes be produced (or at least be influenced) by one or more unconsidered variables. I think that it is important for learning researchers to recognize this, particularly in the context of computing correlations based on two or more groups of subjects. Let me elaborate my concern via our ongoing strategy versus control (two-group) example. Suppose that following administration of the strategy treatment, performance on a recall task is measured. Further suppose that the strategy was effective in producing substantial group mean differences on two measures of performance, total recall and item clustering. In addition to considering the mean differences on each of these measures, the researcher wants to know whether the two measures are related to one another. So, he or she computes the correlation between total recall and item clustering. Sound simple enough?

Not so. As is thoroughly discussed by Marascuilo and Levin (1983, Chapters 2 and 3), in a situation such as this it is possible for one to compute the Pearson correlation coefficient in several different ways. To mention three, one could compute (a) a single correlation based on all subjects, without regard to the group they are in (the "across-groups" correlation); (b) two separate correlations, one based on experimental subjects and one based on control subjects; and (c) an average correlation based on "pooling" the two groups' variances and covariances (the "within-groups" correlation). The bug here typically arises from a researcher's computing and interpreting the *across-groups* correlation coefficient without the apparent realization that the magnitude of that correlation is influenced by the degree to which there are group mean differences on the constituent dependent variable(s). In other words, whenever group mean differences exist the relationship between the two variables is confounded with those between-group differences. In the present example, it would be quite possible to find a substantial across-groups correlation between total recall and item clustering even though the correlation between recall and clustering within each group (or the pooled within-groups correlation) was negligible.

An example of this sort of problem is illustrated in Figure 7-4, where the correlation between recall and clustering within both the control (dots) and strategy (squares) conditions is precisely .00, and yet the across-groups correlation based on both groups combined is equal to .39. For a researcher to conclude that recall and clustering per se are correlated, on the basis of the "spuriously" inflated across-groups correlation, would be quite misleading in this context. Of course, there are instances in which across-groups correlations are meaningful (i.e., when one wishes to generalize across levels of some extraneous grouping or classification variable), but the point being made here is

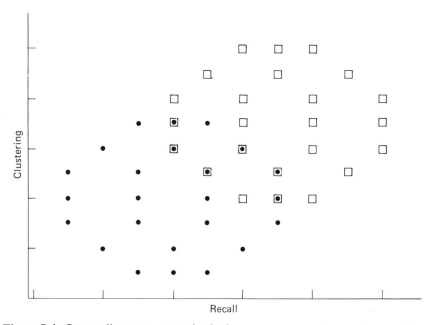

Figure 7-4. Scatter diagram representing both across–groups and separate correlations between recall and clustering.

that a researcher should recognize the various issues and options involved, and behave rationally in light of them.

11. The "recognition" bug. As is now well known by cognitive-developmental researchers, studies in which recognition decisions (typically "yes–no" responses) constitute the dependent variable bring with them a fascinating bug to examine. The bug arises from the fact that differences among conditions in unadjusted correct recognitions are due not only to a subject's ability to *discriminate* between "old" and "new" items, but also to the sheer number of items in the set that a subject is willing to accept as "old" (termed the subject's acceptance *criterion*). When a simple measure such as "percent correct recognitions" is reported (i.e., the percentage of "yes" responses to old items plus the percentage of "no" responses to new items), it is not possible to determine whether an individual's score reflects mainly a discrimination component, mainly a criterion component, or a combination of the two. That is, the two recognition components are confounded in a simple "percent correct" index of performance. To unconfound the two, "signal detection" measures of recognition performance (d')—and simpler z-score proxies of such measures— were developed (see Green & Swets, 1966). Researchers are advised to adopt these standardized measures as replacements for traditional measures such as percentage correct or number correct.[5]

12. The "unit" bug (Species 1). An incredibly persistent bug that has infested the children's learning literature is one associated with the use of inappropriate "experimental units" (see Peckham, Glass, & Hopkins, 1969). An experimental unit is defined as the smallest entity to which treatments are independently administered, and can consist of individual students, small or large groups of students (including classrooms), and even—in the case of large-scale educational- or social-policy treatment studies—communities or geographical regions. An all-too-common faux pas in this context appears in studies where experimental and control subjects are administered their respective treatments and placebos in separate groups or classrooms. In the extreme case, one group of students represents each condition.

From a methodological standpoint, if one experimenter (or teacher) is responsible for one condition and another expermenter for the other condition, then a treatment-by-experimenter confounding exists, and the data are uninterpretable with respect to treatment effects. Fortunately, most contemporary researchers would recognize such an obvious confounding, and so they would mandate that the same experimenter be responsible for administering both the experimental and control treatments. An alternative approach would

---

[5]Other issues related to this discussion include the utility of Markovian analyses of developmental learning data (e.g., Brainerd & Howe, 1980) and that of possible transformations of conditional percentage data in order to meet the assumptions underlying the statistical analysis procedure selected (see, for example, Kirk, 1982, pp. 79–84).

be to enlist two groups or classrooms *per condition* and, with two experimenters, each experimenter could administer *both* treatments.

In addition, however, time-of-day differences in treatment administrations, room differences, and various extraneous incidents that simultaneously affect all members of a group must also be controlled for if the internal validity of treatment-related conclusions is to be preserved. As an example of potential simultaneous treatment contamination, consider Page's (1965) "lawnmower effect" anecdote, where all the students in a particular classroom were disrupted on a weekly basis by the sound of a noisy power lawnmower just outside the classroom window.

If, after all is said and done, such internal validity issues are dealt with satisfactorily, is that all there is to the "unit" bug? Unfortunately, no, because even though the just-noted strategies may alleviate the methodological aspect of the "units" problem, they are unhelpful in alleviating a critical statistical aspect of the same problem. For readers whose curiosity is sufficiently piqued at this point, please take a peek at the points made in the following section on the "unit" bug as a statistical problem.

Statistical Bugs

13. The "unit" bug (Species 2). Once the experimental units have been operationalized, they constitute the "units of analysis" (Barcikowski, 1981; Peckham et al., 1969) for the study. And of critical importance here, virtually all ANOVA-based statistical analyses adopted by behavioral researchers require that the errors associated with the experimental units are mutually independent. As Glass et al. (1972) are careful to point out, in contrast to the normality (related to Bugs 1 and 2) and homogeneity-of-variance (Bug 3) assumptions of the analysis of variance (which can often be compensated for by large and equal samples sizes, respectively), (*a*) nonindependence among experimental units cannot easily be compensated for, and (*b*) the Type I error consequences associated with nonindependence can be devastating.

The implication of the "units-of-analysis" issue for the behavioral researcher is simply that when subjects are treated in groups, then *groups* and not *subjects* constitute the proper units to which the statistical treatment of the data should be applied. Basing the analysis on *individual subjects* in such cases will result in the adoption of an inappropriate error term with inflated degrees of freedom. To be concrete, if an experimental treatment is administered to, say, two independent groups of 15 subjects and a control treatment is administered to another two independent groups of 15 subjects, then each treatment can legitimately furnish only 2 (rather than 30) data points—along with only 1 degree of freedom apiece (rather than 29)—for the statistical analysis. Such data points will typically consist of the group means, medians, or other appropriately selected summary measures that are sensitive to the researcher's hypotheses (see, for example, Levin & Peterson, 1984). The analysis that proceeds as it does in the usual situation with individual scores as the data points, but this time with a single summary "score" representing each *group's* contribution. Lest one be overly concerned about substantial losses in statistical power resulting from this approach, it can be easily shown that with only a moderate number of "groups" per treatment a researcher has respectable chances of detecting nontrivial treatment differences (see, for example, Barcikowski, 1981; Levin et al., 1978; Levin, Pressley, McCormick, Miller, & Shriberg, 1979, Exps. 5 and 6; Levin & Peterson, 1984; and Peckham et al., 1969).

A number of issues bearing on the statistical treatment of the "unit" bug can be, and have been, considered. Unfortunately, space does not permit an accounting of them here. The inquisitive reader is referred to Barcikowski (1981) for the *statistical power* issue, to Cronbach and Snow (1977) and Levin and Peterson (1984) for some *individual-differences* issues, and to Levin et al. (1978) for the analogous issue of nonindependent units in the operant *single-subject research* literature. Suffice it to reiterate here that "units" violations comprise one of the most pervasive—and potentially most serious—hypothesis-testing bugs in the children's-learning literature. Exterminating this bug should certainly be a top priority of cognitive-developmental researchers who care about the soundness of their experimental conclusions.

14. The "matching" bug. This particular bug encompasses a variety of researcher attempts to "equate" noncomparable groups with respect to one or more "antecedent" variables prior to comparing the groups on some dependent measure. Both statistical (viz., ANCOVA) and experimental (viz., blocking) methods of equating have been applied, the latter in both a priori and post hoc forms (for an interesting discussion, see Maxwell, Delaney, & Dill, 1984). Problems arising from attempts to equate preexisting (nonrandomly composed) groups have been well publicized in the behavioral sciences (e.g., Campbell & Boruch, 1975; Campbell & Stanley, 1966; Cook & Campbell, 1976; Elashoff, 1969; Lord, 1967; Porter & Chibucos, 1974). Complications in this context include (among others) regression-toward-the-mean artifacts, covariate mis-adjustments, and treatment-by-covariate confoundings. One particularly interesting manifestation of this last kind of complication occurs in random-assignment experiments when the "control" variable included in an ANCOVA is one that has itself been affected by the treatment manipulation (e.g., when subjects' response latencies are covaried out of an analysis of subjects' response errors)—see, for example, Evans & Anastasio (1968) and rejoinders over the last several years in the *Psychological Bulletin*.

I do not intend the preceding comments to imply that blocking on, or covarying out, relevant antecedent variables is a practice that is to be avoided, for indeed it is not. In contrast to the inclusion of such variables as a "bias-removing" strategy in nonrandom-assignment designs, their inclusion in random-assignment designs as a "variance-reducing" strategy is often both logically defensible and statistically advantageous (e.g., Huitema, 1980; Kirk, 1982; Marascuilo & Levin, 1983). Moreover, when applied and interpreted

judiciously, blocking or ANCOVA designs permit the investigation of substantively interesting aptitude-by-treatment interactions or ATIs (see, for
example, Cronbach & Snow, 1977). As has been true of most of the topics
covered in this chapter, the real message here is that researchers should be able
to use various research strategies *appropriately*, recognizing the inappropriate-
usage occasions.

15. The "multivariate" bug. The increased availability of multiple-regression
and multivariate-analysis-of-variance (MANOVA) computer packages during
the 1970s and now into the 1980s (e.g., *BMDP, SPSS, SAS, Multivariance*) has
been associated with a new breed of statistical bug, the contemporary
"multivariate"bug. Problems range from problems of interpretation (such as
reseachers not being aware of exactly what hypotheses are being tested or how
to interpret the various computer output) to downright questionable or
inappropriate applications of multivariate procedures to a particular data set
(such as when critical distributional assumptions have been violated or when
large variable-to-subject ratios are present). The various statistical assumptions
and other requirements needed for valid application of multivariate analysis are
discussed throughout the recent text by Marascuilo and Levin (1983). I will
briefly mention a few of these bugs that are visibly apparent in the children's-
learning literature.

Perhaps the most prominent multivariate bug is of the Type IV error variety,
which was introduced previously as the inference-leaping bug (Bug 4). In this
context, a researcher performs a MANOVA in which two or more experimental
conditions are compared for their simultaneous equality on two or more
dependent measures. Apart from the fact that the researcher is often unaware of
the particular test criterion to be reported—because unlike the single univariate
F-ratio, in MANOVA four or five different computed test statistics must be
decided among—what often happens is that the reporting of a multivariate "F"
is followed by the reporting of univariate F-ratios associated with each of the
dependent measures.[6]

There are at least three problems with the practice of jumping from
multivariate to univariate statistics: (1) Because the researcher typically
investigates the univariate F-ratios regardless of whether or not the initial
multivariate test was statistically significant, one wonders what purpose the
multivariate test served in the first place. Was it used as a "screening device,"
as an initial omnibus test should be? Obviously not. (2) Typically, each
univariate F-ratio is interpreted with respect to conventional univariate
significance probabilities (e.g., $p < .05$). Doing so defeats a major purpose of

---

[6]The most commonly reported multivariate test statistic is Rao's approximate F-test of Wilks'
lambda criterion. Unfortunately, whether Wilks' lambda is the criterion most appropriate, given the
data and the hypothesis being tested (Olson, 1974), seems to be less important to researchers than
the fact that the "F" on the computer printout is a test statistic with which univariate ANOVA
users are familiar.

multivariate analysis—simultaneous type I error probability protection—because it compounds the researcher's "familywise" Type I error probability (see Marascuilo & Levin, 1983, Chapters 8 and 9, as well as the "unprotected" bug that is discussed next).[7] (3) As the converse of Point 1, obtaining a significant multivariate F in no way guarantees that any of the univariate Fs will be significant. Marascuilo and Levin (pp. 390–394) present an actual research example of how this "dilemma" can trouble and confuse a researcher. Besides the potential frustration associated with this practice, switching from multivariate to univariate Fs without regard for the various logical and statistical issues involved is yet another instance of incoherent (Type IV) research behavior (see Bird & Hadzi-Pavlovic, 1983, for some enlightening additional discussion).

A final note in this domain concerns researchers' reportings of the "stepdown Fs" that often accompany the computer MANOVA and univariate ANOVA results. The use of stepdown Fs also requires consideration of the familywise error issue alluded to in Point 2. But even more importantly, meaningful interpretation of stepdown tests requires that the dependent variables have a logically defensible *order* in which they are to be tested, in the same sense that a "researcher-determined" entry order of independent variables can be defended in stepwise multiple-regression analysis (e.g., Cohen & Cohen, 1975; Marascuilo & Levin, 1983). Unhappily, I have seen research studies in which stepdown tests have been applied to *arbitrarily ordered* dependent variables, thereby negating the whole rationale behind that statistical approach. I therefore figured it was about time that we stepped down on this stepdown bug and other multivariate bugs.

16. The "unprotected" bug. Oh, that researchers would realize that applying statistical tests indiscriminately, as well as applying tests with uncontrolled or questionable "protection properties," is truly an offensive bug! Indeed, it can be reasonably argued that more than any other, this bug has been responsible for the countless nonreplicable findings, dead ends, and wild-goose chases that have been charted in the cognitive-developmental literature. It is so easy to demonstrate that when hypothesis testing gets out of hand (e.g., when every correlation in a 10×10 correlation matrix is tested for significance using as a criterion $p < .05$) one's chances of stumbling down the slippery staircase of spurious significance increases astronomically. In fact, there comes a point where one's chances of doing this become a virtual certainty.

The reason for this diatribe is to convince researchers to conduct an immediate cessation of the following: (*a*) statistical tests of everything in sight in multiple-group or multiple-variable designs; (*b*) nonstatistically based interpretations of differences that look "interesting," both before and after the conduct of an omnibus test that does not *directly* assess the difference being discussed

---

[7]The "familywise" Type I error probability is the probability that *one or more* Type I errors will be made in a given set (or "family") of statistical comparisons (see Kirk, 1982, pp. 104–105).

(e.g., the unwarranted developmental-difference conclusions illustrated in conjunction with Bug 4); and (*c*) "quasi-protected" tests (such as Fisher's LSD test, the Newman-Keuls test, and Duncan's multiple-range test), which are known not to provide their claimed familywise Type I error probability control in most applications (e.g., Jaccard, Becker, & Wood, 1984; Petrinovich & Hardyck, 1969). In contrast, other popular simultaneous multiple-comparison procedures (such as the a priori Dunn-Bonferroni procedure, Dunnett's and Tukey's procedures, and the post hoc Scheffé procedure) *do* control the familywise Type I error probability appropriately, and are therefore to be preferred by the Type I-error-conscious researcher (Kirk, 1982).

As a footnote to this section, let it be recorded that the all-too-common practice of first performing an omnibus *F*-test, and then *following* it with a set of "*planned*" comparisons, has always remained a mystery to me. A planned-comparison approach is an *alternative*, not a companion, to an omnibus test. It represents an alternative, more substantively appealing and statistically powerful, means of answering one's research questions (through the more efficient allocation of the familywise Type I error probability). Inasmuch as in practice researchers usually resort to the ill-conceived version of a "planned" approach when the omnibus test is found *not* to be statistically significant, some very curious (disturbing?) perturbations are being applied to the formal logic of probability theory and classical hypothesis testing. In summary, my philosophy is that if a researcher wishes to increase his or her chances of finding "significant" differences, the researcher should increase those chances *pre*-experimentally; in particular, by testing the specific research hypothesis optimally—via one-degree-of-freedom contrasts, as directional tests (whenever justified), and based on appropriate selected sample sizes (see Bugs 6 and 7). Maximizing one's "significance" chances *post*experimentally (i.e., after looking at the data or after conducting an assortment of "fishing-expedition" tests) is not to make proper use of inferential statistics. So why pretend?

17. The "nonorthogonal" bug. Even though the concept of orthogonality appears in several statistical contexts, the specific usage of "nonorthogonal" here refers to factorial designs that contain unequal and disproportional cell frequencies. The bug refers to the typical reporting of results, where no awareness is apparent on the part of the researcher that his or her conclusions may be due (in either small or large part) to the particular type of unequal-*N* ANOVA conducted. Such types range from an approximate ("unweighted-means") solution, designed for situations with near-equal cell sizes, to a family of exact ("least-squares") solutions. It can be demonstrated that different solution choices can lead to radically different statistical outcomes and interpretations of the data.

Which of the various solutions to select should depend on the researcher's specific hypotheses, including the perceived importance of controlling for various effects (or generalizing across them) when testing for other effects. Issues related to the "proper" application of unequal-*N* approaches have been debated for the last 15 years in the pages of the *Psychological Bulletin*—to which the reader should refer, beginning with the article by Overall & Spiegel (1969)—and elsewhere. My plea here is not that cognitive-developmental researchers resolve to resolve those issues (many of which have not yet been resolved). Instead, it is simply that researchers recognize that there *are* issues involved in the performance of unequal-N analyses, and that a particular solution is selected on rational grounds (rather than on the basis of a computer program's "default" option) so that those selections can be rationally described and defended.

18. The "repeated-measures" bug. One of the most popular designs in the children's-learning literature is the repeated-measures design, in which each subject is tested at two or more different time periods, or is administered and evaluated with respect to two or more different treatments, or is required to study and recall a "mixed list" consisting of two or more different stimulus variations, etc. The common feature here is that each subject in the study produces more than one dependent variable, and if those dependent variables are associated with a common metric, then those variables can be referred to as "repeated measures." With this kind of setup, the reseacher is generally interested in assessing the main effect of the repeated-measures factor, as well as interactions of the repeated-measures factor with other factors in the design.

Let me mention a couple of salient bugs here. One, already noted, is that in order for comparisons among repeated measures to be made, the K measures must be associated with a common metric. It makes no sense, for example, to measure subjects' performance on subtests differing in length, difficulty, or content (or, more generally, on variables representing different constructs) and to regard this as a "repeated-measures" design. Such apples-and-oranges variables should be alternatively conceptualized as multiple dependent measures, and comparisons should not be made *among these dependent measures*. Rather, comparisons *among experimental conditions* with respect to one (univariate ANOVA) or more (MANOVA) of these dependent measures is what one should consider. I can think of isolated instances in which it might be appropriate to adopt a repeated-measures framework even with qualitatively different dependent measures (e.g., with dependent measures that have been standardized across experimental conditions, in order to assess treatment-by-measures interactions); however, such repeated-measures variations represent an atypical application in the literature.

A second critical concern I have in this domain is what I (and other statisticians) view as likely-to-be-incorrect analyses of repeated-measures designs. In particular, virtually everyone conducts what are called "univariate analyses of repeated-measures designs" following the methods associated with the experimental-design textbooks and statistical packages most frequently adopted by psychologists. Yet, univariate analyses of repeated-measures designs have been questioned by many who believe that one or more of the assumptions required for valid application of those analyses is likely to be violated in practice, once again resulting in Type I error probabilities that are unacceptable (e.g., McCall & Appelbaum, 1973; Rogan, Keselman, & Mendoza, 1979; and Romaniuk, Levin, & Hubert, 1977).

Chief among these assumptions is that which is known as "sphericity" or "circularity," which specifies that the variances associated with all pairwise mean differences in levels of the repeated-measures factor are equal (see, for example, Kirk, 1982). Whenever this assumption is violated—and there is empirical evidence to support that its violation is not unlikely in cognitive-developmental research, where the "time-tied" correlations associated with the repeated measures produce a predictable pattern—alternative analysis strategies are to be recommended. These strategies include a univariate "contrast" approach to the repeated-measures design and "multivariate analyses of repeated-measures designs," neither of which depends on the sphericity assumption being met (see Marascuilo & Levin, 1983, pp. 373–390, for details). Of course, valid application of multivariate analyses of repeated-measures designs requires its own set of assumptions, as is discussed in the above sources. A hope for the future is that such alternative repeated-measures analyses will supplant the traditional univariate approach.

Comment

As long as the word "tradition" has come up, let me comment briefly on some unwitting perpetuators of many of the bugs discussed in the chapter. Those perpetuators are the policers of our professional archives, namely the editors and referees of our scholarly journals. Why do I view them as contributors to the problem? Of course, their role in shaping the substantive emphases of the psychological literature (including current fads and fashions) is obvious. What may not be so obvious is the influence they have over the technical (in particular, the statistical) aspects of that literature as well.

One such already-documented influence is the negative bias exhibited by journal reviewers and editors toward nonsignificant results (e.g., Greenwald, 1975). These individuals are also in a unique position to recommend—and often even to *require*—that authors perform specified types of data analysis as a prerequisite to publication. Unfortunately, however, it has been my observation over the years that many of the data-analysis recommendations offered are traditional ones, ones that include the very bugs I would like to see eliminated. To name a few, I have seen editors and reviewers insist that omnibus F-tests be conducted when the researcher has a very specific hypothesis in mind (the unthinking bug), that such tests be followed by various statistically and logically incoherent subsequent analyses (the Type IV, interactive, multivariate and unprotected bugs), and that certain analyses be performed either when nature of the data does not justify them (the trendy and unit bugs) or when necessary statistical assumptions are irreparably violated (the heterogeneous and repeated-measures bugs). I love tradition as much as the next person. But this is one tradition that I would love to see yield to advances in research methodology and statistical sophistication.

A Final Bug and Victual

Permit me to end this excursion with the brief description of a final bug family, one with which in my own stint as a policer of the archives I sadly became too familiar. Exactly what this bug portends for the future of cognitive-developmental psychology I cannot conclude for sure. What I can conclude—and as has been independently concluded by Arthur Jensen and William Rohwer of the University of California, Berkeley—is that the bug is appearing in our journals with such astonishing frequency that the findings reported therein must surely be interpreted from a "caveat emptor" perspective. I am referring to problems of credibility left behind by what I will call the "numbers" bug.

19. The "numbers" bug. This is the bug that permits numerical errors to creep into a journal article or other research report. Anyone who has ever reported a piece of empirical research containing numerical information is well acquainted with the lurking nightmare: "Are the numbers presented there *correct*?" An important point to be made in this regard is that for whatever reasons and from whatever sources these errors may have arisen, the researcher-author bears the ultimate responsibility for them. Given the multiple opportunities for numerical "breakdowns" in the researching and writing and publishing process, this responsibility is an awesome one.

Incorrect numbers result from data-recording errors, typographical and printing errors, computational errors, computer-generated errors, and conceptually based errors, to mention a few that readily come to mind (for more—including *intentionally* committed errors—see Barber, 1973). Briefly stated, data-recording errors refer to a slip-up somewhere between a subject's actual responses, the researcher's interpretation and/or recording of those responses, and the responses that are transferred to coding sheets for manual or computer analysis. Typographical and printing errors occur, respectively, somewhere between an author and a typist, and between a typist and a typesetter. Computational errors result from incorrect calculations made by an animate data analyst, whereas the large variety of potential computer-generated errors emanates from inanimate data-processing devices. Finally, conceptually based errors stem from a researcher's incomplete understanding of statistical concepts and procedures (e.g., error terms, degrees of freedom, or formula values), as well as from misinterpretations of the specific approaches and output associated with the computer package(s) used to analyze the data (e.g., whether biased or unbiased variances are provided, whether stepwise multiple-regression results are based on a user-determined or a data-determined order of variable entry, or what the program default values are for various options).

Can the numbers that appear in published research studies be believed? Jensen and Rohwer—and now add me to the list—are skeptical. In an informal survey that they conducted, it was found that an astonishing number of articles published in several prestigious psychology journals contained at least one numbers bug.[8] But minor numerical errors appearing in an article is not so bad, I can imagine you thinking. Minor, indeed! To quote Jensen (1979):

> ... in *many* cases [the authors'] conclusions were *opposite* to the true outcome of their study! ... [It was estimated that] about one-fourth to one-third of published articles in our top refereed journals have such serious technical defects [including numerical errors of the kind described here] ... that they should never have been published.

How is such a state of affairs possible? How are we to improve our lot? How sad for psychological research (as if we do not have bad enough "press" already)! And what a depressing note on which for me to "bug out" of this chapter!

What I have attempted to do in this essay is to describe a few perceived "eyesores" associated with the methods and analysis of cognitive-developmental research studies. The various bugs that I chose to single out were offered out of a desire to set them free in the research community, with the hope that they will be pondered and puzzled about, and maybe that they will even be persuasive in terms of affecting researchers' current attitudes and behavior. Only time will tell if this hope is fulfilled.

Acknowledgments. Preparation of this chapter was facilitated by a grant from the National Institute of Education through the Wisconsin Center for Education Research, and by a Romnes Faculty Fellowship from the Graduate School of the University of Wisconsin, Madison. I am grateful to Michael Pressley and Ronald Serlin for their initial feedback regarding some of the arguments presented here.

References

Appelbaum, M. I., & McCall, R. B. (1983). Design and analysis in developmental psychology. In P. H. Mussen (Ed.), *Handbook of child psychology* (4th ed.): *Volume 1: History, theory, and methods* (W. Kessen, Ed.). New York: Wiley.

Baltes, P. B., Reese, H. W., & Nesselroade, J. R. (1977). *Life-span developmental psychology: Introduction to research methods*. Monterey: CA: Brooks/Cole.

Barber, T. X. (1973). Pitfalls in research: Nine investigator and experimenter effects. In R. M. W. Travers (Ed.), *Second handbook of research on teaching*. Chicago: Rand McNally.

---

[8]Keep in mind throughout this discussion that the numerical errors discovered include only data-analysis errors that could be easily checked. It is a sobering thought to speculate how many other undiscovered numerical errors were associated with these articles.

Barcikowski, R. S. (1981). Statistical power with group mean as the unit of analysis. *Journal of Educational Statistics, 6*, 267–285.

Betz, M. A., & Levin, J. R. (1982). Coherent analysis-of-variance hypothesis-testing strategies: A general model. *Journal of Educational Statistics, 7*, 192–206.

Bird, K. D., & Hadzi-Pavlovic, D. (1983). Simultaneous test procedures and the choice of a test statistic in MANOVA. *Psychological Bulletin, 93*, 167–178.

Bogartz, R. S. (1976). On the meaning of statistical interactions. *Journal of Experimental Child Psychology, 22*, 178–183.

Brainerd, C. J., & Howe, M. L. (1980). Developmental invariance in a mathematical model of associative learning. *Child Development, 51*, 349–362.

Brown, J. S., & Burton, R. R. (1978). Diagnostic models for procedural bugs in basic mathematical skills. *Cognitive Science, 2*, 153–192.

Campbell, D. T., & Boruch, R. F. (1975). Making the case for randomized assignment to treatments by considering the alternatives: Six ways in which quasi-experimental evaluations in compensatory education tend to underestimate effects. In C. A. Bennett & A. Lumsdaine (Eds.), *Central issues in social program evaluation*. New York: Academic Press.

Campbell, D. T., & Stanley, J. C. (1966). *Experimental and quasi-experimental designs for research*. Chicago: Rand McNally.

Cohen, J. (1977). *Statistical power analysis for the behavioral sciences* (2nd ed.). New York: Academic Press.

Cohen, J., & Cohen, P. (1975). *Applied multiple regression correlation analysis for the behavioral sciences*. Hillsdale, NJ: Erlbaum.

Cook, T. D., & Campbell, D. T. (1976). The design and conduct of quasi-experiments and true experiments in field settings. In M. D. Dunnette & J. P. Campbell (Eds.), *Handbook of industrial and organizational research*. Chicago: Rand McNally.

Cronbach, L. J., & Snow, R. E. (1977). *Aptitudes and instructional methods*. New York: Irvington.

Elashoff, J. D. (1969). Analysis of covariance: A delicate instrument. *American Educational Research Journal, 6*, 381–401.

Evans, S. H., & Anastasio, E. J. (1968). Misuse of analysis of covariance when treatment effect and covariate are confounded. *Psychological Bulletin, 69*, 225–234.

Gabriel, K. R. (1969). Simultaneous test procedures: Some theory of multiple comparisons. *Annals of Mathematical Statistics, 40*, 224–250.

Gaito, J. (1965). Unequal intervals and unequal n in trend analyses. *Psychological Bulletin, 63*, 125–127.

Games, P. A. (1978). Nesting, crossing, Type IV errors and the role of statistical models. *American Educational Research Journal, 15*, 253–258.

Glass, G. V. (1977). Integrating findings: The meta-analysis of research. In L. S. Shulman (Ed.), *Review of Research in Education* (Vol. 5). Itasca, IL: Peacock.

Glass, G. V., Peckham, P. D., & Sanders, J. R. (1972). Consequences of failure to meet assumptions underlying the fixed effects analyses of variance and covariance. *Review of Educational Research, 42*, 237–288.

Green, D. M., & Swets, J. A. (1966). *Signal detection theory and psychophysics*. New York: Wiley.

Greenwald, A. G. (1975). Consequences of prejudice against the null hypothesis. *Psychological Bulletin, 82*, 1–20.

Huitema, B. E. (1980). *The analysis of covariance and alternatives.* New York: Wiley.

Humphreys, L. G. (1980). The statistics of failure to replicate: A comment on Buriel's (1978) conclusions. *Journal of Educational Psychology, 72*, 71–75.

Jaccard, J., Becker, M. A., & Wood, G. (1984). Pairwise multiple comparison procedures: A review. *Psychological Bulletin, 96*, 589–596.

Jensen, A. R. (1979, April). Personal communication.

Kirk, R. E. (1982). *Experimental design* (2nd ed.). Belmont: CA: Brooks/Cole.

Levin, J. R. (1975). Determining sample size for planned and post hoc analysis of variance comparisons. *Journal of Educational Measurement, 12*, 99–108.

Levin, J. R. (1977, April). *Data analysis by the numbers.* Paper presented at the annual meeting of the American Educational Research Association, New York.

Levin, J. R., Marascuilo, L. A., & Hubert, L. J. (1978) N = nonparametric randomization tests. In T. R. Kratochwill (Ed.), *Single subject research: Strategies for evaluating change.* New York: Academic Press.

Levin, J. R., & Peterson, P. L. (1984). Classroom aptitude-by-treatment interactions: An alternative analysis strategy. *Educational Psychologist, 19*, 43–47.

Levin, J. R., & Pressley, M. (1983). Understanding mnemonic imagery effects: A dozen "obvious" outcomes. In M. L. Fleming & D. W. Hutton (Eds.), *Mental imagery and learning.* Englewood Cliffs, NJ: Educational Technology Publications.

Levin, J. R., Pressley, M., McCormick, C. B., Miller, G. E., & Shriberg, L. K. (1979). Assessing the classroom potential of the keyword method. *Journal of Educational Psychology, 71*, 583–594.

Loftus, G. R. (1978). On interpretation of interactions. *Memory & Cognition, 6*, 312–319.

Lord, F. M. (1967). A paradox in the interpretation of group comparisons. *Psychological Bulletin, 68*, 304–305.

Lubin, A. (1961). The interpretation of significant interaction. *Educational and Psychological Measurement, 21*, 807–817.

Marascuilo, L. A., & Levin, J. R. (1970). Appropriate post hoc comparisons for interaction and nested hypotheses in analysis of variance designs: The elimination of Type IV errors. *American Educational Research Journal, 7*, 397–421.

Marascuilo, L. A., & Levin, J. R. (1976). A note on the simultaneous investigation of interaction and nested hypotheses in two-factor analysis of variance designs. *American Educational Research Journal, 13*, 61–65.

Marascuilo, L. A., & Levin, J. R. (1983). *Multivariate statistics in the social sciences: A researcher's guide.* Monterey, CA: Brooks/Cole.

Marascuilo, L. A., & McSweeney, M. (1977). *Nonparametric and distribution-free methods for the social sciences.* Monterey, CA: Brooks/Cole.

Maxwell, S. E., Delaney, H. D., & Dill, C. A. Another look at ANCOVA versus blocking. (1984). *Psychological Bulletin, 95*, 136–147.

McCall, R. B., & Appelbaum, M. I. (1973). Bias in the analysis of repeated-measures designs: Some alternative approaches. *Child Development, 44*, 401–415.

Morrison, D. E., & Henkel, R. E. (Eds.). (1970). *The significance test controversy.* Chicago: Aldine.

Olson, C. L. (1974). Comparative robustness of six tests in multivariate analysis of variance. *Journal of the American Statistical Association, 69*, 894–908.

Overall, J. E., & Spiegel, D. K. (1969). Concerning least squares analysis of experimental data. *Psychological Bulletin, 72*, 311–322.

Page, E. B. (1965, February). *Recapturing the richness within the classroom.* Paper presented at the annual meeting of the American Educational Research Association, Chicago.

Peckham, P. D., Glass, G. V., & Hopkins, K. D. (1969). The experimental unit in statistical analysis. *Journal of Special Education, 3,* 337–349.

Petrinovich, L., & Hardyck, C. D. (1969). Error rates for multiple comparison methods: Some evidence concerning the frequency of erroneous conclusions. *Psychological Bulletin, 71,* 43–54.

Porter, A. C., & Chibucos, T. R. (1974). Analysis issues in summative evaluation. In G. Borich (Ed.), *Evaluating educational programs and products.* Englewood Cliffs, NJ: Educational Technology Press.

Rogan, J. C., Keselman, H. J., & Mendoza, J. L. (1979). Analysis of repeated measurements. *British Journal of Mathematical and Statistical Psychology, 32,* 269–286.

Rohwer, W. D., Jr. (1973). Elaboration and learning in childhood and adolescence: In H. W. Reese (Ed.), *Advances in child development and behavior* (Vol. 8). New York: Academic Press.

Romaniuk, J. G., Levin, J. R., & Hubert, L. J. (1977). Hypothesis-testing procedures in repeated-measures designs: On the road map not taken. *Child Development, 48,* 1757–1760.

Salthouse, T. A., & Kausler, D. H. (1985). Memory methodology in maturity. In C. J. Brainerd & M. Pressley (Eds.), *Basic processes in memory development.* New York: Springer-Verlag.

Serlin, R. C., & Lapsley, D. K. (1983, April). *Rationality in psychological research: The good-enough principle.* Paper presented at the annual meeting of the American Educational Research Association, Montreal, Canada.

Serlin, R. C., & Lapsley, D. K. (1984). *A unified framework for hypothesis testing.* Unpublished manuscript, Department of Educational Psychology, University of Wisconsin, Madison.

Tomarken, A. J., & Serlin, R. C. (in press). A comparison of ANOVA alternatives under variance heterogeneity and with specific noncentrality structures. *Psychological Bulletin.*

Walster, G. W., & Cleary, T. A. (1970). Statistical significance as a decision-making rule. In E. F. Borgatta & G. W. Bohrnstedt (Eds.), *Sociological methodology.* San Francisco: Jossey-Bass.

Winer, B. J. (1971). *Statistical principles in experimental design* (2nd ed.). New York: McGraw-Hill.

Author Index

Subject Index